Hands-On Data Structures and Algorithms with JavaScript

Write efficient code that is highly performant, scalable, and easily testable using JavaScript

Kashyap Mukkamala

BIRMINGHAM - MUMBAI

Hands-On Data Structures and Algorithms with JavaScript

Commissioning Editor: Kunal Chaudhari
Acquisition Editor: Larissa Pinto
Content Development Editor: Arun Nadar
Technical Editor: Leena Patil
Copy Editor: Dhanya Baburaj
Project Coordinator: Sheejal Shah
Proofreader: Safis Editing
Indexers: Aishwarya Gangawane
Graphics: Jason Monteiro
Production Coordinator: Deepika Naik

First published: January 2018

Production reference: 1250118

Published by Packt Publishing Ltd.
Livery Place
35 Livery Street
Birmingham
B3 2PB, UK.

ISBN 978-1-78839-855-8

www.packtpub.com

`mapt.io`

Mapt is an online digital library that gives you full access to over 5,000 books and videos, as well as industry leading tools to help you plan your personal development and advance your career. For more information, please visit our website.

Why subscribe?

- Spend less time learning and more time coding with practical eBooks and Videos from over 4,000 industry professionals

- Improve your learning with Skill Plans built especially for you

- Get a free eBook or video every month

- Mapt is fully searchable

- Copy and paste, print, and bookmark content

PacktPub.com

Did you know that Packt offers eBook versions of every book published, with PDF and ePub files available? You can upgrade to the eBook version at `www.PacktPub.com` and as a print book customer, you are entitled to a discount on the eBook copy. Get in touch with us at `service@packtpub.com` for more details.

At `www.PacktPub.com`, you can also read a collection of free technical articles, sign up for a range of free newsletters, and receive exclusive discounts and offers on Packt books and eBooks.

Contributors

About the author

Kashyap Mukkamala has been a JavaScript enthusiast since he first started working with it back in 2011. Apart from his fun side projects using IoT devices (Arduino, LeapMotion, and AR Drones) and mobile applications (PhoneGap, Ionic, and NativeScript), his corporate experience has been focused around building scalable web SPAs for Fortune 100 companies. Over the past few years, Kashyap has also been a JavaScript instructor for his company and has trained a few hundred students.

I would like to thank my wife, parents, and colleagues at Egen Solutions who have provided me with their support and motivation to write this book. I would also like to thank the amazing team at Packt Publishing who put in a lot of effort behind the scenes to mold this book into its final form.

About the reviewer

Todd Zebert is a full stack web developer, currently at Miles.
He has been a technical reviewer for a number of books and videos, is a frequent presenter at conferences on JavaScript, Drupal, and related technologies, and has a technology blog on Medium.
Todd has a diverse background in technology including infrastructure, network engineering, PM, and IT leadership. He started in web development with the original Mosaic browser.
Todd is an entrepreneur and part of the LA startup community. He's a believer in volunteering, open source, Maker/STEM/STEAM, and contributing back.

> *I'd like to thank the JavaScript community, especially the Node and Angular communities, and also the Drupal community.*
>
> *Finally, I'd like to thank my teen son, Alec, with whom I get to share an interest in technology and science with, while doing Maker-ish things together, with microcontrollers and other electronics.*

Packt is searching for authors like you

If you're interested in becoming an author for Packt, please visit `authors.packtpub.com` and apply today. We have worked with thousands of developers and tech professionals, just like you, to help them share their insight with the global tech community. You can make a general application, apply for a specific hot topic that we are recruiting an author for, or submit your own idea.

Table of Contents

Preface   1

Chapter 1: Building Stacks for Application State Management   7

  Prerequisites   8
  Terminology   8
  API   8
  Don't we have arrays for this?   9
  Creating a stack   10
    Implementing stack methods   10
    Testing the stack   13
    Using the stack   13
  Use cases   14
    Creating an Angular application   14
      Installing Angular CLI   15
      Creating an app using the CLI   15
      Creating a stack   16
    Creating a custom back button for a web application   19
      Setting up the application and its routing   19
      Detecting application state changes   22
      Laying out the UI   23
      Navigating between states   25
      Final application logic   25
    Building part of a basic JavaScript syntax parser and evaluator   28
      Building a basic web worker   28
      Laying out the UI   29
      Basic web worker communication   30
      Enabling web worker communications   31
      Transforming input to machine-understandable expression   32
      Converting infix to postfix expressions   37
      Evaluating postfix expressions   38
  Summary   40

Chapter 2: Creating Queues for In-Order Executions   41

  Types of queue   42
  Implementing APIs   42
  Creating a queue   42
    A simple queue   43
      Testing the queue   44

Priority Queue 45
Testing a priority queue 46
Use cases for queues 49
Creating a Node.js application 49
Starting the Node.js server 51
Creating a chat endpoint 51
Implementing logging using priority queues 57
Comparing performance 61
Running benchmark tests 66
Summary 70

Chapter 3: Using Sets and Maps for Faster Applications 71
Exploring the origin of sets and maps 71
Analyzing set and map types 72
How weak is WeakMap? 73
Memory management 73
API differences 75
Sets versus WeakSets 75
Understanding WeakSets 76
The API difference 77
Use cases 77
Creating an Angular application 77
Creating custom keyboard shortcuts for your application 78
Creating an Angular application 79
Creating states with keymap 81
Activity tracking and analytics for web applications 87
Creating the Angular application 88
Performance comparison 98
Sets and Arrays 99
Maps and Objects 101
Summary 102

Chapter 4: Using Trees for Faster Lookup and Modifications 103
Creating an Angular application 103
Creating a typeahead lookup 104
Creating a trie tree 106
Implementing the add() method 107
The friends' example 108
Implementing the search() method 109
Retaining remainders at nodes 111
The final form 114

Creating a credit card approval predictor   116
   ID3 algorithm   117
      Calculating target entropy   118
      Calculating branch entropy   119
      The final information gain per branch   120
   Coding the ID3 algorithm   122
      Generating training dataset   122
      Generating the decision tree   127
      Predicting outcome of sample inputs   133
      Visualization of the tree and output   134
   Summary   141

Chapter 5: Simplify Complex Applications Using Graphs   143
   Types of graphs   144
   Use cases   147
   Creating a Node.js web server   148
   Creating a reference generator for a job portal   149
      Creating a bidirectional graph   150
      Generating a pseudocode for the shortest path generation   152
      Implementing the shortest path generation 153
      Creating a web server   158
      Running the reference generator   159
   Creating a friend recommendation system for social media   160
      Understanding PageRank algorithm   161
      Understanding Personalized PageRank (PPR) Algorithm   162
      Pseudocode for personalized PageRank   164
      Creating a web server   165
      Implementing Personalized PageRank   166
      Results and analysis   169
   Summary   172

Chapter 6: Exploring Types of Algorithms   173
   Creating a Node.js application   174
   Use cases   174
   Using recursion to serialize data   174
      Pseudocode   175
      Serializing data   175
   Using Dijkstra to determine the shortest path   177
      Pseudo code   178
      Implementing Dijkstra's algorithm   179
   Using BFS to determine relationships   183
      Pseudo code   187
      Implementing BFS   188
   Using dynamic programming to build a financial planner   193

Pseudo code	195
Implementing the dynamic programming algorithm	196
Using a greedy algorithm to build a travel itinerary	201
Understanding spanning trees	203
Pseudo code	203
Implementing a minimum spanning tree using a greedy algorithm	204
Using branch and bound algorithm to create a custom shopping list	208
Understanding branch and bound algorithm	210
Implementing branch and bound algorithm	212
When not to use brute-force algorithm	218
Brute-force Fibonacci generator	219
Recursive Fibonacci generator	220
Memoized Fibonacci generator	220
Summary	221
Chapter 7: Sorting and Its Applications	223
Types of sorting algorithms	224
Use cases of different sorting algorithms	224
Creating an Express server	225
Mocking library books data	226
Insertionsort API	227
What is Insertionsort	227
Pseudo code	227
Implementing Insertionsort API	228
Mergesort API	231
What is Mergesort	231
Pseudo code	232
Implementing Mergesort API	232
Quicksort API	234
What is Quicksort	235
Pseudo code	235
Implementing the Quicksort API	235
Lomuto Partition Scheme	237
Hoare Partition Scheme	239
Performance comparison	241
Summary	243
Chapter 8: Big O Notation, Space, and Time Complexity	245
Terminology	245
Asymptotic Notations	247
Big-O notation	248
Omega notation	249
Theta Notation	251
Recap	251

Examples of time complexity   252
  Constant time   252
  Logarithmic time   252
  Linear time   253
  Quadratic time   254
  Polynomial time   254
    Polynomial time complexity classes   255
  Recursion and additive complexity   256
Space complexity and Auxiliary space   257
  Examples of Space complexity   258
    Constant space   258
    Linear space   258
  Summary   259
Chapter 9: Micro-Optimizations and Memory Management   261
  Best practices   261
  Best practices for HTML   262
    Declaring the correct DOCTYPE   262
    Adding the correct meta-information to the page 262
    Dropping unnecessary attributes   263
    Making your app mobile ready   263
    Loading style sheets in the <head>   263
    Avoiding inline styles   264
    Using semantic markup   264
    Using Accessible Rich Internet Applications (ARIA) attributes 265
    Loading scripts at the end   265
  CSS best practices   266
    Avoiding inline styles   266
    Do not use !important   266
    Arranging styles within a class alphabetically 266
    Defining the media queries in an ascending order 267
  Best practices for JavaScript   268
    Avoiding polluting the global scope   268
    Using 'use strict'   268
    Strict checking (== vs ===)   268
    Using ternary operators and Boolean || or && 268
    Modularization of code   269
    Avoiding pyramid of doom   269
    Keeping DOM access to a minimum   270
    Validating all data   270
    Do not reinvent the wheel   270
  HTML optimizations   271
  DOM structuring   271
  Prefetching and preloading resources   271

<link rel=prefetch >   272
<link rel=preload >   273
Layout and layering of HTML   273
   The HTML layout   274
   HTML layers   282
CSS optimizations   287
   Coding practices   287
     Using smaller values for common ENUM   287
     Using shorthand properties   288
     Avoiding complex CSS selectors   289
   Understanding the browser   290
     Avoiding repaint and reflow   290
     Critical rendering path (CRP)   291
JavaScript optimizations   294
   Truthy/falsy comparisons   294
   Looping optimizations   296
   The conditional function call   296
   Image and font optimizations   298
   Garbage collection in JavaScript   300
     Mark and sweep algorithm   301
     Garbage collection and V8   302
   Avoiding memory leaks   302
     Assigning variables to global scope   303
     Removing DOM elements and references   303
     Closures edge case   304
  Summary   309
  What's next?   310
Other Books You May Enjoy   311
Index   315

Preface

The main focus of this book is employing data structures and algorithms in real-world web applications using JavaScript.

With JavaScript making its way onto the server side and with **Single Page Application** (SPA) frameworks taking over the client side, a lot, if not all, of the business logic, is being ported over to the client side. This makes it crucial to employ hand-crafted data structures and algorithms that are tailor-made for a given use case.

For example, when working on data visualizations such as charts, graphs, and 3D or 4D models, there might be tens or even hundreds of thousands of complex objects being served from the server, sometimes in near real time. There are more ways than one in which this data can be handled and that is what we will be exploring, with real-world examples.

Who this book is for

This book is for anyone who has an interest in and basic knowledge of HTML, CSS, and JavaScript. We will also be using Node.js, Express, and Angular to create some of the web apps and APIs that leverage our data structures.

What this book covers

Chapter 1, *Building Stacks for Application State Management*, introduces building and using stacks for things such as a custom back button for an application and a syntax parser and evaluator for an online IDE.

Chapter 2, *Creating Queues for In-Order Executions*, demonstrates using queues and their variants to create a messaging service capable of handling message failures. Then, we perform a quick comparison of the different types of queues.

Chapter 3, *Using Sets and Maps for Faster Applications*, use sets, and maps to create keyboard shortcuts to navigate between your application states. Then, we create a custom application tracker for recording the analytics information of a web application. We conclude the chapter with a performance comparison of sets and maps with arrays and objects.

Chapter 4, *Using Trees for Faster Lookup and Modifications*, leverages tree data structures to form a typeahead component. Then, we create a credit card approval predictor to determine whether or not a credit card application would be accepted based on historical data.

Chapter 5, *Simplify Complex Applications Using Graphs*, discusses graphs with examples such as creating a reference generator for a job portal and a friend recommendation system on a social media website.

Chapter 6, *Exploring Types of Algorithms*, explores some of the most important algorithms, such as Dijkstra's, knapsack 1/0, greedy algorithms, and so on.

Chapter 7, *Sorting and its Applications*, explores merge sort, insertion sort, and quick sort with examples. Then, we run a performance comparison on them.

Chapter 8, *Big O notation, Space, and Time Complexity*, discusses the notations denoting complexities and then, moves on to discuss what space and time complexities are and how they impact our application.

Chapter 9, *Micro-optimizations and Memory Management*, explores the best practices for HTML, CSS, JavaScript and then, moves on to discuss some of the internal workings of Google Chrome and how we can leverage it to render our applications better and more quickly.

To get the most out of this book

- Basic knowledge of JavaScript, HTML, and CSS
- Have Node.js installed (https://nodejs.org/en/download/)
- Install WebStorm IDE (https://www.jetbrains.com/webstorm/download) or similar
- A next-generation browser such as Google Chrome (https://www.google.com/chrome/browser/desktop/)
- Familiarity with Angular 2.0 or greater is a plus but is not required
- The screenshots in this book are taken on a macOS. There would be little difference (if any) for users of any other OS. The code samples, however, would run without any discrepancies irrespective of the OS. Anywhere we have CMD/cmd/command specified, please use CTRL/ctrl/control key on the windows counterpart. If you see return, please use *Enter* and if you see the term terminal/Terminal please use its equivalent command prompt on windows.

- In this book, the code base is built incrementally as the topic progresses. So, when you compare the beginning of a code sample with the code base in GitHub, be aware that the GitHub code is the final form of the topic or the example that you are referring to.

Download the example code files

You can download the example code files for this book from your account at `www.packtpub.com`. If you purchased this book elsewhere, you can visit `www.packtpub.com/support` and register to have the files emailed directly to you.

You can download the code files by following these steps:

1. Log in or register at `www.packtpub.com`.
2. Select the **SUPPORT** tab.
3. Click on **Code Downloads & Errata**.
4. Enter the name of the book in the **Search** box and follow the onscreen instructions.

Once the file is downloaded, please make sure that you unzip or extract the folder using the latest version of:

- WinRAR/7-Zip for Windows
- Zipeg/iZip/UnRarX for Mac
- 7-Zip/PeaZip for Linux

The code bundle for the book is also hosted on GitHub at `https://github.com/PacktPublishing/Practical-JavaScript-Data-Structures-and-Algorithms`. We also have other code bundles from our rich catalog of books and videos available at `https://github.com/PacktPublishing/`. Check them out!

Download the color images

We also provide a PDF file that has color images of the screenshots/diagrams used in this book. You can download it here:
`https://www.packtpub.com/sites/default/files/downloads/HandsOnDataStructuresandAlgorithmswithJavaScript_ColorImages.pdf`.

Conventions used

There are a number of text conventions used throughout this book.

`CodeInText`: Indicates code words in text, database table names, folder names, filenames, file extensions, pathnames, dummy URLs, user input, and Twitter handles. Here is an example: "The native array operations have varying time complexities. Let's take `Array.prototype.splice` and `Array.prototype.push`."

A block of code is set as follows:

```
class Stack {
    constructor() {
    }
}
```

When we wish to draw your attention to a particular part of a code block, the relevant lines or items are set in bold:

```
var express = require('express');
var app = express();
var data = require('./books.json');
var Insertion = require('./sort/insertion');
```

Any command-line input or output is written as follows:

```
ng new back-button
```

Bold: Indicates a new term, an important word, or words that you see onscreen. For example, words in menus or dialog boxes appear in the text like this. Here is an example: "When the user clicks on the **back** button, we will navigate to the previous state of the application from the stack."

Warnings or important notes appear like this.

Tips and tricks appear like this.

Get in touch

Feedback from our readers is always welcome.

General feedback: Email `feedback@packtpub.com` and mention the book title in the subject of your message. If you have questions about any aspect of this book, please email us at `questions@packtpub.com`.

Errata: Although we have taken every care to ensure the accuracy of our content, mistakes do happen. If you have found a mistake in this book, we would be grateful if you would report this to us. Please visit `www.packtpub.com/submit-errata`, selecting your book, clicking on the Errata Submission Form link, and entering the details.

Piracy: If you come across any illegal copies of our works in any form on the Internet, we would be grateful if you would provide us with the location address or website name. Please contact us at `copyright@packtpub.com` with a link to the material.

If you are interested in becoming an author: If there is a topic that you have expertise in and you are interested in either writing or contributing to a book, please visit `authors.packtpub.com`.

Reviews

Please leave a review. Once you have read and used this book, why not leave a review on the site that you purchased it from? Potential readers can then see and use your unbiased opinion to make purchase decisions, we at Packt can understand what you think about our products, and our authors can see your feedback on their book. Thank you!

For more information about Packt, please visit `packtpub.com`.

1
Building Stacks for Application State Management

Stacks are one of the most common data structures that one can think of. They are ubiquitous in both personal and professional setups. Stacks are a **last in first out** (**LIFO**) data structure, that provides some common operations, such as push, pop, peek, clear, and size.

In most **object-oriented programming** (**OOP**) languages, you would find the stack data structure built-in. JavaScript, on the other hand, was originally designed for the web; it does not have stacks baked into it, yet. However, don't let that stop you. Creating a stacks using JS is fairly easy, and this is further simplified by the use of the latest version of JavaScript.

In this chapter, our goal is to understand the importance of stack in the new-age web and their role in simplifying ever-evolving applications. Let's explore the following aspects of the stack:

- A theoretical understanding of the stack
- Its API and implementation
- Use cases in real-world web

Before we start building a stack, let's take a look at some of the methods that we want our stack to have so that the behavior matches our requirements. Having to create the API on our own is a blessing in disguise. You never have to rely on someone else's library *getting it right* or even worry about any missing functionality. You can add what you need and not worry about performance and memory management until you need to.

Prerequisites

The following are the requirements for the following chapter:

- A basic understanding of JavaScript
- A computer with Node.js installed (downloadable from `https://nodejs.org/en/download/`)

The code sample for the code shown in this chapter can be found at `https://github.com/NgSculptor/examples`.

Terminology

Throughout the chapter, we will use the following terminology specific to Stacks, so let's get to know more about it:

- **Top**: Indicates the top of the stack
- **Base**: Indicates the bottom of the stack

API

This is the tricky part, as it is very hard to predict ahead of time what kinds of method your application will require. Therefore, it's usually a good idea to start off with whatever is the norm and then make changes as your applications demand. Going by that, you would end up with an API that looks something like this:

- **Push**: Pushes an item to the top of the stack
- **Pop**: Removes an item from the top of the stack
- **Peek**: Shows the last item pushed into the stack
- **Clear**: Empties the stack
- **Size**: Gets the current size of the stack

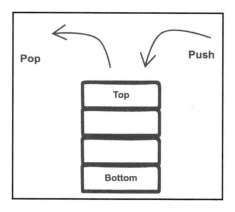

Don't we have arrays for this?

From what we have seen so far, you might wonder why one would need a stack in the first place. It's very similar to an array, and we can perform all of these operations on an array. Then, what is the real purpose of having a stack?

The reasons for preferring a stack over an array are multifold:

- Using stacks gives a more semantic meaning to your application. Consider this analogy where you have a backpack (an array) and wallet (a stack). Can you put money in both the backpack and wallet? Most certainly; however, when you look at a backpack, you have no clue as to what you may find inside it, but when you look at a wallet, you have a very good idea that it contains money. What kind of money it holds (that is, the data type), such as Dollars, INR, and Pounds, is, however, still not known (supported, unless you take support from TypeScript).

- Native array operations have varying time complexities. Let's take `Array.prototype.splice` and `Array.prototype.push`, for example. Splice has a worst-case time complexity of O(n), as it has to search through all the index and readjust it when an element is spliced out of the array. `Push` has a worst case complexity of O(n) when the memory buffer is full but is amortized O(1). Stacks avoid elements being accessed directly and internally rely on a `WeakMap()`, which is memory efficient as you will see shortly.

Creating a stack

Now that we know when and why we would want to use a stack, let's move on to implementing one. As discussed in the preceding section, we will use a `WeakMap()` for our implementation. You can use any native data type for your implementation, but there are certain reasons why `WeakMap()` would be a strong contender. `WeakMap()` retains a weak reference to the keys that it holds. This means that once you are no longer referring to that particular key, it gets garbage-collected along with the value. However, `WeakMap()` come with its own downsides: keys can only be nonprimitives and are not enumerable, that is, you cannot get a list of all the keys, as they are dependent on the garbage collector. However, in our case, we are more concerned with the values that our `WeakMap()` holds rather than keys and their internal memory management.

Implementing stack methods

Implementing a stack is a rather easy task. We will follow a series of steps, where we will use the ES6 syntax, as follows:

1. Define a `constructor`:

```
class Stack {
    constructor() {
    }
}
```

2. Create a `WeakMap()` to store the stack items:

```
const sKey = {};
const items = new WeakMap();

class Stack {
    constructor() {
        items.set(sKey, [])
    }
}
```

3. Implement the methods described in the preceding API in the `Stack` class:

```
const sKey = {};
const items = new WeakMap();

class Stack {
    constructor() {
```

```
        items.set(sKey, []);
    }

    push(element) {
        let stack = items.get(sKey);
        stack.push(element);
    }

    pop() {
        let stack = items.get(sKey)
        return stack.pop()
    }

    peek() {
        let stack = items.get(sKey);
        return stack[stack.length - 1];
    }

    clear() {
        items.set(sKey, []);
    }

    size() {
        return items.get(sKey).length;
    }
}
```

5. So, the final implementation of the `Stack` will look as follows:

```
var Stack = (() => {
    const sKey = {};
    const items = new WeakMap();

    class Stack {

        constructor() {
            items.set(sKey, []);
        }

        push(element) {
            let stack = items.get(sKey);
            stack.push(element);
        }

        pop() {
            let stack = items.get(sKey);
            return stack.pop();
```

```
        }

        peek() {
            let stack = items.get(sKey);
            return stack[stack.length - 1];
        }

        clear() {
            items.set(sKey, []);
        }

        size() {
            return items.get(sKey).length;
        }
    }

    return Stack;
})();
```

This is an overarching implementation of a JavaScript stack, which by no means is comprehensive and can be changed based on the application's requirements. However, let's go through some of the principles employed in this implementation.

We have used a `WeakMap()` here, which as explained in the preceding paragraph, helps with internal memory management based on the reference to the stack items.

Another important thing to notice is that we have wrapped the `Stack` class inside an IIFE, so the constants `items` and `sKey` are available to the `Stack` class internally but are not exposed to the outside world. This is a well-known and debated feature of the current JS Class implementation, which does not allow class-level variables to be declared. TC39 essentially designed the ES6 Class in such a way that it should only define and declare its members, which are prototype methods in ES5. Also, since adding variables to prototypes is not the norm, the ability to create class-level variables has not been provided. However, one can still do the following:

```
constructor() {
    this.sKey = {};
    this.items = new WeakMap();
    this.items.set(sKey, []);
}
```

However, this would make the `items` accessible also from outside our `Stack` methods, which is something that we want to avoid.

Testing the stack

To test the `Stack` we have just created, let's instantiate a new stack and call out each of the methods and take a look at how they present us with data:

```
var stack = new Stack();
stack.push(10);
stack.push(20);

console.log(stack.items); // prints undefined -> cannot be accessed
directly

console.log(stack.size()); // prints 2

console.log(stack.peek()); // prints 20

console.log(stack.pop()); // prints 20

console.log(stack.size()); // prints 1

stack.clear();

console.log(stack.size()); // prints 0
```

When we run the above script we see the logs as specified in the comments above. As expected, the stack provides what appears to be the expected output at each stage of the operations.

Using the stack

To use the `Stack` class created previously, you would have to make a minor change to allow the stack to be used based on the environment in which you are planning to use it. Making this change generic is fairly straightforward; that way, you do not need to worry about multiple environments to support and can avoid repetitive code in each application:

```
// AMD
if (typeof define === 'function' && define.amd) {

    define(function () { return Stack; });

// NodeJS/CommonJS

} else if (typeof exports === 'object') {

    if (typeof module === 'object' && typeof module.exports ===
```

```
    'object') {

        exports = module.exports = Stack;

    }

// Browser

} else {

    window.Stack = Stack;

}
```

Once we add this logic to the stack, it is multi-environment ready. For the purpose of simplicity and brevity, we will not add it everywhere we see the stack; however, in general, it's a good thing to have in your code.

 If your technology stack comprises ES5, then you need to transpile the preceding stack code to ES5. This is not a problem, as there are a plethora of options available online to transpile code from ES6 to ES5.

Use cases

Now that we have implemented a `Stack` class, let's take a look at how we can employ this in some web development challenges.

Creating an Angular application

To explore some practical applications of the stack in web development, we will create an Angular application first and use it as a base application, which we will use for subsequent use cases.

Starting off with the latest version of Angular is pretty straightforward. All you need as a prerequisite is to have Node.js preinstalled in your system. To test whether you have Node.js installed on your machine, go to the Terminal on the Mac or the command prompt on Windows and type the following command:

```
node -v
```

That should show you the version of Node.js that is installed. If you have something like the following:

```
node: command not found
```

This means that you do not have Node.js installed on your machine.

Once you have Node.js set up on your machine, you get access to npm, also known as the node package manager command-line tool, which can be used to set up global dependencies. Using the npm command, we will install the Angular CLI tool, which provides us with many Angular utility methods, including—but not limited to—creating a new project.

Installing Angular CLI

To install the Angular CLI in your Terminal, run the following command:

```
npm install -g @angular/cli
```

That should install the Angular CLI globally and give you access to the ng command to create new projects.

To test it, you can run the following command, which should show you a list of features available for use:

```
ng
```

Creating an app using the CLI

Now, let's create the Angular application. We will create a new application for each example for the sake of clarity. You can club them into the same application if you feel comfortable. To create an Angular application using the CLI, run the following command in the Terminal:

```
ng new <project-name>
```

Replace project-name with the name of your project; if everything goes well, you should see something similar on your Terminal:

```
installing ng
create .editorconfig
create README.md
create src/app/app.component.css
```

```
create src/app/app.component.html
create src/app/app.component.spec.ts
create src/app/app.component.ts
create src/app/app.module.ts
create src/assets/.gitkeep
create src/environments/environment.prod.ts
create src/environments/environment.ts
create src/favicon.ico
create src/index.html
create src/main.ts
create src/polyfills.ts
create src/styles.css
create src/test.ts
create src/tsconfig.app.json
create src/tsconfig.spec.json
create src/typings.d.ts
create .angular-cli.json
create e2e/app.e2e-spec.ts
create e2e/app.po.ts
create e2e/tsconfig.e2e.json
create .gitignore
create karma.conf.js
create package.json
create protractor.conf.js
create tsconfig.json
create tslint.json
Installing packages for tooling via npm.
Installed packages for tooling via npm.
Project 'project-name' successfully created.
```

If you run into any issues, ensure that you have angular-cli installed as described earlier.

Before we write any code for this application, let's import the stack that we earlier created into the project. Since this is a helper component, I would like to group it along with other helper methods under the `utils` directory in the root of the application.

Creating a stack

Since the code for an Angular application is now in TypeScript, we can further optimize the stack that we created. Using TypeScript makes the code more readable thanks to the `private` variables that can be created in a TypeScript class.

So, our TypeScript-optimized code would look something like the following:

```typescript
export class Stack {
    private wmkey = {};
    private items = new WeakMap();

    constructor() {
        this.items.set(this.wmkey, []);
    }

    push(element) {
        let stack = this.items.get(this.wmkey);
        stack.push(element);
    }

    pop() {
        let stack = this.items.get(this.wmkey);
        return stack.pop();
    }

    peek() {
        let stack = this.items.get(this.wmkey);
        return stack[stack.length - 1];
    }

    clear() {
        this.items.set(this.wmkey, []);
    }

    size() {
        return this.items.get(this.wmkey).length;
    }
}
```

To use the `Stack` created previously, you can simply import the stack into any component and then use it. You can see in the following screenshot that as we made the `WeakMap()` and the key private members of the `Stack` class, they are no longer accessible from outside the class:

```typescript
import { Component } from '@angular/core';
import {Stack} from "./utils/stack";

@Component({
    selector: 'app-root',
    templateUrl: './app.component.html',
    styleUrls: ['./app.component.css']
})
export class AppComponent {
    title = 'app works!';

    constructor(private stack: Stack) {
        this.stack.
    }
}
```

Public methods accessible from the Stack class

Creating a custom back button for a web application

These days, web applications are all about user experience, with flat design and small payloads. Everyone wants their application to be quick and compact. Using the clunky browser back button is slowly becoming a thing of the past. To create a custom **Back** button for our application, we will need to first create an Angular application from the previously installed ng cli client, as follows:

```
ng new back-button
```

Setting up the application and its routing

Now that we have the base code set up, let's list the steps for us to build an app that will enable us to create a custom **Back** button in a browser:

1. Creating states for the application.
2. Recording when the state of the application changes.
3. Detecting a click on our custom **Back** button.
4. Updating the list of the states that are being tracked.

Let's quickly add a few states to the application, which are also known as routes in Angular. All SPA frameworks have some form of routing module, which you can use to set up a few routes for your application.

Once we have the routes and the routing set up, we will end up with a directory structure, as follows:

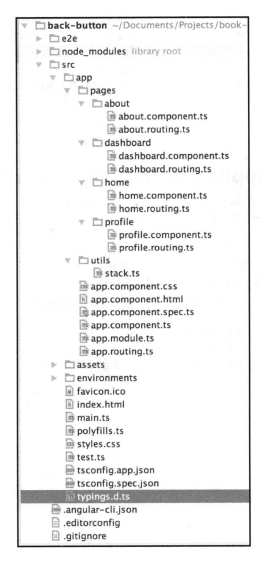

Directory structure after adding routes

Now let's set up the navigation in such a way that we can switch between the routes. To set up routing in an Angular application, you will need to create the component to which you want to route and the declaration of that particular route. So, for instance, your `home.component.ts` would look as follows:

```
import { Component } from '@angular/core';

@Component({
    selector: 'home',
    template: 'home page'
})
export class HomeComponent {

}
```

The `home.routing.ts` file would be as follows:

```
import { HomeComponent } from './home.component';

export const HomeRoutes = [
    { path: 'home', component: HomeComponent },
];

export const HomeComponents = [
    HomeComponent
];
```

We can set up a similar configuration for as many routes as needed, and once it's set up, we will create an app-level file for application routing and inject all the routes and the `navigatableComponents` in that file so that we don't have to touch our main module over and over.

So, your file `app.routing.ts` would look like the following:

```
import { Routes } from '@angular/router';
import {AboutComponents, AboutRoutes} from "./pages/about/about.routing";
import {DashboardComponents, DashboardRoutes} from
"./pages/dashboard/dashboard.routing";
import {HomeComponents, HomeRoutes} from "./pages/home/home.routing";
import {ProfileComponents, ProfileRoutes} from
"./pages/profile/profile.routing";

export const routes: Routes = [
    {
        path: '',
        redirectTo: '/home',
        pathMatch: 'full'
```

```
    },
    ...AboutRoutes,
    ...DashboardRoutes,
    ...HomeRoutes,
    ...ProfileRoutes
];

export const navigatableComponents = [
    ...AboutComponents,
    ...DashboardComponents,
    ...HomeComponents,
    ...ProfileComponents
];
```

You will note that we are doing something particularly interesting here:

```
{
    path: '',
    redirectTo: '/home',
    pathMatch: 'full'
}
```

This is Angular's way of setting default route redirects, so that, when the app loads, it's taken directly to the /home path, and we no longer have to set up the redirects manually.

Detecting application state changes

To detect a state change, we can, luckily, use the Angular router's change event and take actions based on that. So, import the Router module in your app.component.ts and then use that to detect any state change:

```
import { Router, NavigationEnd } from '@angular/router';
import { Stack } from './utils/stack';

...
...

constructor(private stack: Stack, private router: Router) {

    // subscribe to the routers event
    this.router.events.subscribe((val) => {

        // determine of router is telling us that it has ended
        // transition
        if(val instanceof NavigationEnd) {
```

```
            // state change done, add to stack
            this.stack.push(val);
        }
    });
}
```

Any action that the user takes that results in a state change is now being saved into our stack, and we can move on to designing our layout and the back button that transitions the states.

Laying out the UI

We will use angular-material to style the app, as it is quick and reliable. To install angular-material, run the following command:

npm install --save @angular/material @angular/animations @angular/cdk

Once angular-material is saved into the application, we can use the Button component provided to create the UI necessary, which will be fairly straightforward. First, import the MatButtonModule that we want to use for this view and then inject the module as the dependency in your main AppModule.

The final form of app.module.ts would be as follows:

```
import { BrowserModule } from '@angular/platform-browser';
import { NgModule } from '@angular/core';
import { FormsModule } from '@angular/forms';
import { HttpModule } from '@angular/http';
import { BrowserAnimationsModule } from '@angular/platform-
browser/animations';
import { MatButtonModule } from '@angular/material';

import { AppComponent } from './app.component';
import { RouterModule } from "@angular/router";
import { routes, navigatableComponents } from "./app.routing";
import { Stack } from "./utils/stack";

// main angular module
@NgModule({
    declarations: [
        AppComponent,

        // our components are imported here in the main module
        ...navigatableComponents
    ],
```

```
imports: [
    BrowserModule,
    FormsModule,
    HttpModule,

    // our routes are used here
    RouterModule.forRoot(routes),
    BrowserAnimationsModule,

    // material module
    MatButtonModule
],
providers: [
    Stack
],
bootstrap: [AppComponent]
})
export class AppModule { }
```

We will place four buttons at the top to switch between the four states that we have created and then display these states in the `router-outlet` directive provided by Angular followed by the back button. After all this is done, we will get the following result:

```
<nav>
    <button mat-button
        routerLink="/about"
        routerLinkActive="active">
      About
    </button>
    <button mat-button
        routerLink="/dashboard"
        routerLinkActive="active">
      Dashboard
    </button>
    <button mat-button
        routerLink="/home"
        routerLinkActive="active">
      Home
    </button>
    <button mat-button
        routerLink="/profile"
        routerLinkActive="active">
      Profile
    </button>
</nav>

<router-outlet></router-outlet>
```

```
<footer>
    <button mat-fab (click)="goBack()" >Back</button>
</footer>
```

Navigating between states

To add logic to the back button from here on is relatively simpler. When the user clicks on the **Back** button, we will navigate to the previous state of the application from the stack. If the stack was empty when the user clicks the **Back** button, meaning that the user is at the starting state, then we set it back into the stack because we do the pop() operation to determine the current state of the stack.

```
goBack() {
    let current = this.stack.pop();
    let prev = this.stack.peek();

    if (prev) {
        this.stack.pop();

        // angular provides nice little method to
        // transition between the states using just the url if needed.
        this.router.navigateByUrl(prev.urlAfterRedirects);

    } else {
        this.stack.push(current);
    }
}
```

Note here that we are using urlAfterRedirects instead of plain url. This is because we do not care about all the hops a particular URL made before reaching its final form, so we can skip all the redirected paths that it encountered earlier and send the user directly to the final URL after the redirects. All we need is the final state to which we need to navigate our user because that's where they were before navigating to the current state.

Final application logic

So, now our application is ready to go. We have added the logic to stack the states that are being navigated to and we also have the logic for when the user hits the **Back** button. When we put all this logic together in our app.component.ts, we have the following:

```
import {Component, ViewEncapsulation} from '@angular/core';
import {Router, NavigationEnd} from '@angular/router';
import {Stack} from "./utils/stack";
```

```
@Component({
    selector: 'app-root',
    templateUrl: './app.component.html',
    styleUrls: ['./app.component.scss', './theme.scss'],
    encapsulation: ViewEncapsulation.None
})
export class AppComponent {
    constructor(private stack: Stack, private router: Router) {
        this.router.events.subscribe((val) => {
            if(val instanceof NavigationEnd) {
                this.stack.push(val);
            }
        });
    }

    goBack() {
        let current = this.stack.pop();
        let prev = this.stack.peek();

        if (prev) {
            this.stack.pop();
            this.router.navigateByUrl(prev.urlAfterRedirects);
        } else {
            this.stack.push(current);
        }
    }
}
```

We also have some supplementary stylesheets used in the application. These are obvious based on your application and the overall branding of your product; in this case, we are going with something very simple.

For the AppComponent styling, we can add component-specific styles in app.component.scss:

```
.active {
  color: red !important;
}
```

For the overall theme of the application, we add styles to the theme.scss file:

```
@import '~@angular/material/theming';
// Plus imports for other components in your app.

// Include the common styles for Angular Material. We include this here so
that you only
```

```
// have to load a single css file for Angular Material in your app.
// Be sure that you only ever include this mixin once!
@include mat-core();

// Define the palettes for your theme using the Material Design palettes
available in palette.scss
// (imported above). For each palette, you can optionally specify a
default, lighter, and darker
// hue.
$candy-app-primary: mat-palette($mat-indigo);
$candy-app-accent:  mat-palette($mat-pink, A200, A100, A400);

// The warn palette is optional (defaults to red).
$candy-app-warn:    mat-palette($mat-red);

// Create the theme object (a Sass map containing all of the palettes).
$candy-app-theme: mat-light-theme($candy-app-primary, $candy-app-accent,
$candy-app-warn);

// Include theme styles for core and each component used in your app.
// Alternatively, you can import and @include the theme mixins for each
component
// that you are using.
@include angular-material-theme($candy-app-theme);
```

This preceding theme file is taken from the Angular material design documentation and can be changed as per your application's color scheme.

Once we are ready with all our changes, we can run our application by running the following command from the root folder of our application:

ng serve

That should spin up the application, which can be accessed at http://localhost:4200.

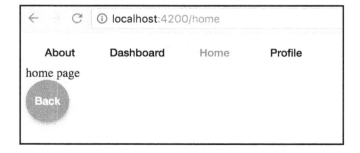

From the preceding screenshot, we can see that the application is up-and-running, and we can navigate between the different states using the **Back** button we just created.

Building part of a basic JavaScript syntax parser and evaluator

The main intent of this application is to show concurrent usage of multiple stacks in a computation-heavy environment. We are going to parse and evaluate expressions and generate their results without having to use the evil eval.

For example, if you want to build your own `plnkr.co` or something similar, you would be required to take steps in a similar direction before understanding more complex parsers and lexers, which are employed in a full-scale online editor.

We will use a similar base project to the one described earlier. To create a new application with angular-cli we will be using the CLI tool we installed earlier. To create the app run the following command in the Terminal:

```
ng new parser
```

Building a basic web worker

Once we have the app created and instantiated, we will create the `worker.js` file first using the following commands from the root of your app:

```
cd src/app
mkdir utils
touch worker.js
```

This will generate the `utils` folder and the `worker.js` file in it.

Note the following two things here:

- It is a simple JS file and not a TypeScript file, even though the entire application is in TypeScript
- It is called `worker.js`, which means that we will be creating a web worker for the parsing and evaluation that we are about to perform

Web workers are used to simulate the concept of **multithreading** in JavaScript, which is usually not the case. Also, since this thread runs in isolation, there is no way for us to provide dependencies to that. This works out very well for us because our main app is only going to accept the user's input and provide it to the worker on every key stroke while it's the responsibility of the worker to evaluate this expression and return the result or the error if necessary.

Since this is an external file and not a standard Angular file, we will have to load it up as an external script so that our application can use it subsequently. To do so, open your .angular-cli.json file and update the scripts option to look as follows:

```
...
"scripts": [
  "app/utils/worker.js"
],
...
```

Now, we will be able to use the injected worker, as follows:

```
this.worker = new Worker('scripts.bundle.js');
```

First, we will add the necessary changes to the app.component.ts file so that it can interact with worker.js as needed.

Laying out the UI

We will use angular-material once more as described in the preceding example. So, install and use the components as you see fit to style your application's UI:

```
npm install --save @angular/material @angular/animations @angular/cdk
```

We will use MatGridListModule to create our application's UI. After importing it in the main module, we can create the template as follows:

```
<mat-grid-list cols="2" rowHeight="2:1">
    <mat-grid-tile>
        <textarea (keyup)="codeChange()" [(ngModel)]="code"></textarea>
    </mat-grid-tile>
    <mat-grid-tile>
        <div>
            Result: {{result}}
        </div>
    </mat-grid-tile>
```

```
</mat-grid-list>
```

We are laying down two tiles; the first one contains the `textarea` to write the code and the second one displays the result generated.

We have bound the input area with `ngModel`, which is going to provide the two-way binding that we need `between` our view and the component. Further, we leverage the `keyup` event to trigger the method called `codeChange()`, which will be responsible for passing our expression into the worker.

The implementation of the `codeChange()` method will be relatively easy.

Basic web worker communication

As the component loads, we will want to set up the worker so that it is not something that we have to repeat several times. So, imagine if there were a way in which you can set up something conditionally and perform an action only when you want it to. In our case, you can add it to the constructor or to any of the lifecycle hooks that denote what phase the component is in such as `OnInit`, OnContentInit, `OnViewInit` and so on, which are provided by Angular as follows:

```
this.worker = new Worker('scripts.bundle.js');

this.worker.addEventListener('message', (e) => {
 this.result = e.data;
});
```

Once initialized, we then use the `addEventListener()` method to listen for any new messages—that is, results coming from our worker.

Any time the code is changed, we simply pass that data to the worker that we have now set up. The implementation for this looks as follows:

```
codeChange() {
    this.worker.postMessage(this.code);
}
```

As you can note, the main application component is intentionally lean. We are leveraging workers for the sole reason that CPU-intensive operations can be kept away from the main thread. In this case, we can move all the logic including the validations into the worker, which is exactly what we have done.

Enabling web worker communications

Now that the app component is set and ready to send messages, the worker needs to be enabled to receive the messages from the main thread. To do that, add the following code to your `worker.js` file:

```
init();

function init() {
    self.addEventListener('message', function(e) {
        var code = e.data;

        if(typeof code !== 'string' || code.match(/.*[a-zA-Z]+.*/g)) {
            respond('Error! Cannot evaluate complex expressions yet. Please
try
            again later');
        } else {
            respond(evaluate(convert(code)));
        }
    });
}
```

As you can see, we added the capability of listening for any message that might be sent to the worker and then the worker simply takes that data and applies some basic validation on it before trying to evaluate and return any value for the expression. In our validation, we simply rejected any characters that are alphabetic because we want our users to only provide valid numbers and operators.

Now, start your application using the following command:

npm start

You should see the app come up at `localhost:4200`. Now, simply enter any code to test your application; for example, enter the following:

```
var a = 100;
```

You would see the following error pop up on the screen:

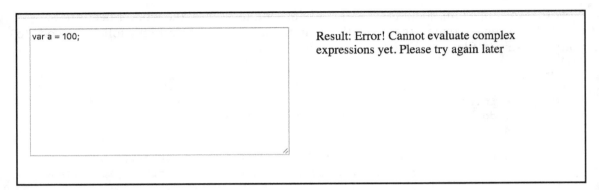

Now, let's get a detailed understanding of the algorithm that is in play. The algorithm will be split into two parts: parsing and evaluation. A step-by-step breakdown of the algorithm would be as follows:

1. Converting input expression to a machine-understandable expression.
2. Evaluating the postfix expression.
3. Returning the expression's value to the parent component.

Transforming input to machine-understandable expression

The input (anything that the user types) will be an expression in the infix notation, which is human-readable. Consider this for example:

```
(1 + 1) * 2
```

However, this is not something that we can evaluate as it is, so we convert it into a postfix notation or reverse polish notation.

To convert an infix to a `postfix` notation is something that takes a little getting used to. What we have is a watered-down version of that algorithm in Wikipedia, as follows:

1. Take the input expression (also known as, the infix expression) and tokenize it, that is, split it.
2. Evaluate each token iteratively, as follows:
   1. Add the token to the output string (also known as the `postfix` notation) if the encountered character is a number
   2. If it is (that is, an opening parenthesis, add it to the output string.
   3. If it is) that is, a closed parenthesis, pop all the operators as far as the previous opening parenthesis into the output string.
   4. If the character is an operator, that is, *, ^, +, –, /, and , then check the precedence of the operator first before popping it out of the stack.
3. Pop all remaining operators in the tokenized list.
4. Return the resultant output string or the `postfix` notation.

Before we translate this into some code, let's briefly talk about the precedence and associativity of the operators, which is something that we need to predefine so that we can use it while we are converting the infix expression to `postfix`.

Precedence, as the name suggests, determines the `priority` of that particular operator whereas associativity dictates whether the expression is evaluated from left to right or vice versa in the absence of a parenthesis. Going by that, since we are only supporting simple operators, let's create a map of operators, their `priority`, and `associativity`:

```
var operators = {
    "^": {
        priority: 4,
        associativity: "rtl" // right to left
    },
    "*": {
        priority: 3,
        associativity: "ltr" // left to right
    },
    "/": {
        priority: 3,
        associativity: "ltr"
    },
    "+": {
        priority: 2,
        associativity: "ltr"
    },
    "-": {
```

```
            priority: 2,
            associativity: "ltr"
        }
    };
```

Now, going by the algorithm, the first step is to tokenize the input string. Consider the following example:

```
(1 + 1) * 2
```

It would be converted as follows:

```
["(", "1", "+", "1", ")", "*", "2"]
```

To achieve this, we basically remove all extra spaces, replace all white spaces with empty strings, and split the remaining string on any of the *, ^, +, -, / operators and remove any occurrences of an empty string.

Since there is no easy way to remove all empty strings "" from an array, we can use a small utility method called clean, which we can create in the same file.

This can be translated into code as follows:

```
function clean(arr) {
    return arr.filter(function(a) {
        return a !== "";
    });
}
```

So, the final expression becomes as follows:

```
expr = clean(expr.trim().replace(/\s+/g, "").split(/([\+\-\*\/\^\(\)])/));
```

Now that we have the input string split, we are ready to analyze each of the tokens to determine what type it is and take action accordingly to add it to the postfix notation output string. This is *Step 2* of the preceding algorithm, and we will use a Stack to make our code more readable. Let's include the stack into our worker, as it cannot access the outside world. We simply convert our stack to ES5 code, which would look as follows:

```
var Stack = (function () {
    var wmkey = {};
    var items = new WeakMap();

    items.set(wmkey, []);

    function Stack() { }
    Stack.prototype.push = function (element) {
```

```
      var stack = items.get(wmkey);
      stack.push(element);
   };
   Stack.prototype.pop = function () {
      var stack = items.get(wmkey);
      return stack.pop();
   };
   Stack.prototype.peek = function () {
      var stack = items.get(wmkey);
      return stack[stack.length - 1];
   };
   Stack.prototype.clear = function () {
      items.set(wmkey, []);
   };
   Stack.prototype.size = function () {
      return items.get(wmkey).length;
   };
   return Stack;
}());
```

As you can see, the methods are attached to the prototype and voilà we have our stack ready.

Now, let's consume this stack in the infix to postfix conversion. Before we do the conversion, we will want to check that the user-entered input is valid, that is, we want to check that the parentheses are balanced. We will be using the simple isBalanced() method as described in the following code, and if it is not balanced we will return an error:

```
function isBalanced(postfix) {
   var count = 0;
   postfix.forEach(function(op) {
      if (op === ')') {
         count++
      } else if (op === '(') {
         count --
      }
   });

   return count === 0;
}
```

We are going to need the stack to hold the operators that we are encountering so that we can rearrange them in the `postfix` string based on their `priority` and `associativity`. The first thing we will need to do is check whether the token encountered is a number; if it is, then we append it to the `postfix` result:

```
expr.forEach(function(exp) {
    if(!isNaN(parseFloat(exp))) {
        postfix += exp + " ";
    }
});
```

Then, we check whether the encountered token is an open bracket, and if it is, then we push it to the operators' stack waiting for the closing bracket. Once the closing bracket is encountered, we group everything (operators and numbers) in between and pop into the `postfix` output, as follows:

```
expr.forEach(function(exp) {
    if(!isNaN(parseFloat(exp))) {
        postfix += exp + " ";
    } else if(exp === "(") {
        ops.push(exp);
    } else if(exp === ")") {
        while(ops.peek() !== "(") {
            postfix += ops.pop() + " ";
        }
        ops.pop();
    }
});
```

The last (and a slightly complex) step is to determine whether the token is one of *, ^, +, −, /, and then we check the `associativity` of the current operator first. When it's left to right, we check to make sure that the priority of the current operator is *less than or equal* to the priority of the previous operator. When it's right to left, we check whether the priority of the current operator is *strictly less* than the priority of the previous operator. If any of these conditions are satisfied, we pop the operators until the conditions fail, append them to the `postfix` output string, and then add the current operator to the operators' stack for the next iteration.

The reason why we do a strict check for a right to left but not for a left to right `associativity` is that we have multiple operators of that `associativity` with the same `priority`.

After this, if any other operators are remaining, we then add them to the `postfix` output string.

Converting infix to postfix expressions

Putting together all the code discussed above, the final code for converting the infix expression to `postfix` looks like the following:

```
function convert(expr) {
    var postfix = "";
    var ops = new Stack();
    var operators = {
        "^": {
            priority: 4,
            associativity: "rtl"
        },
        "*": {
            priority: 3,
            associativity: "ltr"
        },
        "/": {
            priority: 3,
            associativity: "ltr"
        },
        "+": {
            priority: 2,
            associativity: "ltr"
        },
        "-": {
            priority: 2,
            associativity: "ltr"
        }
    };


    expr = clean(expr.trim().replace(/\s+/g, "").split(/([\+\-
\*\/\^\(\)])/));

    if (!isBalanced(expr) {
        return 'error';
    }

    expr.forEach(function(exp) {
        if(!isNaN(parseFloat(exp))) {
            postfix += exp + " ";
        } else if(exp === "(") {
            ops.push(exp);
        } else if(exp === ")") {
            while(ops.peek() !== "(") {
                postfix += ops.pop() + " ";
```

```
            }
            ops.pop();
        } else if("*^+-/".indexOf(exp) !== -1) {
            var currOp = exp;
            var prevOp = ops.peek();
            while("*^+-/".indexOf(prevOp) !== -1 &&
((operators[currOp].associativity === "ltr" && operators[currOp].priority
<= operators[prevOp].priority) || (operators[currOp].associativity ===
"rtl" && operators[currOp].priority < operators[prevOp].priority)))
            {
                postfix += ops.pop() + " ";
                prevOp = ops.peek();
            }
            ops.push(currOp);
        }
    });
    while(ops.size() > 0) {
        postfix += ops.pop() + " ";
    }
    return postfix;
}
```

This converts the infix operator provided into the `postfix` notation.

Evaluating postfix expressions

From here on, executing this `postfix` notation is fairly easy. The algorithm is relatively straightforward; you pop out each of the operators onto a final result stack. If the operator is one of *, ^, +, −, /, then evaluate it accordingly; otherwise, keep appending it to the output string:

```
function evaluate(postfix) {
    var resultStack = new Stack();
    postfix = clean(postfix.trim().split(" "));
    postfix.forEach(function (op) {
        if(!isNaN(parseFloat(op))) {
            resultStack.push(op);
        } else {
            var val1 = resultStack.pop();
            var val2 = resultStack.pop();
            var parseMethodA = getParseMethod(val1);
            var parseMethodB = getParseMethod(val2);
            if(op === "+") {
                resultStack.push(parseMethodA(val1) + parseMethodB(val2));
            } else if(op === "-") {
                resultStack.push(parseMethodB(val2) - parseMethodA(val1));
```

```
        } else if(op === "*") {
            resultStack.push(parseMethodA(val1) * parseMethodB(val2));
        } else if(op === "/") {
            resultStack.push(parseMethodB(val2) / parseMethodA(val1));
        } else if(op === "^") {
            resultStack.push(Math.pow(parseMethodB(val2),
            parseMethodA(val1)));
        }
    }
});

if (resultStack.size() > 1) {
    return "error";
} else {
    return resultStack.pop();
}
}
```

Here, we use some helper methods such as getParseMethod() to determine whether we are dealing with an integer or float so that we do not round any number unnecessarily.

Now, all we need to do is to instruct our worker to return the data result that it has just calculated. This is done in the same way as the error message that we return, so our init() method changes as follows:

```
function init() {
    self.addEventListener('message', function(e) {
        var code = e.data;

        if(code.match(/.*[a-zA-Z]+.*/g)) {
            respond('Error! Cannot evaluate complex expressions yet. Please
try
            again later');
        } else {
            respond(evaluate(convert(code)));
        }
    });
}
```

Summary

There we have it, real-world web examples using stacks. The important thing to note in both examples is that the majority of the logic as expected does not revolve around the data structure itself. It is a supplementary component, that greatly simplifies access and protects your data from unintentional code smells and bugs.

In this chapter, we covered the basics of why we need a specific stack data structure instead of in-built arrays, simplifying our code using the said data structure, and noted the applications of the data structure. This is just the exciting beginning, and there is a lot more to come.

In the next chapter, we will explore the **queues** data structure along the same lines and analyze some additional performance metrics to check whether it's worth the hassle to build and/or use custom data structures.

2
Creating Queues for In-Order Executions

A queue is a programming construct that bears a heavy resemblance to real-world queues, for example, a queue at the movie theater, ATMs, or the bank. Queues, as opposed to stacks, are **first-in first-out** (**FIFO**), so whatever goes in first comes out first as well. This is especially helpful when you would like to maintain data in the same sequence in which it flows in.

A more computer/scientific definition of a queue would be as follows:

An abstract data collection in which the elements can be added to the back called enqueue and removed from the front called dequeue which makes it a FIFO data structure.

Of course, having only *enqueue* and *dequeue* operations may be enough for the majority of cases to cover a wider spectrum of issues that we may encounter; however, we can expand the API and make our queue future-proof.

In this chapter, we will discuss the following topics:

- Types of queue
- Implementation of different types of queue
- Use cases showing the usefulness of queues
- Performance of queues as compared to other native data structures

Types of queue

Before we begin understanding queues, let's quickly take a look at the types of queues that we may want to use in our applications:

- **Simple queue**: In a simple FIFO queue, the order is retained and data leaves in the same order in which it comes in
- **Priority queue**: A queue in which the elements are given a predefined priority
- **Circular queue**: Similar to a simple queue, except that the back of the queue is followed by the front of the queue
- **Double ended queue** (**Dequeue**): Similar to the simple queue but can add or remove elements from either the front or the back of the queue

Implementing APIs

Implementing an API is never as easy as it seems, as discussed earlier. When making generic classes, we can never predict what kinds of a situation our queue is going to be used in. With that in mind, let's create a very generic API for our queue and expand it in future as we see fit. Some of the most common operations that we can add to the queue are as follows:

- `add()`: Pushes an item to the back of the queue
- `remove()`: Removes an item from the start of the queue
- `peek()`: Shows the last item added to the queue
- `front()`: Returns the item at the front of the queue
- `clear()`: Empties the queue
- `size()`: Gets the current size of the queue

Creating a queue

Of the four types of the queue that we have discussed earlier, first, we will implement a simple queue and then move on to modify it for each type of the subsequent queue.

A simple queue

Similar to a stack, we will create a queue using the following steps:

1. Define a `constructor()`:

```
class Queue {
    constructor() {
    }
}
```

2. We will be using `WeakMap()` for in-memory data storage just like we did for stacks:

```
const qKey = {};
const items = new WeakMap();

class Queue {
    constructor() {
    }
}
```

3. Implement the methods described previously in the API:

```
var Queue = (() => {
const qKey = {};
const items = new WeakMap();

class Queue {

    constructor() {
        items.set(qKey, []);
    }

    add(element) {
        let queue = items.get(qKey);
        queue.push(element);
    }

    remove() {
        let queue = items.get(qKey);
        return queue.shift();
    }

    peek() {
        let queue = items.get(qKey);
        return queue[queue.length - 1];
```

```
        }

        front() {
            let queue = items.get(qKey);
            return queue[0];
        }

        clear() {
            items.set(qKey, []);
        }

        size() {
            return items.get(qKey).length;
        }
    }

    return Queue;
})();
```

We have again wrapped the entire class inside an IIFE because we don't want to make ;Queue items accessible from the outside:

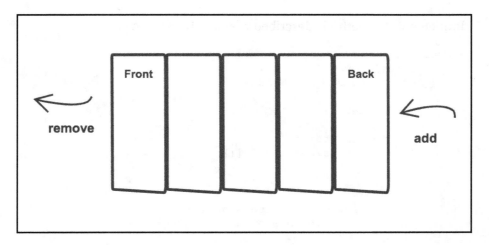

Testing the queue

To test this queue, you can simply instantiate it and add/remove some items to/from the queue:

```
var simpleQueue = new Queue();
simpleQueue.add(10);
```

```
simpleQueue.add(20);

console.log(simpleQueue.items); // prints undefined

console.log(simpleQueue.size()); // prints 2

console.log(simpleQueue.remove()); // prints 10

console.log(simpleQueue.size()); // prints 1

simpleQueue.clear();

console.log(simpleQueue.size()); // prints 0
```

As you can note from the preceding code, all elements are treated the same. Irrespective of the data that they contain, elements are always treated in a FIFO fashion. Although that is a good approach, sometimes we may need something more: the ability to prioritize elements that are coming in and leaving the queue, as we can note in the next section.

Priority Queue

A priority queue is operationally similar the simple queues, that is, they support the same API, but there is a small addition to the data that they hold. Along with the element (your data), they can also persist a priority, which is just a numerical value indicating the priority of your element in the queue.

Addition or removal of these elements from the queue is based on priority. You can either have a minimum priority queue or a maximum priority queue, to help establish whether you are adding elements based on increasing priority or decreasing priority. We will take a look at how the add() method can substitute the add() method of the simple queue that we defined earlier:

```
add(newEl) {
    let queue = items.get(pqkey);
    let newElPosition = queue.length;

    if(!queue.length) {
        queue.push(newEl);
        return;
    }

    for (let [i,v] of queue.entries()) {
        if(newEl.priority > v.priority) {
            newElPosition = i;
```

```
                    break;
            }
        }

    queue.splice(newElPosition, 0, newEl);
}
```

Since we are accounting for the priority of the elements while they are being inserted into the stack, we do not have to concern ourselves with priority while we remove elements from the queue, so the `remove()` method is the same for both simple and priority queues. Other utility methods, such as `front()`, `clear()`, `peek()`, and `size()`, have no correlation with the type of data that is being saved in the queue, so they remain unchanged as well.

 A smart move while creating a priority queue would be to optimize your code and decide whether you would like to determine the priority at the time of addition or removal. That way, you are not overcalculating or analyzing your dataset at each step.

Testing a priority queue

Let's first set up the data for testing the queue:

```
var priorityQueue = new PriorityQueue();

priorityQueue.add({ el : 1, priority: 1});

// state of Queue
// [1]
//  ^

priorityQueue.add({ el : 2, priority: 2});

// state of Queue
// [2, 1]
//  ^

priorityQueue.add({ el : 3, priority: 3});

// state of Queue
// [3, 2, 1]
//  ^

priorityQueue.add({ el : 4, priority: 3});
```

```
// state of Queue
// [3, 4, 2, 1]
//       ^

priorityQueue.add({ el : 5, priority: 2});

// state of Queue
// [3, 4, 2, 5, 1]
//          ^
```

Visually, the preceding steps would generate a queue that looks like the following:

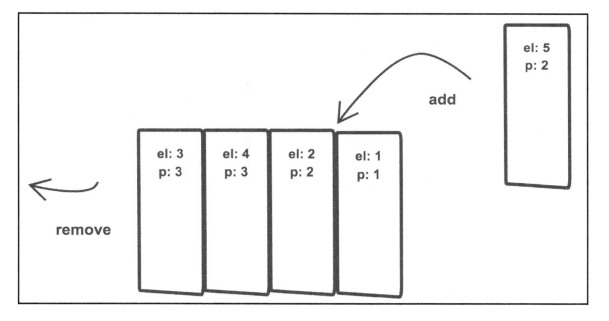

From the preceding figure, we can note how when we add an element with a priority **2** it gets placed ahead of all the elements with priority **1**:

```
priorityQueue.add({ el : 6, priority: 1});

// state of Queue
// [3, 4, 2, 5, 1, 6]
//                 ^
```

And when we add an element with priority 1 (lowest) it gets added to the end of the queue:

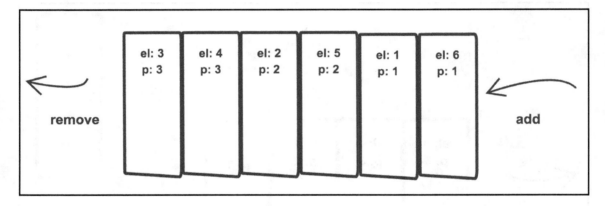

The last element that we add here happens to be the one with the lowest priority as well, which makes it the last element of the queue, thus keeping all the elements ordered based on priority.

Now, let's remove elements from the queue:

```
console.log(priorityQueue.remove());

// prints { el: 3, priority: 3}

// state of Queue
// [4, 2, 5, 1, 6]

console.log(priorityQueue.remove());

// prints { el: 4, priority: 3 }

// state of Queue
// [2, 5, 1, 6]
```

```
console.log(priorityQueue.remove());

// prints { el: 2, priority: 2 }

// state of Queue
// [5, 1, 6]

priorityQueue.print();

// prints { el: 5, priority: 2 } { el: 1, priority: 1 } { el: 6, priority:
1 }
```

There we have it: the creation of simple and priority queues in JavaScript using `WeakMap()`. Let's now take a look at some of the practical applications of these queues.

Use cases for queues

Before we start off with use cases, we will need a base starting point in the form of a Node.js application. To create one, ensure that you have the latest Node.js installed:

node -v

This should show you your currently installed Node.js version; if it does not, then download and install the latest version of Node.js from `https://nodejs.org/en`.

Creating a Node.js application

To start off a sample Node.js project, simply create a project folder first and then run the following command from that folder:

npm init

On running this command, Node will prompt you with a series of questions, which you can either fill or leave blank:

```
Kashyaps-MacBook-Pro:chat kashyapmukkamala$ npm init
This utility will walk you through creating a package.json file.
It only covers the most common items, and tries to guess sensible defaults.

See `npm help json` for definitive documentation on these fields
and exactly what they do.

Use `npm install <pkg> --save` afterwards to install a package and
save it as a dependency in the package.json file.

Press ^C at any time to quit.
name: (chat)
version: (1.0.0)
description: simple chat application
entry point: (index.js)
test command:
git repository:
keywords:
author:
license: (ISC)
About to write to /Users/kashyapmukkamala/Documents/Projects/book-examples/queues/chat/package.json:

{
  "name": "chat",
  "version": "1.0.0",
  "description": "simple chat application",
  "main": "index.js",
  "scripts": {
    "test": "echo \"Error: no test specified\" && exit 1"
  },
  "author": "",
  "license": "ISC"
}


Is this ok? (yes) yes
Kashyaps-MacBook-Pro:chat kashyapmukkamala$
```

Once the blank application is created, all you see is a file called `package.json`. You can now add the dependencies that are needed to create the Node.js application:

```
npm install body-parser express --save
```

The `body-parser` module helps with parsing of the POST request body, whereas the `express` module helps with the creation of the Node.js server.

Starting the Node.js server

Once we have the application shell created, create a file called `index.js`, which will be the main file of your application; you can call it anything you like, but make sure that you update the `main` property accordingly in your `package.json`.

Now, let's add some code to the `index.js` file to start an express server:

```
var express = require('express');
var app = express();

app.listen(3000, function () {
    console.log('Chat Application listening on port 3000!')
});
```

That's it! The server is now up-and-running on the `3000` port. To test it, just add an empty route to tell you whether your application is up or not:

```
app.get('/', function (req, res) {
    res.status(200).send('OK!')
});
```

You can go to your browser and navigate to `localhost:3000`, and that should show you the server status as `OK!` or give you an error if your server is down.

Creating a chat endpoint

Now that we have the server up and running, we can create an in-memory chat endpoint, which would accept a message from two users and forward it to its intended recipient using a queue while retaining the order.

Before we add the logic, we will need to do some groundwork to set up the application in a modular way. First, let's include the `body-parser` and use it in an express middleware so that we can access the `body` of requests easily. So, the updated `index.js` file looks as follows:

```
var express = require('express');
var app = express();
var bodyParser = require('body-parser');

app.use(bodyParser.json());
app.use(bodyParser.urlencoded({ extended: true }));

app.get('/', function (req, res) {
```

```
        res.status(200).send('OK!')
});

app.listen(3000, function () {
    console.log('Chat Application listening on port 3000!')
});
```

Now, to add the endpoint for the message, we can create a new file called `messages.js` under the `routes` folder to which we can add the basic `post` request:

```
var express = require('express');
var router = express.Router();

router.route('/')
    .post(function(req, res) {
        res.send(`Message received from: ${req.body.from} to
${req.body.to} with message ${req.body.message}`);

});

module.exports = router;
```

Then, we can inject it in our `index.js` and make it a part of our application:

```
var message = require('./routes/messages');

...
...
...

app.use('/message', message);
```

Now, to test this, we can start our server and post a message to `localhost:3000/message` using Postman; then we can see the response posted, as follows:

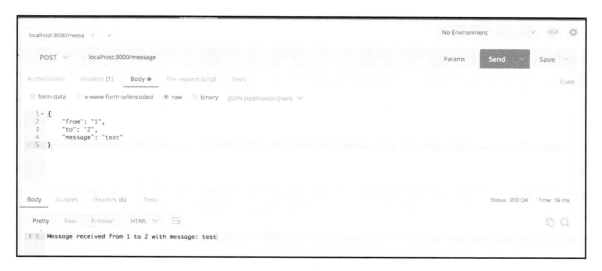

Figure: Sample post message

Now, we can go ahead and start adding the logic to send messages between two users. We are going to abstract, mock, and simplify the chat part of the application and focus more on queue applications in such complex applications.

The workflow itself is relatively straightforward: user A sends a message to user B, which our server tries to forward to user B. If it goes through without any issue, then everything is good, and the message is delivered to user B; but if it fails, then we invoke our `FailureProtocol()`, which retries to send the last failed message per-conversation. For simplicity, we will assume that there is only one channel right now, that is, between user A and user B.

The production counterpart of this would be capable of handling multiple channels simultaneously by creating a new `FailureProtocol()` handler for a particular channel when a message fails on a channel and would have the flexibility of deferring the job over to multiple threads.

Let's now mock out the `sendMessage()` and `getUniqueFailureQueue()` methods in a file called `messaging-utils.js` which will be our wrapper so that we can move them into their own module, as their internal workings are not really important to understand queues in this scenario:

```
var PriorityQueue = require('./priority-queue');

var Utils = (()=> {
    class Utils {
```

```
            constructor() {

            }

            getUniqueFailureQueue(from, to) {
                // use from and to here to determine
                // if a failure queue already
                // exists or create a new one

                return new PriorityQueue();
            }

            sendMessage(message) {
                return new Promise(function(resolve, reject) {
                    // randomize successes and failure of message being
                        sent
                    if(Math.random() < 0.1) {

                        resolve(message)

                    } else {

                        reject(message);

                    }

                });
            }

        }

        return Utils;
    })();

    module.exports = Utils;
```

Now, when we receive a new message, we try to send it to the intended end user:

```
    var express = require('express');
    var router = express.Router();
    var Utils = require('../utils/messaging-utils');
    const msgUtils = new Utils();

    router.route('/')
        .post(function(req, res) {
            const message = req.body.message;
            let failedMessageQueue;
```

```
// try to send the message
msgUtils.sendMessage(req.body)
    .then(function() {

        res.send(`Message received from: ${req.body.from} to
${req.body.to} with message ${req.body.message}`);

    }, function() {

        failedMessageQueue =
            msgUtils.getUniqueFailureQueue(req.body.from,
            req.body.to);

        failedMessageQueue.add(message);

        // trigger failure protocol
        triggerFailureProtocol();

    });
```

If the message is sent successfully, we will need to immediately acknowledge that and send a success message—otherwise, we will get a unique `failedMessageQueue` between the two users—and then add the message to it, which is then followed by triggering the failure protocol.

A failure protocol can mean anything to different applications. While some applications choose to just show a failed message, applications such as ours will retry to send the message until it is sent successfully:

```
function triggerFailureProtocol() {

    var msg = failedMessageQueue.front();

    msgUtils.sendMessage(msg)
        .then(function() {

            failedMessageQueue.remove();

            res.send('OK!');

        }, function(msg) {

            //retry failure protocol
            triggerFailureProtocol();

        });
}
```

We can use the methods available in our Queue to pick the top message and then try to send it. If successful in doing so, then remove it; otherwise, retry. As you can see, using queues greatly simplifies and abstracts the logic of the actual queuing of failed messages and what is even better is that you can upgrade and enhance the queue at any time without having to think twice about what other components would get affected by that change.

Now that we have the API call ready to parse the incoming request, send it to the intended recipient and trigger our custom failure protocol. When we combine all of this logic together, we have the following:

```
var express = require('express');
var router = express.Router();
var Utils = require('../utils/messaging-utils');
const msgUtils = new Utils();

router.route('/')
    .post(function(req, res) {
        const message = req.body.message;
        let failedMessageQueue;

        // try to send the message
        msgUtils.sendMessage(req.body)
            .then(function() {

                console.log("Sent Successfully : " + message);

                res.send(`Message received from: ${req.body.from} to
${req.body.to} with message ${req.body.message}`);

            }, function(msg) {

                console.log('Failed to send: ' + message);

                failedMessageQueue =
                    msgUtils.getUniqueFailureQueue(req.body.from,
                    req.body.to);

                failedMessageQueue.add(message);

                // trigger failure protocol
                triggerFailureProtocol();
            });


        function triggerFailureProtocol() {
```

```
        var msg = failedMessageQueue.front();

    msgUtils.sendMessage(msg)
        .then(function() {

            failedMessageQueue.remove();

            res.send('OK!');

        }, function(msg) {

            //retry failure protocol
            triggerFailureProtocol();

        });
    }
});

module.exports = router;
```

Implementing logging using priority queues

Endpoints fail, it's inevitable. Although we can try to resend failed messages, we need to realize at some point that there is an issue on our end and stop bombarding the server with requests to forward the messages. This is where priority queues can come in handy.

We will replace the existing logic to use a priority queue so that we detect when to stop trying to resend the message and notify the support team instead.

The biggest change is in the triggerFailureProtocol() method where we check whether the message has failed more times than the preset retryThreshold; if it has, then we add the message to the queue with critical priority, which we later use to prevent subsequent bombardment of the server until the support team resolves the issue. This solution although rather naive is very efficient when it comes to preserving server resources.

So, the updated code with the priority queue is as follows:

```
function triggerFailureProtocol() {

    console.log('trigger failure protocol');

    // get front message from queue
    var frontMsgNode = failedMessageQueue.front();
```

```
        // low priority and hasnt hit retry threshold
        if (frontMsgNode.priority === 0
            && failureTriggerCount <= failureTriggerCountThreshold) {

            // try to send message
            msgUtils.sendMessage(frontMsgNode.message)
                .then(function() {

                        console.log('resend success');
                        // success, so remove from queue
                        failedMessageQueue.remove();

                        // inform user
                        res.send('OK!');

                }, function() {

                        console.log('resend failure');
                        // increment counter
                        failureTriggerCount++;

                        //retry failure protocol
                        triggerFailureProtocol();

                });

        } else {

            console.log('resend failed too many times');
            // replace top message with higher priority message
            let prevMsgNode = failedMessageQueue.remove();

            prevMsgNode.priority = 1;

            // gets added to front
            failedMessageQueue.add(prevMsgNode);

            res.status(500).send('Critical Server Error! Failed to send
            message');

        }
    }
```

In the preceding code, we wrapped the same login in an `if-else` block to be able to retry sending the message or create a critical error and stop our retry efforts.

So, the next time a new message for that channel comes in, you can verify that there already exists a critical error and reject the request directly rather than going through the hassle of trying to send the messages and failing, which keeps bloating the failure queue.

This is certainly one approach to solving this problem, but a more suitable approach, which is outside the scope of this example, is to notify the user of any critical errors when the user tries to access the channel rather than doing it when the users posts a message to it.

The following is the complete code including the priority queue:

```
var express = require('express');
var router = express.Router();
var Utils = require('../utils/messaging-utils');
const msgUtils = new Utils();

router.route('/')
    .post(function(req, res) {
        const message = req.body.message;
        let failedMessageQueue;
        let failureTriggerCount = 0;
        let failureTriggerCountThreshold = 3;
        let newMsgNode = {
            message: message,
            priority: 0
        };


        // try to send the message
        msgUtils.sendMessage(req.body)
            .then(function() {
                console.log('send success');

                // success
                res.send(`Message received from: ${req.body.from} to
${req.body.to} with message ${req.body.message}`);

            }, function() {

                console.log('send failed');

                // get unique queue
                failedMessageQueue =
                    msgUtils.getUniqueFailureQueue(req.body.from,
                    req.body.to);

                // get front message in queue
                var frontMsgNode = failedMessageQueue.front();
```

```
                    // already has a critical failure
                    if (frontMsgNode && frontMsgNode.priority === 1) {

                        // notify support

                        // notify user
                        res.status(500)
                            .send('Critical Server Error! Failed to send
                            message');

                    } else {

                        // add more
                        failedMessageQueue.add(newMsgNode);

                        // increment count
                        failureTriggerCount++;

                        // trigger failure protocol
                        triggerFailureProtocol();

                    }
                });


        function triggerFailureProtocol() {

            console.log('trigger failure protocol');

            // get front message from queue
            var frontMsgNode = failedMessageQueue.front();

            // low priority and hasnt hit retry threshold
            if (frontMsgNode.priority === 0
                && failureTriggerCount <= failureTriggerCountThreshold) {

                // try to send message
                msgUtils.sendMessage(frontMsgNode.message)
                    .then(function() {

                        console.log('resend success');
                        // success, so remove from queue
                        failedMessageQueue.remove();

                        // inform user
                        res.send('OK!');

                    }, function() {
```

```
            console.log('resend failure');
            // increment counter
            failureTriggerCount++;

            //retry failure protocol
            triggerFailureProtocol();

         });

    } else {

         console.log('resend failed too many times');
         // replace top message with higher priority message
         let prevMsgNode = failedMessageQueue.remove();

         prevMsgNode.priority = 1;

         // gets added to front
         failedMessageQueue.add(prevMsgNode);

         res.status(500)
            .send('Critical Server Error! Failed to send
            message');

      }
   }
});

module.exports = router;
```

Comparing performance

Earlier, we saw how we can simply swap out a simple queue for a priority queue and not worry about the functional change that it might cause; similarly, we can swap out priority queues for a higher-performant variant of them: circular dequeues.

Before we start working on a comparison, we will need to discuss circular queues and why we need them.

The difference between a circular queue and a simple queue is that the back of the queue is followed by the front of the queue. That being said, they are not functionally different. They still perform the same operations, and produce the same results; you might be wondering where exactly they differ and what's the point if the end result is the same.

In JavaScript arrays, memory locations are contiguous. So, when creating a queue and performing operations such as remove(), we will need to worry about moving the remaining elements to point to the updated *front* instead of *null*, thus increasing the number of operations; it is a memory hit too, unless your queue has an unlimited/dynamic number of slots.

Now, imagine a circular queue—because of its circular nature, this queue has a fixed number of memory locations, and when an element is removed or added, you get to reuse memory locations and reduce the number of operations that are performed, which makes it faster than a regular queue.

Before we can make a similar judgment over the performance of this queue against native arrays in JavaScript, let's take a look under the hood of Chrome's JavaScript engine V8 and check whether it really matters in our case. The reason why we are considering this is because of the frequently overlooked concept of sparse and dense arrays in JavaScript, although this is an under-the-hood implementation and could keep changing every now and then. Most of the time, JavaScript arrays are dense and can easily become sparse if not handled properly. A simple way to test this is to create an array, as follows:

- Consider example 1:

```
const a = [undefined, undefined, 10];
```

When you log it, you see the same:

```
[undefined, undefined, 10];
```

Now, create an array like this:

- Consider example 2:

```
const b = [];
b[3] = 10; // hole as we missed out index 0,1,2
```

When you log it, you get the same result:

```
[undefined x 3, 10];
```

This is interesting, as it shows the difference between the dense (example 1) and sparse (example 2) behavior of JavaScript arrays. When you create these dense arrays, the elements of the array are known to be of specific values, and these values are known at the time of initialization, which gives JavaScript the option of keeping these values in contiguous memory.

The V8 code for the JavaScript array implementation has the following comment, which makes for another interesting observation that is in line with what we have discussed so far

```
// The JSArray describes JavaScript Arrays
// Such an array can be in one of two modes:
//          - fast, backing storage is a FixedArray and length <=
elements.length();
//          Please note: push and pop can be used to grow and shrink the
array.
//          - slow, backing storage is a HashTable with numbers as keys.
class JSArray: public JSObject {
```

So, arrays internally are treated differently based on the type and size of data that is being saved in the array. As a rule of thumb, always create an empty array using an array literal and incrementally assign values to elements starting from the 0 index while leaving no gaps or holes in the array. This keeps the array fast, and it does not go into the dictionary mode unless the sheer size of the data demands it.

A double-ended circular queue, also known as circular dequeue, is also similar to a simple queue, except that the add() and remove() can be done from either the front or the back of the queue.

This is basically the same API as your array, and we can build an example of the class that would provide this functionality, but let's go one better and take a look at how we can implement everything we discussed previously using a circular queue and make it as performant as possible:

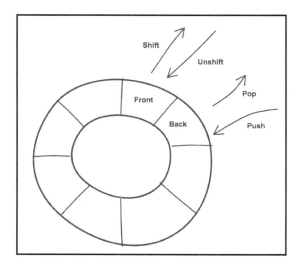

First, we will make an assumption that this queue has a limited size; it can be extended later to be of a dynamic nature, but that's not a concern right now. Until now, `WeakMap()` has been used as the in-memory data store in which we persisted the data necessary for the queue, but when it comes to performance it just adds another layer of retrieval to our data structure, so we will move over to a standard array in this case, as that is what we will be comparing against in our benchmark tests anyway. Translating this into some code, we can get our `CircularDequeue`, as follows:

```
var CircularDequeue = (() => {
    class CircularDequeue {
        constructor() {
            // pseudo realistic 2^x value
            this._size = 1024;
            this._length = 0;
            this._front = 0;
            this._data = [];
        }

        push (item) {
            // get the length of the array
            var length = this._length;

            // calculate the end
            var i = (this._front + length) & (this._size - 1);

            // assign value to the current end of the data
            this._data[i] = item;

            // increment length for quick look up
            this._length = length + 1;

            // return new length
            return this._length;
        }

        pop () {
            // get the length of the array
            var length = this._length;

            // calculate the end
            var i = (this._front + length - 1) & (this._size - 1);

            // copy the value to return
            var ret = this._data[i];

            // remove the value from data
```

```
    this._data[i] = undefined;

    // reduce length for look up
    this._length = length - 1;

    // return value
    return ret;
}

shift () {
    // get the current front of queue
    var front = this._front;

    // capture return value
    var ret = this._data[front];

    // reset value in the data
    this._data[front] = undefined;

    // calculate the new front of the queue
    this._front = (front + 1) & (this._size - 1);

    // reduce the size
    this._length = this._length - 1;

    // return the value
    return ret;

}

unshift (item) {
    // get the size
    var size = this._size;

    // calculate the new front
    var i = (((( this._front - 1 ) & ( size - 1) ) ^ size ) -
    size );

    // add the item
    this._data[i] = item;

    // increment the length
    this._length = this._length + 1;

    // update the new front
    this._front = i;

    // return the acknowledgement of the addition of the new
```

```
                item
                return this._length;
            }
        }

    return CircularDequeue;
})();

module.exports = CircularDequeue;
```

Of course, this is only one way of implementing a circular dequeue; you can get better performance by adding the properties to the class's constructor itself instead of wrapping them inside an IIFE (that is, avoid scope chain lookups) and also further simplify the code if you are using TypeScript, which allows private class members as discussed with stacks.

Running benchmark tests

Before we run the benchmark, it is important to understand our intention of comparing our queue with native arrays. We are not trying to prove that the queue is faster than arrays and that's why we should be using them. At the same time, we do not want to use something, that is ridiculously slow. The goal of these tests is to help us understand where queues lie with respect to native data structures and whether we can rely on them to provide a performant custom data structure if needed.

Now, let's run some benchmark tests to compare a circular dequeue and an array. We will use benchmark.js to set up and run our benchmark tests. The setup is pretty straightforward; we will be comparing the circular dequeue API with a regular array's native operations.

To start with the testing, let's first include the benchmark node module in our project. To install it, run the following command on your Terminal in the project root:

```
npm install benchmark --save-dev
```

Once it is installed, we are ready to create our test suite. Create a tests folder and add a file called benchmark.js under it. To create a test suite, we will first set up the data. As discussed earlier, we will compare our CircularDequeue against an array:

```
var Benchmark = require("benchmark");
var suite = new Benchmark.Suite();
var CircularDequeue = require("../utils/circular-dequeue.js");

var cdQueue = new CircularDequeue();
var array = [];
```

```
for(var i=0; i < 10; i++) {
    cdQueue.push(i);
    array.push(i);
}
```

Here, we start off with a small dataset in both the circular dequeue and array. This will allow the arrays to be dense and thus allow V8 engine will run in fast mode and apply internal optimizations.

Now, we can go ahead and add tests to our testing suite:

```
suite
    .add("circular-queue push", function(){
        cdQueue.push(cdQueue.shift());
    })
    .add("regular array push", function(){
        array.push(array.shift());
    })
    .add("circular-queue pop", function(){
        cdQueue.pop();
    })
    .add("regular array pop", function(){
        array.pop();
    })
    .add("circular-queue unshift", function(){
        cdQueue.unshift(cdQueue.shift());
    })
    .add("regular array unshift", function(){
        array.unshift( array.shift());
    })
    .add("circular-queue shift", function(){
        cdQueue.shift();
    })
    .add("regular array shift", function(){
        array.shift();
    })
    .on("cycle", function(e) {
        console.log("" + e.target);
    })
    .run();
```

One thing to note in the previous tests is that we always couple two operations together, as follows:

```
.add("regular array push", function(){
    array.push(array.shift());
});
```

If we do not do a `shift()` method before doing the `push()` method and push a number instead, for example, 1 or 2, then we will quickly run into an `out of memory` error, as the number of iterations of the tests internally is too large for the arrays to handle; circular queues, on the other hand, will be fine because of their circular nature: they would just overwrite the previous values.

Now, add the test to your `package.json` scripts for an easier access:

```
"scripts": {
    "start": "node index.js",
    "test": "node tests/benchmark.js"
},
```

To run the benchmark test suite, run the following command:

npm run test

The result will be as follows:

```
> node tests/benchmark.js

Running Fast Elements Array
circular-queue push x 49,093,818 ops/sec ±0.83% (90 runs sampled)
regular array push x 42,568,260 ops/sec ±0.93% (90 runs sampled)
circular-queue pop x 67,985,077 ops/sec ±0.87% (88 runs sampled)
regular array pop x 95,477,009 ops/sec ±1.04% (91 runs sampled)
circular-queue unshift x 45,205,363 ops/sec ±1.93% (87 runs sampled)
regular array unshift x 14,003,505 ops/sec ±2.07% (79 runs sampled)
circular-queue shift x 59,707,783 ops/sec ±2.28% (83 runs sampled)
regular array shift x 82,651,984 ops/sec ±2.09% (79 runs sampled)
```

As you can note from the preceding screenshot, the push and the unshift for the circular queues are much faster than the native push and unshift operations, whereas the pop and shift operations are almost 30% slower.

Now, let's make the arrays sparse so that we force V8 to run the array methods in dictionary mode (this can be a real use case for some and also a possibility sometimes when dealing with arrays of mixed data types):

```
var i = 1000;

while(i--){
    cdQueue.push(i);
    array.push(i);
}
```

When we run similar tests but with sparse arrays, the results are as follows:

```
> node tests/benchmark.js

Running Dictionary Mode Array
circular-queue push x 48,317,225 ops/sec ±1.24% (86 runs sampled)
regular array push x 10,610,772 ops/sec ±1.49% (91 runs sampled)
circular-queue pop x 61,889,374 ops/sec ±1.97% (84 runs sampled)
regular array pop x 90,028,316 ops/sec ±1.70% (84 runs sampled)
circular-queue unshift x 45,178,523 ops/sec ±1.29% (83 runs sampled)
regular array unshift x 15,658,060 ops/sec ±1.55% (85 runs sampled)
circular-queue shift x 64,574,793 ops/sec ±1.29% (86 runs sampled)
regular array shift x 91,389,686 ops/sec ±1.36% (85 runs sampled)
```

You can see that the performance greatly varies from that of the fast mode for the push() operation, whereas the other pretty much remains the same. This is a great way to understand the consequences of adopting a particular coding practice. You will need to understand the requirements of your application and pick the right tool for the right job accordingly.

For example, when memory is a priority, we will use the simple queue instead, which works with WeakMap(), instead of regular array. We can create two new tests, which we can run separately to track their individual memory usage:

```
suite
    .add("regular array push", function(){
        array.push(array.shift());
    })
    .on("cycle", function(e) {
        console.log("" + e.target);
        console.log(process.memoryUsage());
    })
    .run();
```

It produces the following result:

```
> node tests/benchmark.js

regular array push x 42,192,977 ops/sec ±1.25% (89 runs sampled)
{ rss: 50614272,
  heapTotal: 33640448,
  heapUsed: 23483576,
  external: 8748 }
```

We can note from the preceding screenshot that it logs the result of our test run, which is the ops/sec, and also logs the total memory usage of that cycle.

Similarly, we can run the benchmark for a `remove` operation on the simple queue, which is very similar to what we did with the shift operation:

```
suite
    .add("simple queue push", function(){
        simpleQueue.add(simpleQueue.remove());
    })
    .on("cycle", function(e) {
        console.log("" + e.target);
        console.log(process.memoryUsage());
    })
    .run();
```

This produces the following result:

```
> node tests/benchmark.js

simple queue push x 10,422,721 ops/sec ±0.62% (91 runs sampled)
{ rss: 50716672,
  heapTotal: 33640448,
  heapUsed: 22201776,
  external: 8748 }
```

You can see that the simple queue is obviously slower than the array by a factor of 4, but what is important here is to note that the `heapUsed` for both scenarios. This is another factor that lets you decide when and how to pick a particular type of data structure.

Summary

With that, we conclude this chapter on queues. We learned about simple, priority, and circular queues and it's double-ended variant. We also learned when to apply them based on use cases and we saw with example, how we can leverage the power of benchmarking any algorithm or data structure as needed. In the next chapter, we will be putting sets, maps, and hashes under the microscope to understand their internal workings and see what situations they can be useful in.

3
Using Sets and Maps for Faster Applications

Sets and **maps** are two notoriously simple-looking data structures, that have been standardized in the latest version of ES6.

In this chapter, we will cover the following topics:

- Why do we need sets and maps?
- When and how to use sets and maps
- ES6 API of sets and maps
- Use cases
- A performance comparison

Exploring the origin of sets and maps

Before we try and understand how to use sets and maps in real-world applications, it is more meaningful to understand the origin of sets and maps and why we need them in JavaScript in the first place.

Traditional arrays, until ES5, did not support a few major features, that developers usually want to leverage:

- Acknowledging that it contains a particular element
- Adding new elements without having duplicates

This led to developers implementing their own versions of sets and maps, which were available in other programming languages. A common implementation of a set and map using JavaScript's `Object` is as follows:

```
// create an empty object
var setOrMap = Object.create(null);

// assign a key and value
setOrMap.someKey = someValue;

// if used as a set, check for existence
if(setOrMap.someKey) {
    // set has someKey
}

// if used as a map, access value
var returnedValue = setOrMap.someKey;
```

Although a lot of prototype headaches can be avoided by using `Object.create` to create the set or map, it still does not resolve the fact that the main `Key` that is being held can only be a `string` because `Object` only allows keys as strings, so we could unintentionally end up with values overwriting each other:

```
// create a new map object
let map = Object.create(null);

// add properties to the new map object
let b = {};
let c = {};
map[b] = 10
map[c] = 20

// log map
Object [object Object]: 20
```

Analyzing set and map types

Before actually using sets and maps, we will need to understand when and where we need to use them. Each data structure whether native or custom has its own strengths and weaknesses.

Not only is it important to utilize these strengths, it's much more important to avoid their weaknesses. To understand some of these, we will explore set and map types and why they are needed and where to employ them.

There are primarily four different set and map types:

- **Map**: A key-value pair in which the key can either be an `Object` or a primitive and can hold any arbitrary value.
- **WeakMap**: A key-value pair in which the key can only be an `Object` and can hold any arbitrary value. The Keys are weakly referenced; this means that they are not prevented from being garbage-collected if not in use.
- **Set**: Data type that allows a user to store unique values of any type.
- **WeakSet**: Similar to set, but maintains a weak reference.

How weak is WeakMap?

By now, we all know what a map is and how to add keys and values, at least in theory. However, how do you determine when to use a map and when to use a `WeakMap`?

Memory management

The official definition of a `WeakMap` as per MDN (https://developer.mozilla.org/en-US/docs/Web/JavaScript/Reference/Global_Objects/WeakMap) is as follows:

> The WeakMap object is a collection of key/value pairs in which the keys are weakly referenced. The keys must be objects and the values can be arbitrary values.

The key emphasis is on *weakly referenced.*

Before comparing `Map` and `WeakMap`, it is crucial to understand when to use a particular data structure. If you need to know the keys of the collection at any time or if you need to iterate over your collection, then you will need to use a `Map` over a `WeakMap` because keys are not enumerable, that is, you cannot get a list of the keys available in the latter, as it only maintains a weak reference.

So, naturally, the preceding statement should raise two questions in your mind:

- What happens if I always use a map?
  - Nothing really, life goes on. You may or may not end up with memory leaks, depending on how well you have used your map. For the most part, you will be fine.
- What is a weak reference?
  - A weak reference is something that allows everything an object refers to be garbage-collected in the event all the referrers are removed. Confused? Good. Let's take a look at the following example to understand it better:

```
var map = new Map();

(function() {
    var key = {}; <- Object

    map.set(key, 10); <- referrer of the Object

    // other logic which uses the map

})(); <- IIFE which is expected to remove the referrer once
executed
```

We all know that the IIFE is primarily used so that we can immediately execute a function and remove its scope so that we can avoid memory leaks. In this case, although we have wrapped the key and map setter in an IIFE, the key does not get garbage-collected because internally the Map still holds a reference to the key and its value:

```
var myWeakMap = new WeakMap();

(function() {
    var key = {};<- Object
    myWeakMap.set(key, 10);<- referrer of the Object
    // other logic which uses the weak map
})(); <- IIFE which is expected to remove the referrer once executed
```

When the same code is written with a WeakMap, once the IIFE is executed, the key and the value of that key are removed from memory because the key is taken out of scope; this helps to keep memory usage to a minimum.

API differences

The API for `Map` and `WeakMap` is very similar when it comes to standard operations, such as `set()` and `get()`. This makes the API very straightforward and contains the following:

- `Map.prototype.size`: Returns the size of the map; not available on typical objects unless you loop and count
- `Map.prototype.set`: Sets a value for a given key and returns the entire new map
- `Map.prototype.get`: Gets a value for a given key and returns undefined if not found
- `Map.prototype.delete`: Deletes a value for a given key and returns `true` if deletion was successful, otherwise `false`
- `Map.prototype.has`: Checks the map for the presence of an element with the key provided; returns boolean
- `Map.prototype.clear`: Clears the map; returns nothing
- `Map.prototype.forEach`: Loops over the map and gives access to each element
- `Map.prototype.entries`: Returns an iterator on which you can apply the `next()` method to get the value of the next element in `Map`, for example, `mapIterator.next().value`
- `Map.prototype.keys`: Similar to `entries`; returns an iterator that can be used to get access to the next value
- `Map.prototype.values`: Similar to `key`; returns access to values

The main difference comes in when accessing anything related to keys and the values for a `WeakMap`. As described earlier, because of the enumeration challenge in case of the `WeakMap`, methods such as `size()`, `forEach()`, `entries()`, `keys()`, and `values()` are not available in `WeakMap`.

Sets versus WeakSets

Now, we understand the fundamental meaning of weak in the term `WeakMap` or `WeakSet`. It is not very complex to predict how sets work and how `WeakSet` differs from them. Let's take a quick look at the functional difference and then move on to the API.

Understanding WeakSets

`WeakSet` is very similar to `WeakMap`; the values that a `WeakSet` can hold are only objects and cannot be primitives just like in the case of a `WeakMap`. The `WeakSet`s are also not enumerable, so you do not have direct access to the values available inside the set.

Let's create a small example and understand the difference between a `Set` and a `WeakSet`:

```
var set = new Set();
var wset = new WeakSet();

(function() {
  var a = {a: 1};
  var b = {b: 2};
  var c = {c: 3};
  var d = {d: 4};
  set.add(1).add(2).add(3).add(4);
  wset.add(a).add(b).add(b).add(d);
})();

console.dir(set);
console.dir(wset);
```

One important thing to note is that `WeakSet` does not accept primitives and can only accept objects similar to the `WeakMap` keys.

The output of the preceding code is as follows, which is what was expected from the `WeakSet`. `WeakSet` does not retain elements beyond the lifespan of the variables that were holding them:

```
▼ Set(4)
    size: (...)
  ▶ __proto__: Set
  ▼ [[Entries]]: Array(4)
    ▶ 0: 1
    ▶ 1: 2
    ▶ 2: 3
    ▶ 3: 4
      length: 4
▼ WeakSet
  ▶ __proto__: WeakSet
  ▼ [[Entries]]: Array(0)
      length: 0
```

As expected, the `WeakSet` is empty once the IIFE is terminated.

The API difference

The API difference as documented in `WeakMap` case of maps is pretty close to what you can find for Sets as well:

- `Set.prototype.size`: Returns the size of the set
- `Set.prototype.add`: Adds a value for a given element and returns the entire new set
- `Set.prototype.delete`: Deletes an element and returns `true` if delete was successful, otherwise `false`
- `Set.prototype.has`: Checks the set for the presence of an element and returns a Boolean
- `Set.prototype.clear`: Clears the set and returns nothing
- `Set.prototype.forEach`: Loops over the set and gives access to each element
- `Set.prototype.values`: Returns an iterator, which can be used to get access to the next value
- `Set.prototype.keys`: Similar to values—returns access to values in the set

`WeakSet`, on the other hand, does not contain the `forEach()`, `keys()`, and `values()` methods for reasons discussed previously.

Use cases

Before we start off with use cases, let's create a base application, that will be reused for each of the examples just like we did in `Chapter 1`, *Building Stacks for Application State Management*.

The following section is a quick recap of creating a base Angular application:

Creating an Angular application

Before moving on to the individual use cases, we will first create the Angular application which will work as the base for our examples.

Follow the given commands to get up and running with the application:

1. Install the Angular CLI:

   ```
   npm install -g @angular/cli
   ```

2. Create a new project in the folder of your choice by running the following command:

   ```
   ng new <project-name>
   ```

3. After these two steps, you should be able to see the new project created and all the corresponding node modules installed and ready to go.
4. To run your application, run the following command from a Terminal:

   ```
   ng serve
   ```

Creating custom keyboard shortcuts for your application

In most cases, creating a web application means having a beautiful UI with unobstructed data. You want your user to have a fluid experience without having to go through the hassle of clicking through multiple pages, which can become quite a hassle sometimes.

Take any IDE, for example. As useful as they are and as easy as they make our lives on a day-to-day basis, imagine not having simple shortcuts in them, such as code indentation. Sorry for the scare, but it is true that having minor details like these can make the user experience very fluid, making users come back for more.

Let's now create a simple set of keyboard shortcuts that you can provide to your application to make things a lot easier for your end user. To create this, you will need the following things:

- A web application (we created one earlier)
- A set of features, which you want to be able to control with the keyboard
- An implementation simple enough to make adding new features to it very simple

If you remember the *custom back button* from `Chapter 1`, *Building Stacks for Application State Management*, we are going to create an application that is something similar. Let's quickly put together the example application again. For detailed instructions, you can follow the same example (Creating an Angular Application) from `Chapter 1`, *Building Stacks for Application State Management*.

Creating an Angular application

1. Create the application:

```
ng new keyboard-shortcuts
```

2. Create multiple states (**About, Dashboard, Home,** and **Profile**) with basic templates under `src/pages` folder:

```
import { Component } from '@angular/core';

@Component({
    selector: 'home',
    template: 'home page'
})
export class HomeComponent {

}
```

3. Create the routing for that state under `<component_name>.routing.ts`:

```
import { HomeComponent } from './home.component';

export const HomeRoutes = [
    { path: 'home', component: HomeComponent },
];

export const HomeComponents = [
    HomeComponent
];
```

4. Add the new `routes` and `Components` to the application's main routing file `app.routing.ts` next to `app.module.ts`:

```
import { Routes } from '@angular/router';
import {AboutComponents, AboutRoutes} from
"./pages/about/about.routing";
import {DashboardComponents, DashboardRoutes} from
```

```
"./pages/dashboard/dashboard.routing";
import {HomeComponents, HomeRoutes} from
"./pages/home/home.routing";
import {ProfileComponents, ProfileRoutes} from
"./pages/profile/profile.routing";

export const routes: Routes = [
    {
        path: '',
        redirectTo: '/home',
        pathMatch: 'full'
    },
    ...AboutRoutes,
    ...DashboardRoutes,
    ...HomeRoutes,
    ...ProfileRoutes
];

export const navigatableComponents = [
    ...AboutComponents,
    ...DashboardComponents,
    ...HomeComponents,
    ...ProfileComponents
];
```

5. Register the routes with your application using `RouterModule` and declare your `navigatableComponents` in the `app.module.ts` file:

```
@NgModule({
    declarations: [
        AppComponent,
        ...navigatableComponents
    ],
    imports: [
        BrowserModule,
        FormsModule,
        RouterModule.forRoot(routes)
    ],
    providers: [],
    bootstrap: [AppComponent]
})
export class AppModule { }
```

6. Create the HTML template to load the four routes in `app.component.html`:

```
<nav>
    <button mat-button
```

```
            routerLink="/about"
            routerLinkActive="active">
        About
    </button>
    <button mat-button
            routerLink="/dashboard"
            routerLinkActive="active">
        Dashboard
    </button>
    <button mat-button
            routerLink="/home"
            routerLinkActive="active">
        Home
    </button>
    <button mat-button
            routerLink="/profile"
            routerLinkActive="active">
        Profile
    </button>
</nav>

<router-outlet></router-outlet>
```

Once you have performed all the steps listed previously, run the following command in your Terminal; the web app should be up-and-running with four states for you to toggle:

```
ng serve
```

Creating states with keymap

So far, what we have declared in the states (or routes) is the path and the component that we want to go with them. What Angular does allow us to do is add a new property called **data** to the route configuration. This allows us to add any data that we would like regarding any route. In our case, it works out very well because we want to be able to toggle routes based on the keys a user presses.

So, let's take an example route that we have defined previously:

```
import { HomeComponent } from './home.component';

export const HomeRoutes = [
  { path: 'home', component: HomeComponent },
];

export const HomeComponents = [
  HomeComponent
```

```
];
```

We will now modify this and add the new `data` property to the route configuration:

```
import { HomeComponent } from './home.component';

export const HomeRoutes = [
  { path: 'home', component: HomeComponent, data: { keymap: 'ctrl+h'} },
];

export const HomeComponents = [
  HomeComponent
];
```

You can see that we have added a property called `keymap` and its value `ctrl+h`; we will do the same for all the other routes defined as well. One important thing to nail down in the very beginning is the anchor key (`ctrl`, in this case) that is going to be used alongside a secondary identifying key (`h` for the home route). This really helps filter down key presses that the user may making within your application.

Once we have the keymaps associated with each of the routes, we can register all of these keymaps when the app loads and then start tracking user activity to determine whether they have selected any of our predefined keymaps.

To register the keymaps, in the `app.component.ts` file, we will first define the `Map` in which we are going to hold all the data and then extract the data from the routes before adding it to `Map`:

```
import {Component} from '@angular/core';
import {Router} from "@angular/router";

@Component({
    selector: 'app-root',
    templateUrl: './app.component.html',
    styleUrls: ['./app.component.scss',  './theme.scss']
})
export class AppComponent {

    // defined the keyMap
    keyMap = new Map();
    constructor(private router: Router) {
        // loop over the router configuration
        this.router.config.forEach((routerConf)=> {
            // extract the keymap
            const keyMap = routerConf.data ? routerConf.data.keymap :
            undefined;
```

```
            // if keymap exists for the route and is not a duplicate,
            add
            // to master list
            if (keyMap && !this.keyMap.has(keyMap)) {
                this.keyMap.set(keyMap, `/${routerConf.path}`);
            }
        })
    }

}
```

Once the data is added to the `keyMap`, we will need to listen to user interactions and determine where the user wants to navigate. To do that, we can use the `@HostListener` decorator provided by Angular, listen for any keypress events, and then filter item down based on the application's requirements, as follows:

```
import {Component, HostListener} from '@angular/core';
import {Router} from "@angular/router";

@Component({
    selector: 'app-root',
    templateUrl: './app.component.html',
    styleUrls: ['./app.component.scss',  './theme.scss']
})
export class AppComponent {

    // defined the keyMap
    keyMap = new Map();

    // add the HostListener
    @HostListener('document:keydown', ['$event'])
    onKeyDown(ev: KeyboardEvent) {
        // filter out all non CTRL key presses and
        // when only CTRL is key press
        if (ev.ctrlKey && ev.keyCode !== 17) {
            // check if user selection is already registered
            if (this.keyMap.has(`ctrl+${ev.key}`)) {

                // extract the registered path
                const path = this.keyMap.get(`ctrl+${ev.key}`);

                // navigate
                this.router.navigateByUrl(path);
            }
        }
    }
}
```

```
constructor(private router: Router) {
    // loop over the router configuration
    this.router.config.forEach((routerConf)=> {

        // extract the keymap
        const keyMap = routerConf.data ? routerConf.data.keymap :
        undefined;

        // if keymap exists for the route and is not a duplicate,
        add
        // to master list
        if (keyMap && !this.keyMap.has(keyMap)) {
            this.keyMap.set(keyMap, `/${routerConf.path}`);
        }
    })
}
}
```

There we have it! We can now define and navigate to routes easily whenever a user makes a keypress. However, before we move on, we will need to take another perspective here to understand the next step. Consider you are the end user and not the developer. How do you know what the bindings are? What do you do when you want to bind not just the routes on a page but also the buttons? How do you know whether you are pressing the wrong keys?

All of this can be fixed with a very simple UX review of what we have so far and what we need instead. One thing that is clear is that we need to show the user what they are selecting so that they do not keep pounding our application with incorrect key combinations.

First, to inform our users of what they can select, let's modify the navigation in such a way that the first character of each of the route names is highlighted. Let's also create a variable to hold the value that the user is selecting, display that on the UI, and clear it out after a few milliseconds.

We can modify our `app.component.scss` to that effect, as follows:

```
.active {
    color: red;
}

nav {
    button {
        &::first-letter {
            font-weight:bold;
            text-decoration: underline;
            font-size: 1.2em;
```

```
        }
      }
  }

.bottom-right {
  position: fixed;
  bottom: 30px;
  right: 30px;
  background: rgba(0,0,0, 0.5);
  color: white;
  padding: 20px;
}
```

Our template gets an addition at the very end to show the key the user has pressed:

```
<nav>
    <button mat-button
            routerLink="/about"
            routerLinkActive="active">
        About
    </button>
    <button mat-button
            routerLink="/dashboard"
            routerLinkActive="active">
        Dashboard
    </button>
    <button mat-button
            routerLink="/home"
            routerLinkActive="active">
        Home
    </button>
    <button mat-button
            routerLink="/profile"
            routerLinkActive="active">
        Profile
    </button>
</nav>

<router-outlet></router-outlet>

<section [class]="keypress? 'bottom-right': ''">
    {{keypress}}
</section>
```

Our app.component.ts in its final form is as follows:

```
import {Component, HostListener} from '@angular/core';
import {Router} from "@angular/router";
```

```
@Component({
    selector: 'app-root',
    templateUrl: './app.component.html',
    styleUrls: ['./app.component.scss',  './theme.scss']
})
export class AppComponent {

    // defined the keyMap
    keyMap = new Map();

    // defined the keypressed
    keypress: string = '';

    // clear timer if needed
    timer: number;

    // add the HostListener
    @HostListener('document:keydown', ['$event'])
    onKeyDown(ev: KeyboardEvent) {

        // filter out all non CTRL key presses and
        // when only CTRL is key press
        if (ev.ctrlKey && ev.keyCode !== 17) {

            // display user selection
            this.highlightKeypress(`ctrl+${ev.key}`);
            // check if user selection is already registered
            if (this.keyMap.has(`ctrl+${ev.key}`)) {

                // extract the registered path
                const path = this.keyMap.get(`ctrl+${ev.key}`);

                // navigate
                this.router.navigateByUrl(path);
            }
        }
    }

    constructor(private router: Router) {
        // loop over the router configuration
        this.router.config.forEach((routerConf)=> {

            // extract the keymap
            const keyMap = routerConf.data ? routerConf.data.keymap :
            undefined;

            // if keymap exists for the route and is not a duplicate,
            add
```

```
                // to master list
                if (keyMap && !this.keyMap.has(keyMap)) {
                    this.keyMap.set(keyMap, `/${routerConf.path}`);
                }
            })
        }

        highlightKeypress(keypress: string) {
            // clear existing timer, if any
            if (this.timer) {
                clearTimeout(this.timer);
            }

            // set the user selection
            this.keypress = keypress;
            // reset user selection
            this.timer = setTimeout(() => {
                this.keypress = '';
            }, 500);
        }

    }
```

This way, the user is always informed of their options and what they are selecting, making the overall usability of your application a lot higher.

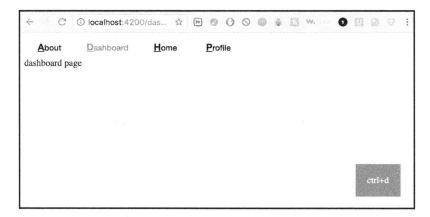

Irrespective of what the user selects, they will always see their selection at the bottom-right side of the screen as long as the *Ctrl* key is pressed.

Activity tracking and analytics for web applications

Whenever someone mentions analytics, especially for web applications, the first thing that usually comes to mind is something such as Google analytics or new relic. Although they do an amazing job at collecting analytics, such as page views and custom events, these tools keep the data with them and do not let you download/export the raw data. It becomes necessary to build your own custom modules to track user actions and activity.

Activity tracking and analytics are complex and can quickly get out of hand with growing application size. In this use case, we will build a simple web application in which we will be tracking custom actions that a user is taking and lay down some groundwork for syncing application data with the server.

Before we jump into coding, let's discuss briefly what our approach is going to be and how we are going to take advantage of the Angular components that are available to us. In our application, we will build a basic form for the user, which they get to fill out and submit. As and when the user interacts with the different components available on the form, we will start tracking the user activity and then extract some custom data based on the events generated. This custom data is obviously going to change based on the application that is being built. For brevity, we will simply track the time of the event, the x and y coordinates, and custom values (if any).

Creating the Angular application

First, let's create an Angular application like we did in the preceding use case:

```
ng new heatmap
```

This should create the app and it should be ready to go. Just go into your project folder and run the following command to see your app running:

```
ng serve
```

Once the application is up, we will include Angular material just so we can quickly have a nice form up and running. To install material in your Angular application, run the following command:

```
npm install --save @angular/material @angular/animations @angular/cdk
```

Once `material` is installed, include the module of your choice in your main `app.module.js`, which, in this case, is going to be `MatInputModule` and `ReactiveFormsModule` because we will need them to create the forms. After this, your `app.module.js` will look something like this:

```
import { BrowserModule } from '@angular/platform-browser';
import { NgModule } from '@angular/core';
import {FormsModule, ReactiveFormsModule} from '@angular/forms';
import {BrowserAnimationsModule} from '@angular/platform-
browser/animations';
import { MatInputModule } from '@angular/material';


import { AppComponent } from './app.component';

@NgModule({
    declarations: [
        AppComponent
    ],
    imports: [
        BrowserModule,
        FormsModule,
        ReactiveFormsModule,
        BrowserAnimationsModule,
        MatInputModule
    ],
    providers: [
    ],
    bootstrap: [AppComponent]
})
export class AppModule { }
```

Now that we have the application set up, we can set up our template, which is going to be fairly straightforward, so let us add the following template to our `app.component.html` file:

```
<form>
    <mat-input-container class="full-width">
        <input matInput placeholder="Company Name">
    </mat-input-container>

    <table class="full-width" cellspacing="0">
        <tr>
            <td>
                <mat-input-container class="full-width">
                    <input matInput placeholder="First Name">
                </mat-input-container>
```

```
                    </td>
                    <td>
                        <mat-input-container class="full-width">
                            <input matInput placeholder="Last Name">
                        </mat-input-container>
                    </td>
                </tr>
            </table>
            <p>
                <mat-input-container class="full-width">
                    <textarea matInput placeholder="Address"></textarea>
                </mat-input-container>
                <mat-input-container class="full-width">
                    <textarea matInput placeholder="Address 2"></textarea>
                </mat-input-container>
            </p>

            <table class="full-width" cellspacing="0">
                <tr>
                    <td>
                        <mat-input-container class="full-width">
                            <input matInput placeholder="City">
                        </mat-input-container>
                    </td>
                    <td>
                        <mat-input-container class="full-width">
                            <input matInput placeholder="State">
                        </mat-input-container>
                    </td>
                    <td>
                        <mat-input-container class="full-width">
                            <input matInput #postalCode maxlength="5"
                            placeholder="Postal Code">
                            <mat-hint align="end">{{postalCode.value.length}} /
5</mat-
                            hint>
                        </mat-input-container>
                    </td>
                </tr>
            </table>
    </form>
```

This is a simple form with standard fields for user details; we will style it a little bit so that it's centered on the page so we can update our `app.component.scss` file to contain our styles:

```
body {
```

```
  position: relative;
}

form {
  position: absolute;
  top: 50%;
  left: 50%;
  transform: translate(-50%, -50%);
}

.full-width {
  width: 100%;
}
```

Here's the end result on the UI:

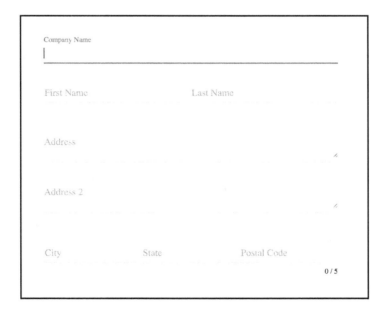

Now that we have the form ready, we want an activity tracker, which is going to be extremely lightweight as we will be calling this quite frequently.

 A good practice is to have the tracker logic moved into a web worker; that way, your tracker will not take up the only available thread, thus freeing up your application from any extra load.

Before we actually start creating a web worker, we will need something to invoke our worker; for this, we will create a tracker service. Also, to make the worker includable in an Angular project, we will add it to the scripts option of the .angular-cli.json file, which will allow us to use this as an external script called scripts.bundle.js which is generated from the file utils/tracker.js by webpack.

Let's create a folder called tracker under a folder called services, then create a tracker.service.ts file:

```
import {Injectable} from '@angular/core';

@Injectable()
export class TrackerService {
    worker: any;

    constructor() {
        this.setupTracker();
    }

    setupTracker () {
        this.worker = new Worker('scripts.bundle.js');
    }

    addEvent(key: string, event: any, customValue ?: string) {
        this.worker.postMessage({
            key: key,
            user: 'user_id_here'
            event: {
                pageX: event.pageX,
                pageY: event.pageY
            },
            customValue : customValue
        });
    }
}
```

Nothing out of the ordinary here; we initialized the worker when we triggered the service and added an addEvent() method, which takes in a few parameters such as the name of the event (key), the event data (or parts of it), and custom values (if any). The rest of the logic we defer to the worker so that our application is seamless.

However, to trigger the constructor of the service, we will need to add the service to the providers of the main module. So, our app.module.ts now updates to the following:

```
....
import {TrackerService} from "./service/tracker/tracker.service";
```

```
@NgModule({
    ....,
    providers: [
        TrackerService
    ],
    bootstrap: [AppComponent]
})
export class AppModule { }
```

Good, we now have the application bootstrapped and the worker set up. However, what is actually calling the addEvent() method to track these custom events? You can do one or both of the following things:

- Inject the TrackerService into your component/service and call the addEvent() method with the right parameters
- Create a directive to capture clicks and sync data using the addEvent() method on the TrackerService

We will take the second approach for this example as we have a form and do not want to add a click handler to each and every element. Let's create a directives folder and another folder called tracker, which will contain our tracker.directive.ts:

```
import {Directive, Input, HostListener} from '@angular/core';
import {TrackerService} from "../../service/tracker/tracker.service";

@Directive({
    selector: '[tracker]',
})
export class tracker {

    @Input('tracker') key: string;

    constructor(private trackerService: TrackerService) {}

    @HostListener('click', ['$event'])
    clicked(ev: MouseEvent) {
        this.trackerService.addEvent(this.key, ev);
    }
}
```

You can see that the directive is pretty lean; it injects the TrackerService and then triggers the addEvent() method on a click.

To consume this, all we need is to add the directive to the input elements on the form that we created earlier, like so:

```
<input matInput placeholder="First Name" tracker="first-name">
```

Now, when the user interacts with any field on the form, our worker is notified of the change, and it's now up to our worker to basically batch the events and save them on the server.

Let's quickly recap what we have done so far:

1. We set up the worker and invoked it via the constructor of our `TrackerService`, which gets instantiated on app start.
2. We created a simple directive capable of detecting clicks, extracting event information, and passing it on to the `TrackerService` to be forwarded to our worker:

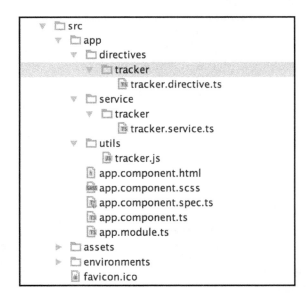

The preceding screenshot shows the directory structure of the application so far.

Our next step will be to update our worker so that we can easily handle the data that is coming in and send it to the server based on whatever logic your application sees fit.

Let's break this worker under `utils/tracker.js` down into simple steps it's made up of:

- The worker receives the message from the `TrackerService`, and this message is then forwarded to be added to the master list of events:

```
var sessionKeys = new Set();
var sessionData = new Map();
var startTime = Date.now();
var endTime;

self.addEventListener('message', function(e) {
 addEvent(e.data);
});
```

We will do something different here by maintaining two lists, one for just the keys that are being saved and another that maps the keys to the collection of data that we are receiving.

- The `addEvent()` method then decomposes the incoming data and stores it in a master list of items being collected to be synced up with the database:

```
function addEvent(data) {
   var key = data.key || '';
   var event = data.event || '';
   var customValue = data.customValue || '';
   var currentOccurrences;
   var newItem = {
      eventX: event.pageX,
      eventY: event.pageY,
      timestamp: Date.now(),
      customValue: customValue ? customValue : ''
   };

   if (sessionKeys.has(key)) {
      currentOccurrences = sessionData.get(key);
      currentOccurrences.push(newItem);

      sessionData.set(key, currentOccurrences);
   } else {
      currentOccurrences = [];
      currentOccurrences.push(newItem);

      sessionKeys.add(key);
      sessionData.set(key, currentOccurrences);
   }
```

```
        if (Math.random() > 0.7) {
            syncWithServer(data.user);
        }
    }
```

We will try to check whether the user has already interacted with the provided key's element. If that's true, we will just append it to the existing collection of events; otherwise, we will create a new one. This check is where we leverage sets and their extremely fast `has()` method, which we will explore in the next section.

Apart from this, the only logic that we will need now is to sync this data with the server based on predetermined logic. As you can see, right now we are just doing this based on a random number but, of course, that is not recommended for a production application. What you can do instead is learn based on how much your user is interacting with the application, and sync accordingly. For some application tracking services, this is way too much, so they go with the simpler approach of either syncing at a regular interval (in the order of a few seconds) or syncing based on the payload size. You can take up any of these approaches as your application demands.

However, once you have that nailed down, everything is pretty straightforward:

```
function syncWithServer(user) {
    endTime = Date.now();

    fakeSyncWithDB({
        startTime: startTime,
        endTime: endTime,
        user: user,
        data: Array.from(sessionData)
    }).then(function () {
        setupTracker();
    });
}

function fakeSyncWithDB(data) {
    //fake sync with DB
    return new Promise(function (resolve, reject) {
        console.dir(data);
        resolve();
    });
}

function setupTracker() {
    startTime = Date.now();
    sessionData.clear();
    sessionKeys.clear();
```

```
}
```

One peculiar thing to note here is the way we are transforming data to an array before we send it to the server. Could we have just passed the entire sessionData here? Perhaps, but it's a Map, which means the data is not accessible as-is and you would have to use .entires() or .values() to get an Iterator Object on which you can iterate to get the data from the map. Having worked with arrays a lot, it may seem a little backward to have to transform data before sending it to the server, but it's well worth the effort given the other benefits that Maps provide to our applications.

Let's now take a look at how it all comes together in our tracker.js file:

```
var sessionKeys = new Set();
var sessionData = new Map();
var startTime = Date.now();
var endTime;

self.addEventListener('message', function(e) {
    addEvent(e.data);
});

function addEvent(data) {
    var key = data.key || '';
    var event = data.event || '';
    var customValue = data.customValue || '';
    var currentOccurrences;
    var newItem = {
        eventX: event.pageX,
        eventY: event.pageY,
        timestamp: Date.now(),
        customValue: customValue ? customValue : ''
    };

    if (sessionKeys.has(key)) {
        currentOccurrences = sessionData.get(key);
        currentOccurrences.push(newItem);

        sessionData.set(key, currentOccurrences);
    } else {
        currentOccurrences = [];

        currentOccurrences.push(newItem);
        sessionKeys.add(key);

        sessionData.set(key, currentOccurrences);
    }
```

```
    if (Math.random() > 0.7) {
        syncWithServer(data.user);
    }
}


function syncWithServer(user) {
    endTime = Date.now();

    fakeSyncWithDB({
        startTime: startTime,
        endTime: endTime,
        user: user,
        data: Array.from(sessionData)
    }).then(function () {
        setupTracker();
    });
}

function fakeSyncWithDB(data) {
    //fake sync with DB
    return new Promise(function (resolve, reject) {
        resolve();
    });
}

function setupTracker() {
    startTime = Date.now();
    sessionData.clear();
    sessionKeys.clear();
}
```

As you can note in the preceding code, sets and maps silently, yet effectively, change how we designed our application. Instead of having a simple array and an object, we will actually get to use some concrete data structures with fixed set of APIs, which allows us to simplify our application logic.

Performance comparison

In this section, we will compare the performance of sets and maps against their counterparts: arrays and objects. As mentioned in earlier chapters, the main goal of doing a comparison is not to know that the data structures are superior to their native counterparts but to understand their limitations and ensure that we make an informed decision when trying to use them.

It's very important to take benchmarks with a grain of salt. Benchmarking tools often use engines such as V8, which are built and optimized to run in a way that is very different from some other web-based engines. This may cause the results to be a little skewed based on the environment in which your application runs.

We will need to do some initial set up to run our performance benchmark. To create a Node.js project, go to a Terminal and run the following command:

```
mkdir performance-sets-maps
```

This will set up an empty directory; now, go into the directory and run the npm initialization command:

```
cd performance-sets-maps
npm init
```

This step will ask you a series of questions, and all of them can be filled out or left blank, as you wish.

Once the project is set up, next we will need the benchmarking tool, which we can install using npm:

```
npm install benchmark --save
```

Now, we are ready to start running some benchmark suites.

Sets and Arrays

Creating and running suites is very easy thanks to the benchmark tool. All we will need is to set up our sets-arr.js file, and we are good-to-go:

```
var Benchmark = require("benchmark");
var suite = new Benchmark.Suite();

var set = new Set();
var arr = [];

for(var i=0; i < 1000; i++) {
    set.add(i);
    arr.push(i);
}

suite
```

```
        .add("array #indexOf", function(){
            arr.indexOf(100) > -1;
        })
        .add("set #has", function(){
            set.has(100);
        })
        .add("array #splice", function(){
            arr.splice(99, 1);
        })
        .add("set #delete", function(){
            set.delete(99);
        })
        .add("array #length", function(){
            arr.length;
        })
        .add("set #size", function(){
            set.size;
        })
        .on("cycle", function(e) {
            console.log("" + e.target);
        })
        .run();
```

You can see that the setup is pretty self-explanatory. Once we create the new `suite`, we set up some data for the initial load and then we can add our tests to the `suite`:

```
var set = new Set();
var arr = [];

for(var i=0; i < 1000; i++) {
    set.add(i);
    arr.push(i);
}
```

To execute this `suite`, you can run the following command from a Terminal:

`node sets-arr.js`

The results of the `suite` are as follows:

```
Kashyaps-MacBook-Pro:performance-sets-maps kashyapmukkamala$ node sets-arr.js
array #indexOf x 12,980,029 ops/sec ±0.85% (87 runs sampled)
set #has x 27,372,744 ops/sec ±0.95% (89 runs sampled)
array #splice x 9,994,447 ops/sec ±0.86% (92 runs sampled)
set #delete x 30,538,077 ops/sec ±1.27% (89 runs sampled)
array #length x 89,741,212 ops/sec ±1.55% (85 runs sampled)
set #size x 58,543,894 ops/sec ±1.32% (84 runs sampled)
Kashyaps-MacBook-Pro:performance-sets-maps kashyapmukkamala$ []
```

Note that the sets are a little faster than the arrays in this setup. Of course, the data that we are using in the tests can also cause variations in the results; you can try this out by switching between the data types that are being stored in the array and the set.

Maps and Objects

We will have a similar setup for Maps and Objects in a file called `maps-obj.js`, which will give us something like the following:

```
var Benchmark = require("benchmark");
var suite = new Benchmark.Suite();

var map = new Map();
var obj = {};

for(var i=0; i < 100; i++) {
    map.set(i, i);
    obj[i] = i;
}


suite
    .add("Object #get", function(){
        obj[19];
    })
    .add("Map #get", function(){
        map.get(19);
    })
    //
    .add("Object #delete", function(){
        delete obj[99];
    })
    .add("Map #delete", function(){
        map.delete(99);
    })
    .add("Object #length", function(){
        Object.keys(obj).length;
    })
    .add("Map #size", function(){
        map.size;
    })
    .on("cycle", function(e) {
        console.log("" + e.target);
    })
    .run();
```

Now, to run this `suite`, run the following command on a Terminal:

```
node maps-obj.js
```

This will give us the following result:

```
Kashyaps-MacBook-Pro:performance-sets-maps kashyapmukkamala$ node maps-obj.js
Object #get x 85,607,409 ops/sec ±1.57% (84 runs sampled)
Map #get x 6,452,224 ops/sec ±0.95% (87 runs sampled)
Object #delete x 19,291,361 ops/sec ±1.10% (86 runs sampled)
Map #delete x 6,353,435 ops/sec ±1.08% (86 runs sampled)
Object #length x 240,602 ops/sec ±1.06% (85 runs sampled)
Map #size x 55,984,048 ops/sec ±1.05% (87 runs sampled)
Kashyaps-MacBook-Pro:performance-sets-maps kashyapmukkamala$ []
```

You can see that the `Object` hugely outperforms the map and is clearly the better of the two here, but it does not provide the syntactical sugar and some features that the map is capable of.

Summary

In this chapter, we delved into sets and maps, their weaker counterparts, and their APIs. Then, we used sets and maps in few real-world examples such as applications with keyboard shortcuts for navigation powered by sets and an application analytics tracker powered by sets and maps. Then, we concluded the chapter with a performance comparison between objects and arrays.

In the next chapter, we will be exploring trees and how we can leverage them to make our web applications faster with reduced code complexity.

4
Using Trees for Faster Lookup and Modifications

Trees are one of the most advanced and complex data structures out there. It opens doors to graph theory, which is used to represent a relationship between objects. The objects can be of any type, and as long as they have an established relationship, it can be represented in the form of a tree.

Although there are tens of trees out there, it is not possible to cover them all in the chapter, so we will take a different approach and learn about trees in a more practical way when we go through the examples, instead of doing it upfront like in previous chapters.

In this chapter, we will be exploring the following topics:

- Creating a base angular application,
- Creating a typeahead lookup component using **trie trees**
- Creating a credit card approval predictor using the ID3 algorithm.

So, let's dig into it.

Creating an Angular application

Before we implement any trees, let's set up a base application, which we can use in our subsequent examples.

Like we did in previous chapters, we will be creating an Angular application using the Angular CLI using the following steps:

1. Install the Angular CLI using the following command (if not done already):

    ```
    npm install -g @angular/cli
    ```

2. Create the new project in the folder of your choice by running the following command:

    ```
    ng new <project-name>
    ```

After these two steps, you should be able to see the new project created and all the corresponding node modules installed and ready to go.

3. To run your application, run the following command from Terminal:

    ```
    ng serve
    ```

Creating a typeahead lookup

Imagine this, you have a form for user signup, and your users have to fill out their information, including their country. Lucky for us, there are only a fixed number of countries, so the user experience around populating and selecting can be made extremely fun and easy rather than having them scroll through hundreds of options.

In this example, we will be creating a trie tree and prepopulating it with a list of all the countries. The users can then type the name of their country and our component will work as a typeahead and show the available options to the user.

Let's now discuss why we need a trie tree. According to Wikipedia, the following is the definition of a simple trie tree:

> *In computer science, a trie, also called digital tree and sometimes radix tree or prefix tree (as they can be searched by prefixes), is a kind of search tree — an ordered tree data structure that is used to store a dynamic set or associate array where the keys are usually strings*

In other words, a trie tree is an optimized search tree where the keys are strings. Let's illustrate this with a simple example:

Let's consider that we have an array of strings:

```
var friends = [ 'ross', 'rachel', 'adam', 'amy', 'joey'];
```

This, when converted into a `trie` tree, would look as follows:

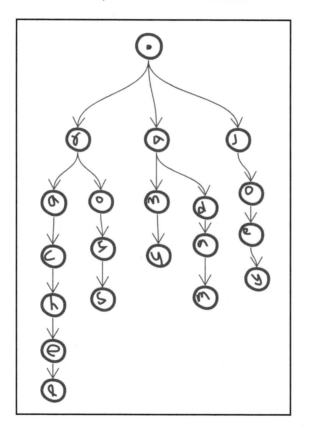

From the preceding diagram, we can note that the tree starts at the root and then, based on the input strings, the tree gets constructed. While inserting the strings into the `trie` tree, the words are broken into individual characters and then the duplicate nodes are not reinserted but rather reused to construct the rest of the tree.

Creating a trie tree

Let's now create the `trie` tree, which we will be using within our application. Within our application, let's first create the directory called `utils` under the `src` folder in which we will be adding our `trie.ts` file.

The API for our tree will be quite concise with only two methods:

- `add()` : Adds elements to the `trie` tree
- `search()` : Accepts an input string and returns the subtree that matches the query string:

```
import {Injectable} from "@angular/core";

@Injectable()
export class Trie {
    tree: any = {};

    constructor() {}

}
```

Once created, let's inject it into the list of providers in our main module listed in `app.module.ts` so that our components have access to the tree, as follows:

```
import { BrowserModule } from '@angular/platform-browser';
import { NgModule } from '@angular/core';
import { FormsModule } from '@angular/forms';

import { AppComponent } from './app.component';
import {Trie} from "./utils/trie";

@NgModule({
  declarations: [
    AppComponent
  ],
  imports: [
    BrowserModule,
    FormsModule
  ],
  providers: [
      Trie
  ],
  bootstrap: [AppComponent]
})
export class AppModule { }
```

Implementing the add() method

Now, our tree is ready to have its first method implemented. Our tree starts off with no elements in it (that is, an empty object). You can use any data structure for your implementation, but we will use objects as our data store for simplicity:

```
add(input) {
    // set to root of tree
    var currentNode = this.tree;

    // init next value
    var nextNode = null;

    // take 1st char and trim input
    // adam for ex becomes a and dam
    var curChar = input.slice(0,1);
    input = input.slice(1);

    // find first new character, until then keep trimming input
    while(currentNode[curChar] && curChar){
        currentNode = currentNode[curChar];

        // trim input
        curChar = input.slice(0,1);
        input = input.slice(1);
    }

    // while next character is available keep adding new branches and
    // prune till end
    while(curChar) {
        // new reference in each loop
        nextNode = {};

        // assign to current tree node
        currentNode[curChar] = nextNode;

        // hold reference for next loop
        currentNode = nextNode;

        // prepare for next iteration
        curChar = input.slice(0,1);
        input = input.slice(1);
    }
}
```

As you can see in the preceding code, this method is made up of the following two steps:

1. Determine what level the tree is already built to and ignore those characters.
2. Add the remainder as a new subtree and continue till the end.

The friends' example

Let's put our knowledge to use in an example in which our user wants to add two elements to this tree, **Adam**, and **Adrian**. First, we will add **Adam** to the tree so we have nodes **a**, **d**, **a**, and **m**. Then, when adding **Adrian**, we check what is already added—**a** and **d**, in this case—and thus the rest of the word **rian** is added as a new subtree.

When logged, the following is what we see:

```
{
    "a": {
        "d": {
            "a": {
                "m": {}
            },
            "r": {
                "i": {
                    "a": {
                        "n": {}
                    }
                }
            }
        }
    }
}
```

As you can see from the preceding screenshot, **a** and **d** are common for both the words and then the rest are two subtrees for each string that we added.

Implementing the search() method

The `search()` method is even simpler and highly efficient with a complexity of O(n), where n is the length of the search input. The big O notation is something that will be covered in detail in a later chapter:

```
search(input) {
    // get the whole tree
    var currentNode = this.tree;
    var curChar = input.slice(0,1);
    // take first character
    input = input.slice(1);

    // keep extracting the sub-tree based on the current character
    while(currentNode[curChar] && curChar){
        currentNode = currentNode[curChar];
        curChar = input.slice(0,1);
        input = input.slice(1);
    }

    // reached the end and no sub-tree found
    // e.g. no data found
    if (curChar && !currentNode[curChar]) {
        return {};
    }

    // return the node found
    return currentNode;
}
```

Let's take the friends example described in the preceding code. If the user types **a**, for example, we extract the subtree using the `search()` method just implemented. We get the subtree below **a**.

The more input character the user provides, the more granular the response object:

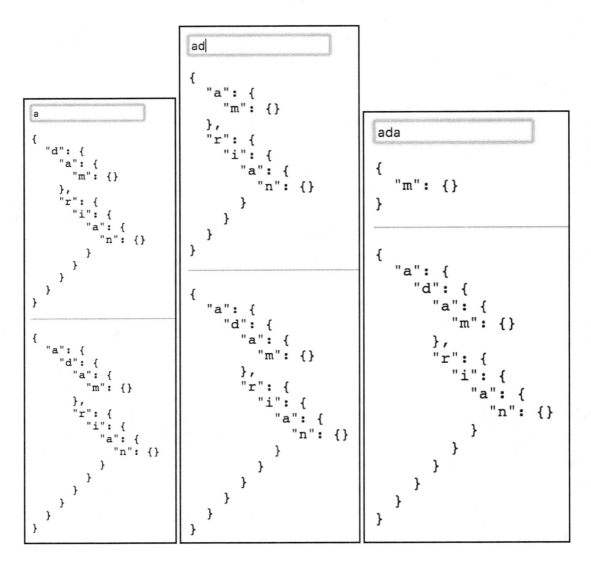

As we can see from the preceding screenshots, as the user types more, our `search()` method keeps returning the sub-tree of the node that matches with it while the entire tree can be seen below it. And to render it on the screen we are using the following code.

In our `app.component.ts` file we add the following, which queries the `search()` method on the `Trie` class:

```
import { Component } from '@angular/core';
import {Trie} from "../utils/trie";

@Component({
    selector: 'app-root',
    templateUrl: './app.component.html',
    styleUrls: ['./app.component.css']
})
export class AppComponent {
    countries =
["Afghanistan","Albania","Algeria",...,"Yemen","Zambia","Zimbabwe"];
    searchResp = [];
    constructor(private trie : Trie) {
        this.countries.forEach((c) => {
            this.trie.add(c);
        });
    }
    search(key) {
        this.searchResp = this.trie.search(key).remainder;
    }
}
```

Then this search result is bound to the template using a simple `pre` tag:

```
<pre>{{searchResp}}</pre>
```

Retaining remainders at nodes

The `search()` method that we implemented earlier works great; however, as a developer, you would now need to loop over the returned sub-tree and construct the remainder of the word out of it to be displayed on the UI. That's kind of a hassle, isn't it? What if we can simplify it so that the tree would return the sub-tree along with the remainder of the words that they form? Actually, it's quite easy to achieve this.

We will need to make a small change to our algorithm and add remainders set at each node; that way, whenever a node is recognized, we can add the remainder to that set and also push new elements into this set while creating new nodes. Let's take a look at how this modifies our code:

```
add(input) {
```

```
    // set to root of tree
    var currentNode = this.tree;

    // init value
    var nextNode = null;

    // take 1st char and trim input
    var curChar = input.slice(0,1);
    input = input.slice(1);

    // find first new character, until then keep triming input
    while(currentNode[curChar] && curChar){
        currentNode = currentNode[curChar];

        // update remainder array, this will exist as we added the node
        earlier
        currentNode.remainder.push(input);

        // trim input
        curChar = input.slice(0,1);
        input = input.slice(1);
    }

    // while next character is available keep adding new branches and
    prune till end
    while(curChar) {
        // new reference in each loop
        // create remainder array starting with current input
        // so when adding the node `a` we add to the remainder `dam`
        and so on
        nextNode = {
            remainder: [input]
        };

        // assign to current tree node
        currentNode[curChar] = nextNode;

        // hold reference for next loop
        currentNode = nextNode;

        // prepare for next iteration
        curChar = input.slice(0,1);
        input = input.slice(1);
    }
}
```

As you can see in the preceding code, adding two lines has made our job a lot easier than earlier. No more unnecessary looping over the subtree objects, and we have the remainder of the words at each node of the sub-tree returned:

```
ad|

{
    "remainder": [
        "am",
        "rian"
    ],
    "a": {
        "remainder": [
            "m"
        ],
        "m": {
            "remainder": [
                ""
            ]
        }
    },
    "r": {
        "remainder": [
            "ian"
        ],
        "i": {
            "remainder": [
                "an"
            ],
            "a": {
                "remainder": [
                    "n"
                ],
                "n": {
                    "remainder": [
                        ""
                    ]
                }
            }
        }
    }
}
```

This would also mean that we have to update our `search()` method's failure condition to return an empty object with a `remainder` set instead of an empty object, unlike earlier:

```
search(input) {
    var currentNode = this.tree;
    var curChar = input.slice(0,1);
```

```
    input = input.slice(1);

    while(currentNode[curChar] && curChar){
        currentNode = currentNode[curChar];
        curChar = input.slice(0,1);
        input = input.slice(1);
    }

    if (curChar && !currentNode[curChar]) {
        return {
            remainder: []
        };
    }

    return currentNode;
}
```

The final form

Putting this all together and adding simple changes to our UI, we can finally search through a list and show the results in a very fast and efficient manner.

With the previous changes incorporated, our `app.component.ts` is ready to take its final form:

```
import { Component } from '@angular/core';
import {Trie} from "../utils/trie";

@Component({
    selector: 'app-root',
    templateUrl: './app.component.html',
    styleUrls: ['./app.component.css']
})
export class AppComponent {
    countries =
["Afghanistan","Albania","Algeria","Andorra","Angola","Anguilla","Antigua &
Barbuda","Argentina","Armenia","Aruba","Australia","Austria","Azerbaijan","
Bahamas","Bahrain","Bangladesh","Barbados","Belarus","Belgium","Belize","Be
nin","Bermuda","Bhutan","Bolivia","Bosnia &
Herzegovina","Botswana","Brazil","British Virgin
Islands","Brunei","Bulgaria","Burkina
Faso","Burundi","Cambodia","Cameroon","Cape Verde","Cayman
Islands","Chad","Chile","China","Colombia","Congo","Cook Islands","Costa
Rica","Cote D Ivoire","Croatia","Cruise Ship","Cuba","Cyprus","Czech
Republic","Denmark","Djibouti","Dominica","Dominican
Republic","Ecuador","Egypt","El Salvador","Equatorial
```

Guinea", "Estonia", "Ethiopia", "Falkland Islands", "Faroe
Islands", "Fiji", "Finland", "France", "French Polynesia", "French West
Indies", "Gabon", "Gambia", "Georgia", "Germany", "Ghana", "Gibraltar", "Greece", "
Greenland", "Grenada", "Guam", "Guatemala", "Guernsey", "Guinea", "Guinea
Bissau", "Guyana", "Haiti", "Honduras", "Hong
Kong", "Hungary", "Iceland", "India", "Indonesia", "Iran", "Iraq", "Ireland", "Isle
of
Man", "Israel", "Italy", "Jamaica", "Japan", "Jersey", "Jordan", "Kazakhstan", "Ken
ya", "Kuwait", "Kyrgyz
Republic", "Laos", "Latvia", "Lebanon", "Lesotho", "Liberia", "Libya", "Liechtenst
ein", "Lithuania", "Luxembourg", "Macau", "Macedonia", "Madagascar", "Malawi", "Ma
laysia", "Maldives", "Mali", "Malta", "Mauritania", "Mauritius", "Mexico", "Moldov
a", "Monaco", "Mongolia", "Montenegro", "Montserrat", "Morocco", "Mozambique", "Na
mibia", "Nepal", "Netherlands", "Netherlands Antilles", "New Caledonia", "New
Zealand", "Nicaragua", "Niger", "Nigeria", "Norway", "Oman", "Pakistan", "Palestin
e", "Panama", "Papua New
Guinea", "Paraguay", "Peru", "Philippines", "Poland", "Portugal", "Puerto
Rico", "Qatar", "Reunion", "Romania", "Russia", "Rwanda", "Saint Pierre &
Miquelon", "Samoa", "San Marino", "Satellite", "Saudi
Arabia", "Senegal", "Serbia", "Seychelles", "Sierra
Leone", "Singapore", "Slovakia", "Slovenia", "South Africa", "South
Korea", "Spain", "Sri Lanka", "St Kitts & Nevis", "St Lucia", "St Vincent", "St.
Lucia", "Sudan", "Suriname", "Swaziland", "Sweden", "Switzerland", "Syria", "Taiwa
n", "Tajikistan", "Tanzania", "Thailand", "Timor
L'Este", "Togo", "Tonga", "Trinidad &
Tobago", "Tunisia", "Turkey", "Turkmenistan", "Turks &
Caicos", "Uganda", "Ukraine", "United Arab Emirates", "United
Kingdom", "Uruguay", "Uzbekistan", "Venezuela", "Vietnam", "Virgin Islands
(US)", "Yemen", "Zambia", "Zimbabwe"];

```
    searchResp = [];
    constructor(private trie : Trie) {
        this.countries.forEach((c) => {
            this.trie.add(c);
        });
    }
    search(key) {
        this.searchResp = this.trie.search(key).remainder;
    }
}
```

Similarly, update the app.component.html template to show the search results:

```html
<input type="text" placeholder="search countries" #searchInp
(keyup)="search(searchInp.value)" />

<div *ngFor="let resp of searchResp">
    <strong>{{searchInp.value}}</strong>{{resp}}
</div>
```

```
<div *ngIf="searchInp.value && !searchResp.length">
    No results found for {{searchInp.value}}
</div>
```

The result is as follows:

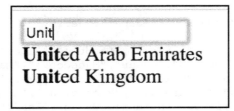

Creating a credit card approval predictor

Trees are ubiquitous. No matter what application you are using, chances are that there are trees in play internally. Having said that, not all trees are data structures. In this example, we will explore something different, which is a really popular but not a typical data structure, that is, a decision tree.

At some stage, you would have come across some sort of an automatic prediction system. Whether it is a sports website that predicts the winner of a game or credit scoring websites that tell you which credit card you should apply for to get a quick approval. In this example, we will go with a credit card approval predictor, but this can be easily transferred to any application of your choice.

In a majority of the cases, we have a complex Machine Learning model running behind the scenes to generate an accurate prediction, but, because we know that the number of factors affecting the approval or rejection is finite, we can use a decision tree to determine the chances of approval based on the past patterns exhibited. The following is the list of tasks that we will have to achieve in this example:

1. Creating the decision tree by implementing **Iterative Dichotomiser 3 (ID3)** algorithm to classify future samples.
2. Creating a training dataset.
3. Running new inputs through the algorithm and validating responses.

ID3 algorithm

So far, the algorithms that we have seen were not very complex; they were rather trivial, and most of our focus was on implementing the API for a particular data structure. In this example, there is no data structure to implement; the algorithm itself generates the decision tree that we would be using for our application.

First, let's take a look at how a table of historical data can be converted into a decision tree. The tree that is formed primarily is made up of **decision nodes** (which indicate a decision) and **leaf nodes** (which indicates the final response, such as yes or no). The decision nodes can have two or more subnodes, depending on the dataset. However, the tree has to start from somewhere, right? What would be the root node and how do we get it?

To determine the root node, we will first need to know some basics of Information Theory here:

- **Entropy**: Entropy is the measure of uncertainty of a series of inputs—the more uncertain the number of input messages, the more inputs are needed to determine what the message is; for example, if our input series always sends the same message, there is no uncertainty, and thus the entropy is zero. Such an input series is also known as pure. However, if the same series sends n different types of inputs with the same probability, then the entropy becomes high and the receiver needs to ask $\log_2 n$ Boolean questions to determine the message. The average number of bits needed to identify a message is a measure of the sender's entropy.

- **Information gain**: To determine the root node, first we will need to split the dataset based on the attributes provided, and then determine the entropy at each attribute, the difference of entropy at each attribute and that of the target determines the information gain or loss of each attribute.

The attribute with the highest information gain becomes the root attribute. Then, we repeat the process for each subtree until we get no entropy. Let's take a look at this with an example and then start off with the code.

For the following example, we will take a simple input and popular dataset to decide whether a game is going to be played or not based on the weather conditions:

Outlook	Temperature	Humidity	Wind	Play Soccer
Sunny	Hot	High	Weak	No
Sunny	Hot	High	Strong	No
Overcast	Hot	High	Weak	Yes
Rain	Mild	High	Weak	Yes
Rain	Cool	Normal	Weak	Yes
Sunny	Cool	Normal	Weak	Yes
Rain	Mild	Normal	Weak	Yes
Sunny	Mild	Normal	Strong	Yes
Overcast	Mild	High	Strong	Yes
Overcast	Hot	Normal	Weak	Yes
Rain	Cool	Normal	Strong	No
Overcast	Cool	Normal	Strong	Yes
Sunny	Mild	High	Weak	No

In the preceding example, the target is the *Play Soccer* attribute. Let's assume that our input source has a capability of sending n messages and the probability of sending each message is P_n, then the entropy of the source is the summation over n of the probabilities $E = -p_i * log_2(p_i)$.

Calculating target entropy

Since we have two possible outputs for the *Play Soccer* (target) attribute, we will calculate the entropy using the frequency table (indicating how many times a particular value was received) of the target attribute:

The probability of receiving yes is the total times it was received divided by the total number of messages received and so on.

Play Soccer	
Yes	No
9	4

So, the entropy of the target would be as follows:

```
targetEntropy =  -( (9/13) log₂ (9/13) ) - ( (4/13) log₂ (4/13) );
targetEntropy = 0.89049164021;
```

Calculating branch entropy

Now, let's break the dataset down further and calculate the entropy based on each branch. We have the following four main branches here:

- Outlook
- Temperature
- Humidity
- Wind

Let's first start with the branch for Outlook:

		Play		
		Yes	No	Total
Outlook	Sunny	2	3	5
	Overcast	4	0	4
	Rain	3	1	4
				13

To calculate the entropy of the branch, we will first calculate the probability of each sub-branch and then multiply it with the entropy of that branch. We will then add the resultant entropy for each sub-branch to get the total entropy of the branch; then, we can calculate the information gain for the branch:

*P(Play, Outlook) = P(Outcast) * E(4,0) + P(Sunny) * E(2,3) + P(Rain) * E(3,1)*

$$= (4/13) * 0 + (5/13) * 0.970 + (4/13) * 0.811$$

$$= 0.62261538461$$

So, *the total Information gain for Outlook branch = targetEntropy - branchEntropy*

$$= 0.89049164021 - 0.62261538461$$

$$= 0.2678762556 \ or \ \mathbf{0.27}$$

The final information gain per branch

Now, we can calculate the entropy of all the branches using a frequency table of two attributes for the rest of the columns, similar to what we did for Outlook, and get the following result:

For the branch Humidity, there are two possible sub-branches, which have the following results breakup:

		yes	no	total
Humidity	high	3	3	6
	normal	6	1	7
				13

Similarly, for Wind, the breakup is as follows:

		yes	no	total
Wind	weak	6	2	8
	strong	3	2	5
				13

For Temperature, it is as follows:

		yes	no	total
Temperature	Hot	2	2	4
	Mild	4	1	5
	Cool	3	1	4
				13

We calculate the *branchEntropy* and the *Information gain* for each branch, and here are the results following similar steps as we did for the Outlook branch:

	Outlook	Temperature	Humidity	Wind
Gain	0.27	0.055510642	0.110360144	0.017801027

Since Outlook has the highest information gain, we can make it the root decision node and split the tree based on its branches and then recursively continue the process until we get all the leaf nodes, for example, entropy 0.

With the root node selected, our input data looks as follows from left to right:

	Overcast	Hot	High	Weak	Yes
	Overcast	Mild	High	Strong	Yes
	Overcast	Hot	Normal	Weak	Yes
	Overcast	Cool	Normal	Strong	Yes
	Sunny	Hot	High	Weak	No
Outlook	Sunny	Hot	High	Strong	No
	Sunny	Cool	Normal	Weak	Yes
	Sunny	Mild	Normal	Strong	Yes
	Sunny	Mild	High	Weak	No
	Rain	Mild	High	Weak	Yes
	Rain	Cool	Normal	Weak	Yes
	Rain	Mild	Normal	Weak	Yes
	Rain	Cool	Normal	Strong	No

Now, we can see that the branch Overcast always yields response as *Yes* (rightmost column), so we can leave that branch out, as the entropy is always 0, that is, node Overcast is a leaf node.

Now, at the branch Outlook -> Sunny, we will need to determine the next decision node by repeating the process that we did similar to the root. Basically, the steps we did previously will continue recursively until we determine all the leaf nodes. Let's translate this into code for our credit card example and see it in action.

Coding the ID3 algorithm

First, we would need to have an application; let's go ahead and create an Angular application as shown previously.

From the previous example, we have seen that the first thing we will need is to list out our training data, which will be fed into our algorithm. In this case, we will need to first identify the different attributes that are affecting our target attribute (approved). Without going in too deep, the following are the major factors (and their possible values), which we are taking as an example of something, which can affect your approval chances:

- Credit score: Overall score of your credit (Excellent, Good, Average, and Poor)
- Credit age: Age of your credit history in years (>10, >5, >2, >=1)
- Derogatory remarks: If there are any remarks on your account (0, 1, 2, >=3)
- Utilization: How much of your approved credit you use (High, Medium, and Low)
- Hard inquiries: How many new accounts did you open recently (0, 1, 2, >=3)

Because of the fixed number of combinations of the preceding list, we can, in theory, generate a dataset that comprises all scenarios and then we can predict with 100% accuracy using that dataset, but where is the fun in that. We will instead be only taking half of the generated dataset and use it to predict the outcome of the other half.

Generating training dataset

Although generating the training dataset can be done manually, it's not fun. So, let's write a small script, which will help us to create the dataset:

```
// input attributes and the target values

var _ = require('lodash');

var creditScore = ['Excellent', 'Good', 'Average', 'Poor'];
var creditAge = ['>10', '>5', '>2', '>=1'];
var remarks = ['0', '1', '2', '>=3'];
var utilization = ['Low', 'Medium', 'High'];
```

```javascript
var hardInquiries = ['0', '1', '2', '>=3'];

// expected output structure
/* {
 "creditScore": "",
 "creditAge": "",
 "remarks": "",
 "utilization": "",
 "hardInquiries": "",
 "approval": ""
 } */


var all = [];
var even = [];
var odd = [];

// does not have to be optimal, this is a one time script
_.forEach(creditScore, function(credit) {

  // generate new object on each loop at top

  var resp = {};

  resp.creditScore = credit;

  _.forEach(creditAge, function(age) {

    resp.creditAge = age;

    _.forEach(remarks, function(remark) {

      resp.remarks = remark;

      _.forEach(utilization, function(util) {

        resp.utilization = util;

        _.forEach(hardInquiries, function(inq) {

          resp.hardInquiries = inq;

          // looping is by reference so persist a copy

          all.push(_.cloneDeep(resp));

        });
      });
```

```
      });
    });
  });


  for (var i = 0; i < all.length; i++) {

    // index is even
    if (i % 2 === 0) {

      // training data set
      even.push(all[i]);

    } else {

      // prediction data set (input)
      odd.push(all[i])

    }
  }

  // apply our fake algorithm to detect which application is approved
  var trainingDataWithApprovals = applyApprovals(even);

  // apply approval logic so that we know what to expect
  var predictionDataWithApprovals = applyApprovals(odd);


  function applyApprovals(data) {
    return _.map(data, function(d) {

      // Excellent credit score is approved, no questions asked

      if (d.creditScore === 'Excellent') {
        d.approved = 'Yes';
        return d;
      }

      // if credit score is good, then account should have a decent age
      // not very high utilization, less remarks and less inquiries

      if (d.creditScore === 'Good' &&
        (d.creditAge != '>=1') &&
        (d.remarks == '1' || d.remarks == '0') &&
        d.utilization !== 'High' &&
        (d.hardInquiries != '>=3')) {
        d.approved = 'Yes';
        return d;
```

```
    }

    // if score is average, then age should be high, no remarks, not
    very high
    // utilization and little to no inquiries.

    if (d.creditScore === 'Average' &&
      (d.creditAge == '>5' || d.creditAge == '>10') &&
      d.remarks == '0' &&
      d.utilization !== 'High' &&
      (d.hardInquiries == '1' || d.hardInquiries == '0')) {
      d.approved = 'Yes';
      return d;
    }

    // reject all others including all Poor credit scores
    d.approved = 'No';
    return d;

  });
}

console.log(trainingDataWithApprovals);
console.log(predictionDataWithApprovals);
```

To run the preceding script, let's create a small Node.js project within our credit-card project. At the root of the project, from Terminal, run the following commands to create the project:

```
// create folder for containing data
mkdir training-data

// move into the new folder
cd training-data

// create a new node project (answer the questions and hit return)
npm init

// install lodash to use helper methods
npm install lodash --save

// create the js file to generate data and copy paste the code above
// into this file
touch data.js

// run the script
node data.js
```

Running the script above logs the `trainingDataWithApprovals`
and `predictionDataWithApprovals`.

Next, copy the `trainingDataWithApprovals` into a file at the following
path: `src/utils/training-data/credit-card.ts`. The data that is logged from the
preceding code logs the data, an example of which can be seen in the following screenshot:

```
export class CreditCard {
    /*
     *
     * creditScore: Excellent, Good, Average, Poor
     * creditAge: 10, 5, 2, 1 (or above)
     * remarks: 0, 1, 2, 3 (or more)
     * utilization: Low, Medium, High
     * hardInquiries: 0, 1, 2, 3 (or more)
     *
     */

    public static data = [{"creditScore":"Excellent","creditAge":">10","remarks":"0","utilization":"Low","hardInquiries":"0",
"approved":"Yes"},{"creditScore":"Excellent","creditAge":">10","remarks":"0","utilization":"Low","hardInquiries":"2","approved":"Yes"},
{"creditScore":"Excellent","creditAge":">10","remarks":"0","utilization":"Medium","hardInquiries":"0","approved":"Yes"},
{"creditScore":"Excellent","creditAge":">10","remarks":"0","utilization":"Medium","hardInquiries":"2","approved":"Yes"},
{"creditScore":"Excellent","creditAge":">10","remarks":"0","utilization":"High","hardInquiries":"0","approved":"Yes"},
{"creditScore":"Excellent","creditAge":">10","remarks":"0","utilization":"High","hardInquiries":"2","approved":"Yes"},
{"creditScore":"Excellent","creditAge":">10","remarks":"1","utilization":"Low","hardInquiries":"0","approved":"Yes"},
{"creditScore":"Excellent","creditAge":">10","remarks":"1","utilization":"Low","hardInquiries":"2","approved":"Yes"},
{"creditScore":"Excellent","creditAge":">10","remarks":"1","utilization":"Medium","hardInquiries":"0","approved":"Yes"},
{"creditScore":"Excellent","creditAge":">10","remarks":"1","utilization":"Medium","hardInquiries":"2","approved":"Yes"},
{"creditScore":"Excellent","creditAge":">10","remarks":"1","utilization":"High","hardInquiries":"0","approved":"Yes"},
```

We can now move the `predictionDataWithApprovals` into the `app.component.ts` file
and rename the `approved` attribute to `expected` as that is what we expect the output to
be. We will compare the actual output against this later:

```
import { Component, OnInit } from '@angular/core';
import {ID3} from "../utils/id3";
import {without, keys, filter} from "lodash";

@Component({
    selector: 'app-root',
    templateUrl: './app.component.html',
    styleUrls: ['./app.component.scss']
})
export class AppComponent implements OnInit {
    tests: any;

    constructor(private id3: ID3) {

    }

    ngOnInit() {
        this.tests = [{"creditScore":"Excellent","creditAge":">10","remarks":"0","utilization":"Low","hardInquiries":"1","expected":"Yes"},
{"creditScore":"Excellent","creditAge":">10","remarks":"0","utilization":"Low","hardInquiries":">=3","expected":"Yes"},
{"creditScore":"Excellent","creditAge":">10","remarks":"0","utilization":"Medium","hardInquiries":"1","expected":"Yes"},
{"creditScore":"Excellent","creditAge":">10","remarks":"0","utilization":"Medium","hardInquiries":">=3","expected":"Yes"},
{"creditScore":"Excellent","creditAge":">10","remarks":"0","utilization":"High","hardInquiries":"1","expected":"Yes"},
{"creditScore":"Excellent","creditAge":">10","remarks":"0","utilization":"High","hardInquiries":">=3","expected":"Yes"},
{"creditScore":"Excellent","creditAge":">10","remarks":"1","utilization":"Low","hardInquiries":"1","expected":"Yes"},
{"creditScore":"Excellent","creditAge":">10","remarks":"1","utilization":"Low","hardInquiries":">=3","expected":"Yes"},
{"creditScore":"Excellent","creditAge":">10","remarks":"1","utilization":"Medium","hardInquiries":"1","expected":"Yes"},
{"creditScore":"Excellent","creditAge":">10","remarks":"1","utilization":"Medium","hardInquiries":">=3","expected":"Yes"},
```

Now that we have the training data ready and imported into the project, let's create the rest
of the algorithm to complete the tree.

Generating the decision tree

To keep the code complexity to a minimum, we will be extracting all the helper methods that we would be recursively calling, as seen in the previous example. We can start with the `train()` method because that is going to be called first to determine the root decision node.

Before we do that, let's create an Injectable service for our ID3 algorithm in the `utils` folder which we will be injecting where we wish to use it. This logic can live anywhere you wish, server or client side. One thing to note is that the dataset, in this case, is relatively small, so training the dataset and predicting the outcomes are an okay thing to do on the client side. With larger datasets, which take much longer to train, it is recommended to do this on the server side, as follows:

```
import {Injectable} from "@angular/core";

@Injectable()
export class ID3 {
    constructor() {

    }

}
```

At each step of the algorithm, we will be relying heavily on helper methods to keep the implementation details clear; most of these would be provided by `lodash`, so let's install and import it so that we can implement the `train()` method:

npm install lodash --save

Once `lodash` is installed, we can start with the `train()` method, which accepts three parameters: the training dataset, the target attribute, and the list of all the attributes extracted from the training dataset sans the target:

```
import {Injectable} from "@angular/core";
import { } from "lodash";

@Injectable()
export class ID3 {
    constructor() {

    }

    public train(trainingData, target, attributes) {

    }
```

```
    }
```

To use this service, mark it as a `provider` in the main module and then inject it in the `app.component`:

```
...
import { ID3 } from '../utils/id3';
...

@NgModule({
    ...
    providers: [
        ID3
    ],
    ...
})
export class AppModule { }
```

Then, to consume it in the main component, we can just import the ID3 service we have just created and then call the `train()` method on the service instance:

```
import { Component, OnInit } from '@angular/core';
import {ID3} from "../utils/id3";
import {without, keys, filter} from "lodash";
import {CreditCard} from "../utils/training-data/credit-card";

@Component({
    selector: 'app-root',
    templateUrl: './app.component.html',
    styleUrls: ['./app.component.scss']
})
export class AppComponent implements OnInit {
    tree;
    tests: any;

    constructor(private id3: ID3) {
        this.tree = this.id3.train(
                        CreditCard.data,
                        'approved',
                        without(keys(CreditCard.data[0]),
                        'approved'));
    }

    ngOnInit() {
        this.tests = ... // testing data
    }
```

```
}
```

Let us also add some styles to our page to make it look nice, so update the
app.component.scss file:

```scss
.split {
    width: 50%;
    float: left
}

table, td, th {
  text-align: center;
  border: 1px solid black;
}

table {
  border-collapse: collapse;
  width: 100%;
}

th {
  height: 50px;
}


.true {
  background: #bcf9bc;
}

.false {
  background: #ffa2a7;
}
```

As discussed in the preceding algorithm, the first thing that we do in our application is to
determine the root decision node, for example, the attribute with the highest information
gain:

```typescript
import {Injectable} from "@angular/core";
import { maxBy, uniq, map, filter, without, keys, size, chain, find,
countBy } from "lodash";

@Injectable()
export class ID3 {
    constructor() {

    }
```

```
public train(trainingData, target, attributes) {

    // calculate root node from current list of attributes
    var currentRootNode = this.getCurrentRootNode(
                            trainingData, target, attributes);

}

private getCurrentRootNode(trainingData, target, attributes) {

    // get max extropy attribute
    return maxBy(attributes, (attr) => {

        // calculate information gain at each attribute
        // e.g. 'creditScore', 'creditAge' etc
        return this.gain(trainingData, target, attr);
    });
}

private gain(trainingData, target, attr) {
    // calculate target branches entropy e.g. approved
    var targetEntropy = this.entropy(map(trainingData, target));

    // calculate the summation of all branches entropy
    var sumOfBranchEntropies =
        chain(trainingData)

            // extract branches for the given attribute
            // e.g creditScore has the branches Excellent, Good,
            // Average, Poor
            .map(attr)

            // make the values unique
            .uniq()

            // for each unique branch calculate the branch entropy
            // e.g. calculate entropy of Excellent, Good, Average,
            Poor
            .map((branch) => {

                // extract only the subset training data
                // which belongs to current branch
                var branchTrainingData = filter(trainingData,
                [attr, branch]);

                // return (probability of branch) * entropy of
                branch
                return (branchTrainingData.length /
```

```
                        trainingData.length)
                            * this.entropy(map(branchTrainingData,
                            target));
                    })

                    // add all branch entropies
                    // e.g. add entropy of Excellent, Good, Average, Poor
                    .reduce(this.genericReducer, 0)

                    // return the final value
                    .valueOf();

        // return information gain
        return targetEntropy - sumOfBranchEntropies;
    }

private entropy(vals) {

        // take all values
        return chain(vals)

            // make them unique
            // e.g. an array of Yes and No
            .uniq()

            // calculate probability of each
            .map((x) => this.probability(x, vals))

            // calculate entropy
            .map((p) => -p * Math.log2(p))

            // reduce the value
            .reduce(this.genericReducer, 0)

            // return value
            .valueOf();
    }

private probability(val, vals){

        // calculate total number of instances
        // e.g. Yes is 100 out of the 300 values
        var instances = filter(vals, (x) => x === val).length;

        // total values passed e.g. 300
        var total = vals.length;

        // return 1/3
```

```
        return instances/total;
    }

    private genericReducer(a, b) {

        // add and return
        return a + b;
    }
```

From the preceding code, you can see that we calculate the root decision node of the tree first by calculating the branch entropies of each attribute and determining the maximum information gain.

Now that we have the root, we can recursively repeat the process for each branch of the node and then continue to find the decision nodes until we hit the entropy of 0, that is, leaf nodes.

This modifies our `train()` method as follows :

```
public train(trainingData, target, attributes) {
    // extract all targets from data set e.g.
    // Yes or No
    var allTargets = uniq(map(trainingData, target));

    // only Yes or No is remaining e.g. leaf node found
    if (allTargets.length == 1){
        return { leaf: true, value: allTargets[0] };
    }

    // calculate root node from current list of attributes
    var currentRootNode = this.getCurrentRootNode(
                            trainingData, target, attributes);

    // form node for current root
    var node: any = { name: currentRootNode, leaf: false };

    // remove currentRootNode from list of all attributes
    // e.g. remove creditScore or whatever the root node was
    // from the entire list of attributes
    var remainingAttributes = without(attributes, currentRootNode);

    // get unique branch names for currentRootNode
    // e.g creditScore has the branches Excellent, Good,
    // Average, Poor
    var branches = uniq(map(trainingData, currentRootNode));

    // recursively repeat the process for each branch
```

```
node.branches = map(branches, (branch) => {

    // take each branch training data
    // e.g. training data where creditScore is Excellent
    var branchTrainingData = filter(trainingData, [currentRootNode,
    branch]);

    // create node for each branch
    var branch: any = { name: branch, leaf: false };

    // initialize branches for node
    branch.branches = [];

    // train and push data to subbranch
    branch.branches.push(this.train(
            branchTrainingData, target, remainingAttributes));

    // return branch as a child of parent node
    return branch;
});

return node;
}
```

With that, the `train()` method:

1. Takes the input training data, the target attribute, and the attributes list.
2. Gets the current root attribute by calculating the maximum information gain at each of the branch of the attribute and creates the root node of the tree.
3. Pushes the recursively generated sub-tree into the branches of the root node.

Predicting outcome of sample inputs

Now that our tree is ready and returned, we can use this in our `app.component` to determine whether the prediction matches that of the expected outcome using the `predict()` method:

```
public predict(tree, input) {
    var node = tree;

    // loop over the entire tree
    while(!node[0].leaf){

        // take node name e.g. creditScore
        var name = node[0].name;
```

```
            // take value from input sample
            var inputValue = input[name];

            // check if branches for given input exist
            var childNode = filter(node[0].branches, ['name', inputValue]);

            // if branches exist return branches or default to No
            node = childNode.length ?
                childNode[0].branches : [{ leaf: true, value: 'No'}];
        }

        // return final leaf value
        return node[0].value;
    }
```

Then, in the `app.component`, we consume the `predict()` method:

```
    ...
        accuracyPct: any;

        ngOnInit() {

            this.tests = // test data set;

            this.tests.forEach((test) => {
                test.actual = this.id3.predict([this.tree], test);
                test.accurate = test.expected === test.actual;
            });
            this.accuracyPct =  (filter(this.tests, { accurate: true }).length
    /
                                this.tests.length) *100;
        }

    }
```

Visualization of the tree and output

Although we have generated the tree and the expected/actual results of the input dataset based on training set, it's really difficult to visualize this data right now. So, to do that, let's create a small component that accepts the tree and renders the nested format of the tree on the UI. This is pretty minimal and is only for the purpose of understanding our data in the form of the decision tree.

Under the utils folder, let's first create the folder called treeview to contain our component. Let's call it treeview, as we create the component and inject it into the main module.

For the treeview, let's first create the treeview.ts file:

```
import {Component, Input} from '@angular/core';

@Component ({
    selector: 'tree-view',
    templateUrl:'./treeview.html',
    styleUrls: ['./treeview.scss']
})
export class TreeView {
    @Input() data;
}
```

Then, we will create the template that goes with the component and add it as treeview.html:

```
<ul *ngFor="let node of data">
    <li *ngIf="node.name">
        <!-- show name when available -->
        <span class="name">{{node.name}}</span>
    </li>

    <!-- is not root node, render branches recursively -->
    <tree-view *ngIf="!node.leaf" [data]="node.branches"></tree-view>
    <!-- if leaf node render node value -->
    <li *ngIf="node.leaf">
        <span class="leaf {{node.value}}">{{node.value}}</span>
    </li>
</ul>
```

Let's style the treeview to make it more legible, treeview.scss:

```
ul {
  list-style: none;
  line-height: 40px;
  position: relative;

  &::before{
    content: "";
    height: calc(100% - 60px);
    display: block;
    top: 40px;
    left: 60px;
```

```
      border-left: 1px solid #333;
      position: absolute;
    }
  }

  li {
    position: relative;

    &::before{
      content: "";
      width: 20px;
      display: block;
      top: 50%;
      left: -20px;
      border-bottom: 1px solid #333;
      position: absolute;
      transform: translateY(-50%);
    }
  }

  .name {
    padding: 10px;
    background: #e1f4ff;
  }

  .leaf {
    padding: 10px;
    position: relative;

    &.Yes {
      background: #bcf9bc;
    }

    &.No {
      background: #ffa2a7;
    }
  }
```

Now, to consume the `treeview` component, let's add it to the declarations in `app.module.ts`:

```
...
import {TreeView} from "../utils/treeview/treeview";

@NgModule({
    declarations: [
        ...
```

```
        TreeView
    ],
    ...
})
export class AppModule { }
```

To use this, we just have to bind the tree that we generated in our app.component to the
tree-view component:

With the treeview added, app.component.html gets updated as follows:

```
<div *ngIf="tree">
    <tree-view [data]="[tree]"></tree-view>
</div>
```

This renders the tree on the UI as expected:

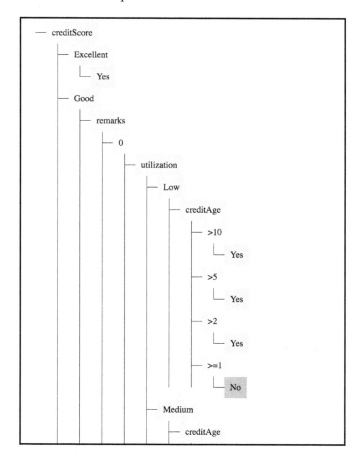

However, this is only a part of the big tree that is generated, which is tough to read and visualize. Let's try the same with the Soccer example by switching the training and testing data with Soccer data instead, which we saw in the previous sections:

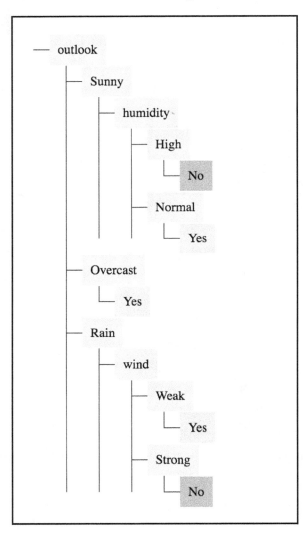

Let's render the input data that we passed in for testing our decision tree. For that, we can modify our `app.component.html` to show the table and visualization simultaneously:

```html
<div class="split">
    <div *ngIf="tree">
        <tree-view [data]="[tree]"></tree-view>
    </div>
</div>
<div class="split">
    <h3>Overall accuracy {{accuracyPct | number}}%</h3>

    <table>
        <thead>
            <th>Credit Score</th>
            <th>Credit Age</th>
            <th>Remarks</th>
            <th>Utilization</th>
            <th>Hard Inquiries</th>
            <th>Expected</th>
            <th>Actual</th>
            <th>Accurate</th>
        </thead>
        <tbody>
            <tr *ngFor="let test of tests">
                <td>{{test.creditScore}}</td>
                <td>{{test.creditAge}}</td>
                <td>{{test.remarks}}</td>
                <td>{{test.utilization}}</td>
                <td>{{test.hardInquiries}}</td>
                <td>{{test.expected}}</td>
                <td>{{test.actual}}</td>
                <td [class]="test.accurate">{{test.accurate}}</td>
            </tr>
        </tbody>
    </table>
</div>
```

To style the table, we can add the following to our `app.component.scss` file:

```scss
.split {
    width: 50%;
    float: left
}

table, td, th {
  text-align: center;
  border: 1px solid black;
```

```
    }

    table {
      border-collapse: collapse;
      width: 100%;
    }

    th {
      height: 50px;
    }


    .true {
      background: #bcf9bc;
    }

    .false {
      background: #ffa2a7;
    }
```

The expected output is as follows:

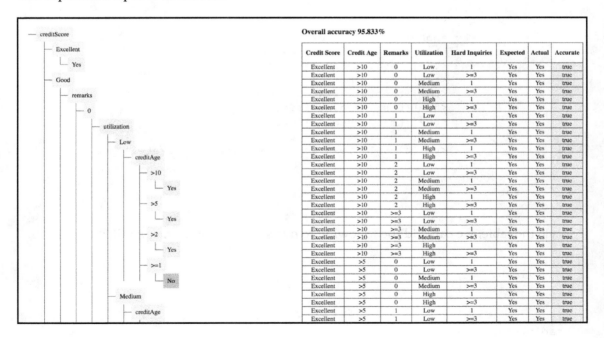

For the Soccer example:

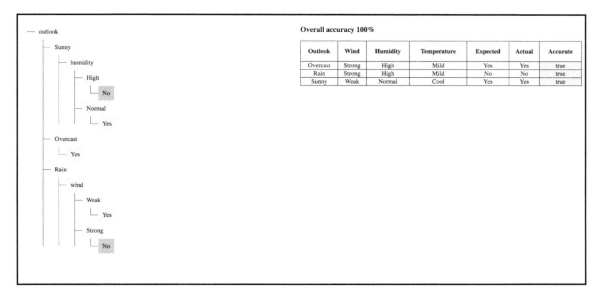

Summary

In this chapter, we took a rather orthodox approach to understanding trees as data structures, where we deviated from the standard process of learning about a tree and implementing its methods. We instead took some real-world example and implemented the trees as we see fit, based on the use case at hand. This will be the case where you are provided the data and are challenged to implement it in a generic way to expand the use cases. In the next chapter, we will expand this approach and take it one step further, where we will note how it expands into graph theory.

5
Simplify Complex Applications Using Graphs

The simplest way to define a graph would be anything that is a collection of nodes in which the nodes are connected by edges. Graphs are one of the most popular mathematical concepts that are used in computer science. Popular examples of graph implementations would be any social media website these days. Facebook use *friends* as nodes and *friendship* as edges; Twitter, on the other hand, defines *followers* as nodes and *following* as an edge, and so on. Take a look at the following image:

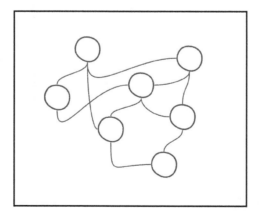

In the preceding image, you can see a typical graph with *nodes* and *edges*. As you can note, there are no directions listed out to our edges, and there are no details mentioned on our nodes. This is because there are different types of graphs, and the nodes and edges vary slightly between these different types of graphs, which we will see in the subsequent sections.

In this chapter, we will first go over the following topics:

1. Types of graphs
2. Creating a reference generator for a job portal
3. Creating a friend recommendation system

Types of graphs

From the preceding description, we can speculate on the types of graphs. There are way too many to cover in this chapter or even in this book. However, let's take a look at some of the most important and popular graphs, which we will be exploring with examples in this chapter:

- **Simple graphs**: A simple graph is an undirected, unweighted graph that contains no loops or multi-edge (that is multiple edges between the two nodes also known as parallel edges) nodes:

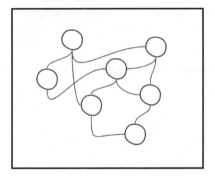

- **Undirected graphs**: This is a graph in which the edge definitions are interchangeable. For example, in the following image, the edge between nodes **1** and **2** can be represented as (1,2) or (2,1). The nodes are thus joined by a line without the arrows pointing towards any of the nodes:

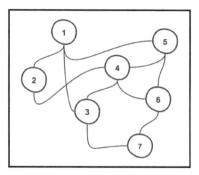

- **Directed graphs**: This is a graph in which the edges are given predefined direction based on a functional or logical condition. The edges are drawn with arrows, indicating the direction of the flow, for example, one user following another user on Twitter. Take a look at the following image:

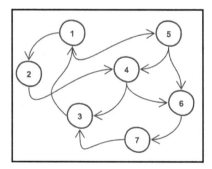

- **Cyclic graphs**: This is a graph in which the edges form a circular connection between nodes, that is, the start and end nodes are the same. For example, in the following image, we can note that the nodes **1 >> 5 >> 6 >> 7 >> 3 >> 1** form the cycle within the graph:

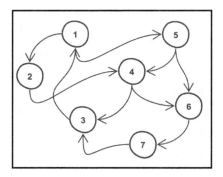

- **Directed acyclic graphs**: This is a directed graph with no cycles. These are the most common kind of graphs. In the following example, nodes are **1, 2, 3, 4, 5, 6, 7** and edges are {(1, 2), (1, 3), (1, 5), (2, 4), (4, 3), (4, 6), (5, 4), (5, 6), (6, 7), (7, 3)}:

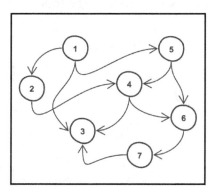

- **Weighted graphs**: This is a graph in which the edges are assigned numeric weights based on how expensive or inexpensive it can be to traverse that edge. The usage of the weight of each edge can vary based on the use cases. In the following example, you can note that the graphs are assigned weights (0, 1, 3, or 5) based on the edges between them:

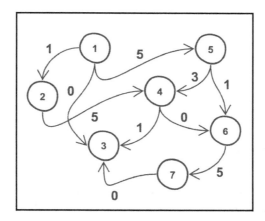

Fortunately, or unfortunately, the problems that we face in our day-to-day challenges do not directly tell us whether we can solve them with a graph, and if so, what kind of graph it needs to be or what kind of parsing algorithm we will need to employ. This is something that we take upon a case-by-case basis, which is what we will be doing with the following use cases.

Use cases

Implementing a graph is similar to that of trees; there is no set way of creating one. However, based on your use case, you can structure your graphs as directed, cyclic, or any other form as explained earlier. Doing this can make their traversal easier, which would, in turn, make data retrieval easier and faster.

Let's take a look at some examples for which we will be needing a base application first.

Creating a Node.js web server

Let's first create a web server using Node.js, which we will use to create endpoints later on to access our graph-based applications:

1. The first step is to create your application's project folder; to do so, run the following command from the Terminal:

```
mkdir <project-name>
```

2. Then, to initialize a Node.js project, run the init command in the root folder of your project. This will prompt a series of questions to generate the package.json file. You can fill out the answers you want or just click on return to accept default values for the prompts:

```
cd <project-name>
npm init
```

3. Next, since we want to create a web server, we will use express, which is a very powerful and popular framework available for Node.js. We will also use another library called body-parser, which helps us parse the incoming JSON body requests with ease. Lastly, we will also use lodash to help out with some complex data manipulations. To install lodash, express, and body-parser, run the following command:

```
npm install express body-parser lodash --save
```

4. Once we have the application setup done, we will need to start the application server using express and include our body-parser middleware. So, we can now create a server.js file at the root and then add the following code to it:

```
var express = require('express');
var app = express();
var bodyParser = require('body-parser');

// middleware to parse the body of input requests
app.use(bodyParser.json());


// test url
app.get('/', function (req, res) {
    res.status(200).send('OK!')
});
```

```
// start server
app.listen(3000, function () {
    console.log('Application listening on port 3000!')
});
```

5. Now, the app is ready to be launched. Under the `scripts` tag of your `package.json` file, add the following and then run `npm start` from the terminal to bring your server up:

```
{

...

"scripts": {
  "start": "node server.js",
  "test": "echo \"Error: no test specified\" && exit 1"
},

...

}
```

Creating a reference generator for a job portal

In this example, we will create a reference generator for a job portal. For instance, we have a few users who are friends with each other, we will create nodes for each of the users and associate each of the nodes with data, such as their name and the company at which they work.

Once we create all these nodes, we will join them based on some predefined relationships between the nodes. Then, we will use these predefined relationships to determine who a user would have to talk to to get referred for a job interview at a company of their choice. For example, A who works at company X and B who works at company Y are friends, B and C who works at company Z are friends. So, if A wants to get referred to company Z, then A talks to B, who can introduce them to C for a referral to company Z.

In most production-level apps, you will not be creating the graphs in such a fashion. You can simply use a graph database, which can perform a lot of features out of the box.

Returning to our example, in more technical terms, we have an undirected graph (think of users as nodes and friendship as edges between them), and we want to determine the shortest path from one node to another.

To do what we have described so far, we will be using a technique known as **Breadth First Search** (**BFS**). BFS is a graph traversal mechanism in which the neighboring nodes are examined or evaluated first before moving on to the next level. This helps to ensure that the number of links found in the resulting chain is always minimum, hence we always get the shortest possible path from node A to node B.

Although there are other algorithms, such as **Dijkstra**, to achieve similar results, we will go with BFS because Dijkstra is a more complex algorithm that is well suited when each edge has an associated cost with it. For example, in our case, we would go with Dijkstra if our user's friendships have a weight associated with it such as *acquaintance*, *friend*, and *close friend*, which would help us associate weights with each of those paths.

A good use case to consider Dijkstra would be for something such as a Maps application, which would give you directions from point A to B based on the traffic (that is, the weight or cost associated with each edge) in between.

Creating a bidirectional graph

We can start with logic for our graph by creating a new file under `utils/graph.js`, which will hold the edges and then provide a simple `shortestPath` method to access the Graph and apply the BFS algorithm on the graph that is generated, as shown in the following code:

```
var _ = require('lodash');

class Graph {

    constructor(users) {
        // initialize edges
        this.edges = {};

        // save users for later access
        this.users = users;

        // add users and edges of each
        _.forEach(users, (user) => {
            this.edges[user.id] = user.friends;
        });
    }
}

module.exports = Graph;
```

Once we add the edges to our graph, it has nodes (user IDs), and edges are defined as the relationship between each user ID and friend in the `friends` array, which is available for each user. Forming the graph was an easy task, thanks to the way our data is structured. In our example dataset, each user has a set of friends list, which is listed in the following code:

```
[
    {
        id: 1,
        name: 'Adam',
        company: 'Facebook',
        friends: [2, 3, 4, 5, 7]
    },
    {
        id: 2,
        name: 'John',
        company: 'Google',
        friends: [1, 6, 8]
    },
    {
        id: 3,
        name: 'Bill',
        company: 'Twitter',
        friends: [1, 4, 5, 8]
    },
    {
        id: 4,
        name: 'Jose',
        company: 'Apple',
        friends: [1, 3, 6, 8]
    },
    {
        id: 5,
        name: 'Jack',
        company: 'Samsung',
        friends: [1, 3, 7]
    },
    {
        id: 6,
        name: 'Rita',
        company: 'Toyota',
        friends: [2, 4, 7, 8]
    },
    {
        id: 7,
        name: 'Smith',
        company: 'Matlab',
        friends: [1, 5, 6, 8]
```

```
    },
    {
        id: 8,
        name: 'Jane',
        company: 'Ford',
        friends: [2, 3, 4, 6, 7]
    }
]
```

As you can note in the preceding code, we did not really have to establish a bidirectional edge exclusively here because if user 1 is a friend of user 2 then user 2 is also a friend of user 1 .

Generating a pseudocode for the shortest path generation

Before its implementation, let's quickly jot down what we are about to do so that the actual implementation becomes a lot easier:

```
INITIALIZE tail to 0 for subsequent iterations

MARK source node as visited

WHILE result not found

    GET neighbors of latest visited node (extracted using tail)

    FOR each of the node

        IF node already visited
            RETURN

        Mark node as visited

        IF node is our expected result

            INITIALIZE result with current neighbor node

            WHILE not source node

                BACKTRACK steps by popping users
                from previously visited path until
                the source user

            ADD source user to the result
```

```
        CREATE and format result variable


    IF result found return control

    NO result found, add user to previously visited path

    ADD friend to queue for BFS in next iteration

  INCREMENT tail for next loop


RETURN NO_RESULT
```

Implementing the shortest path generation

Let's now create our customized BFS algorithm to parse the graph and generate the shortest possible path for our user to get referred to company A:

```javascript
var _ = require('lodash');

class Graph {

    constructor(users) {
        // initialize edges
        this.edges = {};

        // save users for later access
        this.users = users;

        // add users and edges of each
        _.forEach(users, (user) => {
            this.edges[user.id] = user.friends;
        });
    }


    shortestPath(sourceUser, targetCompany) {
        // final shortestPath
        var shortestPath;

        // for iterating along the breadth
        var tail = 0;

        // queue of users being visited
        var queue = [ sourceUser ];
```

```
// mark visited users
var visitedNodes = [];

// previous path to backtrack steps when shortestPath is found
var prevPath = {};
// request is same as response
if (_.isEqual(sourceUser.company, targetCompany)) {
    return;
}

// mark source user as visited so
// next time we skip the processing
visitedNodes.push(sourceUser.id);

// loop queue until match is found
// OR until the end of queue i.e no match
while (!shortestPath && tail < queue.length) {

    // take user breadth first
    var user = queue[tail];

    // take nodes forming edges with user
    var friendsIds = this.edges[user.id];

    // loop over each node
    _.forEach(friendsIds, (friendId) => {
        // result found in previous iteration, so we can stop
        if (shortestPath) return;

        // get all details of node
        var friend = _.find(this.users, ['id', friendId]);

        // if visited already,
        // nothing to recheck so return
        if (_.includes(visitedNodes, friendId)) {
            return;
        }

        // mark as visited
        visitedNodes.push(friendId);

        // if company matched
        if (_.isEqual(friend.company, targetCompany)) {

            // create result path with the matched node
            var path = [ friend ];

            // keep backtracking until source user and add to path
```

```
    while (user.id !== sourceUser.id) {

        // add user to shortest path
        path.unshift(user);

        // prepare for next iteration
        user = prevPath[user.id];
    }

    // add source user to the path
    path.unshift(user);

    // format and return shortestPath
    shortestPath = _.map(path, 'name').join(' -> ');
    }

    // break loop if shortestPath found
    if (shortestPath) return;

    // no match found at current user,
    // add it to previous path to help backtracking later
    prevPath[friend.id] = user;

    // add to queue in the order of visit
    // i.e. breadth wise for next iteration
    queue.push(friend);
    });

    // increment counter
    tail++;
    }

    return shortestPath ||
        `No path between ${sourceUser.name} & ${targetCompany}`;
    }

}


module.exports = Graph;
```

The most important part of the code is when the match is found, as shown in the following code block from the preceding code:

```
// if company matched
if (_.isEqual(friend.company, targetCompany)) {

    // create result path with the matched node
```

```
    var path = [ friend ];

    // keep backtracking until source user and add to path
    while (user.id !== sourceUser.id) {

        // add user to shortest path
        path.unshift(user);

        // prepare for next iteration
        user = prevPath[user.id];
    }

    // add source user to the path
    path.unshift(user);

    // format and return shortestPath
    shortestPath = _.map(path, 'name').join(' -> ');
}
```

Here, we are employing a technique called backtracking, which helps us retrace our steps when the result is found. The idea here is that we add the current state of the iteration to a map whenever the result is not found—the key as the node being visited currently, and the value as the node from which we are visiting.

So, for example, if we visited node 1 from node 3, then the map would contain { 1: 3 } until we visit node 1 from some other node, and when that happens, our map will update to point to the new node from which we got to node 1, such as { 1: newNode }. Once we set up these previous paths, we can easily trace our steps back by looking at this map. By adding some log statements (available only in the GitHub code to avoid confusion), we can easily take a look at the long but simple flow of the data. Let us take an example of the data set that we defined earlier, so when Bill tries to look for friends who can refer him to Toyota, we see the following log statements:

```
starting the shortest path determination
added 3 to the queue
marked 3 as visited
    shortest path not found, moving on to next node in queue: 3
    extracting neighbor nodes of node 3 (1,4,5,8)
        accessing neighbor 1
        mark 1 as visited
        result not found, mark our path from 3 to 1
        result not found, add 1 to queue for next iteration
        current queue content : 3,1
        accessing neighbor 4
        mark 4 as visited
        result not found, mark our path from 3 to 4
```

```
        result not found, add 4 to queue for next iteration
        current queue content : 3,1,4
        accessing neighbor 5
        mark 5 as visited
        result not found, mark our path from 3 to 5
        result not found, add 5 to queue for next iteration
        current queue content : 3,1,4,5
        accessing neighbor 8
        mark 8 as visited
        result not found, mark our path from 3 to 8
        result not found, add 8 to queue for next iteration
        current queue content : 3,1,4,5,8
increment tail to 1
shortest path not found, moving on to next node in queue: 1
extracting neighbor nodes of node 1 (2,3,4,5,7)
        accessing neighbor 2
        mark 2 as visited
        result not found, mark our path from 1 to 2
        result not found, add 2 to queue for next iteration
        current queue content : 3,1,4,5,8,2
        accessing neighbor 3
        neighbor 3 already visited, return control to top
        accessing neighbor 4
        neighbor 4 already visited, return control to top
        accessing neighbor 5
        neighbor 5 already visited, return control to top
        accessing neighbor 7
        mark 7 as visited
        result not found, mark our path from 1 to 7
        result not found, add 7 to queue for next iteration
        current queue content : 3,1,4,5,8,2,7
increment tail to 2
shortest path not found, moving on to next node in queue: 4
extracting neighbor nodes of node 4 (1,3,6,8)
        accessing neighbor 1
        neighbor 1 already visited, return control to top
        accessing neighbor 3
        neighbor 3 already visited, return control to top
        accessing neighbor 6
        mark 6 as visited
        result found at 6, add it to result path ([6])
        backtracking steps to 3
            we got to 6 from 4
            update path accordingly: ([4,6])
        add source user 3 to result
        form result [3,4,6]
        return result
increment tail to 3
```

```
return result Bill -> Jose -> Rita
```

What we basically have here is an iterative process using BFS to traverse the tree and backtracking the result. This forms the core of our functionality.

Creating a web server

We can now add a route to access this graph and its corresponding `shortestPath` method. Let's first create the route under `routes/references` and add it as a middleware to the web server:

```
var express = require('express');
var app = express();
var bodyParser = require('body-parser');

// register endpoints
var references = require('./routes/references');

// middleware to parse the body of input requests
app.use(bodyParser.json());

// route middleware
app.use('/references', references);

// start server
app.listen(3000, function () {
    console.log('Application listening on port 3000!');
});
```

Then, create the route as shown in the following code:

```
var express = require('express');
var router = express.Router();
var Graph = require('../utils/graph');
var _ = require('lodash');
var userGraph;

// sample set of users with friends
// same as list shown earlier
var users = [...];

// middleware to create the users graph
router.use(function(req) {
    // form graph
    userGraph = new Graph(users);
```

```
    // continue to next step
    req.next();
});

// create the route for generating reference path
// this can also be a get request with params based
// on developer preference
router.route('/')
    .post(function(req, res) {

        // take user Id
        const userId = req.body.userId;

        // target company name
        const companyName = req.body.companyName;

        // extract current user info
        const user = _.find(users, ['id', userId]);

        // get shortest path
        const path = userGraph.shortestPath(user, companyName);

        // return
        res.send(path);
    });

module.exports = router;
```

Running the reference generator

To test this, simply start the web server by running the `npm start` command from the root of the project as shown earlier.

Once the server is up and running, you can use any tool you wish to post the request to your web server, as shown in the following screenshot:

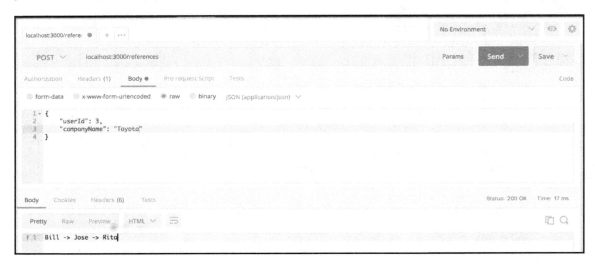

As you can see in the preceding screenshot, we get the response back as expected. This can, of course, be changed in a way to return all the user objects instead of just the names. That could be a fun extension of the example for you to try on your own.

Creating a friend recommendation system for social media

You cannot simply deny the fact that social networking sites are all about the data. This is why a majority of the features built in these websites rely on the data that you provide to them. One such example of these is a *people you might know* or a *who to follow* component that you can find on many of the websites.

From the previous example, we know that the data can be grouped into `nodes` and `edges`, in which the nodes are the people and the edges are the relationships that you want to establish between the nodes.

We could simply form a bidirected graph and then apply a BFS algorithm to determine the connected nodes at *n*th degree, which we can then de-duplicate to show the friend or node recommendations. However, considering that we already did this in the preceding example, and also that the actual list of users and friends of each of these users is huge in a production application, we will take a different approach. We will go with the assumption that our dataset is stored in a graph database, such as **neo4j**, and then we will use an algorithm called **Personalized PageRank**, that is a BFS and PageRank combination which we will explore in the next section.

Understanding PageRank algorithm

At some point in our lives, we must have come across this term, PageRank. PageRank is one of the many ways in which Google ranks the web pages for searching and indexing. A simple Google search (pun totally intended) will return results that tell you how it basically involves a collection of nodes from which we can walk in a random direction. However, what does that really mean?

Given that the control is dropped on any node within a graph, we are saying that the control can jump to any node on the graph unbiased with a probability of `alpha`, and when it does land on any node, it shares a portion of its rank equally with all of its connected nodes before traversing along one of these nodes edges randomly with a probability of `(1 - alpha)`.

How and why does this matter? It's just jumping from one node to another and then randomly traversing to some other connected node, right?

If you do this for long enough, you would land on all the nodes and some of the nodes more times than the other. You see where I am going with this? This would end up telling you which nodes are more frequented compared to others, which could happen for the following two reasons :

- We just happened to jump to the same node multiple times
- That node is connected to multiple nodes

The first scenario can happen, but, since we know that our jumps are unbiased and the Law of Large Numbers dictates that this would yield the normalized value when done for long enough, we can safely rule it out.

The second scenario, on the other hand, is not only possible but also very important to PageRank. Once you land on one of these nodes, that's when we calculate the PageRank for that node-based on alpha and on the rank inherited from the preceding node.

We were talking in abstract terms of nodes and edges; however, for a brief time, let's take a look at a statement made in the very first publication of PageRank by Sergey Brin and Lawrence Page (`http://infolab.stanford.edu/~backrub/google.html`):

> We assume page A has pages T1...Tn which point to it (i.e., are citations). The parameter d is a damping factor which can be set between 0 and 1. We usually set d to 0.85. There are more details about d in the next section. Also, C(A) is defined as the number of links going out of page A. The PageRank of page A is given as follows:
>
> PR(A) = (1-d) + d (PR(T1)/C(T1) + ... + PR(Tn)/C(Tn))
>
> Note that the PageRanks form a probability distribution over web pages, so the sum of all web pages' PageRanks will be one.

From the preceding statement, we can see that the PageRank *(PR)* of a given page/node is derived from the *PR* of its citations *(T1...Tn)*, but how does one know where to start since we need to know its citations to calculate the PR for *T1*. The simple answer is that we do not need to know the value of the *PR(T1)* or any other citation as a matter of fact. What we can do instead is to simply guess a value for *PR(T1)* and recursively apply the values that are derived from the preceding step.

However, why on earth would that work, you ask? The answer is simple, remember the Law of Large Numbers? If you repeat an action for long enough, the result of the said action will converge to the median value. Then, there are questions about how you can do it for the millions and billions of web pages and be effective? There are ways and means, which are beyond the scope of this chapter and book; however, for those interested, this book that explains Google's Page Rank is a great read, available at `https://press.princeton.edu/titles/8216.html`. I hope that this book sheds some light on the basic principle involved.

Understanding Personalized PageRank (PPR) Algorithm

Now that we have a brief understanding of PageRank, what is Personalized PageRank? It's quite simple actually, instead of jumping to a random node every time, we jump to a predefined node and then recursively accumulate the probability of hitting each node while traversing using BFS.

Let's assume that we have a few friends who are structured as shown in the following diagram:

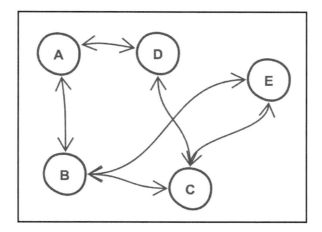

This is straightforward; we have bidirectional edges between the nodes, indicating a friendship between them. In this problem, we can assume that we want to suggest new friends to User **A**.

The simplest part is also the important thing that we need to talk about before moving onto the code for PPR. We will always be starting out from our target node, that is, the jumps are no longer started at random. We start at our target node, assume that the control traverses all edges equally, and then come back to the parent. Then, we recursively repeat this process while expanding the degree by one edge at a time until we meet our target degree.

Also, every time we increase our search by one degree from the target node, we are sharing the probability of the node with the neighbors, but if we share all of it, the node becomes 0 so what we would do instead is to apply a damping factor (alpha).

For example, assume that we are at the node X, which has a probability of 1 (that is, it is the target node), and that this node X has two neighbors, Y, and Z. The alpha that we set (for example, 0.5) will be applied here, so after the first iteration, X would have the probability as 0.5, and then Y and Z would have an equal probability of 0.25. Then, the process would be repeated recursively to the next degree with this new map of probabilities that we have just created.

Pseudocode for personalized PageRank

Let's convert what we discussed in the earlier section into the pseudocode for an easier implementation:

```
START at root node

    assign it a probability of 1 in the probabilityMap

    trigger CALC_PPR with current node, probabilityMap and iterations count

FUNCTION CALC_PPR

    IF number of iteration left is 0

        remove target and its neighbors from probabilityMap

        return rest of probabilityMap

    ELSE
        determine an ALPHA

        extract all nodes at the current degree

        FOR each nodes at current degree
            extract neighbors

            calculate the probability to propagate to neighbor

            IF neighbor already has a probability

                add to existing probability

            ELSE

                assign new probability

        CALC_PPR with decreased iteration count
```

Now that was not scary, was it? Implementing the PPR algorithm now is going to be easy.

Creating a web server

Before we write any code for our Personalized PageRank, let's first create a Node.js application, as explained earlier.

Once the application is ready, let's create a route that will be serving us our user suggestions. Similar to the example from the preceding example, we can quickly piece together the following route under routes/suggestions.js:

```
const express = require('express');
const router = express.Router();
const _ = require('lodash');

// sample set of users with friends extracted from some grapgh db
const users = {
    A: { neighbors: [ 'B', 'D' ] },
    B: { neighbors: [ 'A', 'C', 'E' ] },
    C: { neighbors: [ 'B', 'D', 'E' ] },
    D: { neighbors: [ 'A', 'C' ] },
    E: { neighbors: [ 'B', 'C' ] }
};

// middleware
router.use(function(req) {
    // intercept, modify and then continue to next step
    req.next();
});

// route
router.route('/:userId')
    .get(function(req, res) {
        var suggestions;

        // take user Id
        const userId = req.params.userId;

        // generate suggestions

        // return suggestions
        res.send(userId);
    });

module.exports = router;
```

We can also quickly piece together our express server:

```
var express = require('express');
var app = express();
var bodyParser = require('body-parser');

// suggestion endpoints
var suggestions = require('./routes/suggestions');

// middleware to parse the body of input requests
app.use(bodyParser.json());

// route middleware
app.use('/suggestions', suggestions);

// start server
app.listen(3000, function () {
    console.log('Application listening on port 3000!');
});
```

Implementing Personalized PageRank

Now, let's move over to creating our **Personalized PageRank** (**PPR**) algorithm. We will be creating an `ES6` class, which will handle all of the logic to generate the suggestions once we provide the graph and target node to it. Note that in the preceding code, I have already shown you what the graph looks like:

```
const users = {
    A: { neighbors: [ 'B', 'D' ] },
    B: { neighbors: [ 'A', 'C', 'E' ] },
    C: { neighbors: [ 'B', 'D', 'E' ] },
    D: { neighbors: [ 'A', 'C' ] },
    E: { neighbors: [ 'B', 'C' ] }
};
```

We have established a bidirectional relationship by specifying two nodes as each other's neighbors. Now, we can start with the code for PPR:

```
const _ = require('lodash');

class PPR {

    constructor(data) {
        this.data = data;
    }
```

```
getSuggestions(nodeId) {
    return this.personalizedPageRankGenerator(nodeId);
};
}


module.exports = PPR;
```

We will first accept the graph as the input to our `constructor`. Next, we will define our `getSuggestions` method, which will accept the input `nodeId` and then pass it to calculate the PPR. This is also the first step of our preceding pseudo code, as shown in the following code:

```
personalizedPageRankGenerator(nodeId) {
    // Set Probability of the starting node as 1
    // because we will start from that node
    var initProbabilityMap = {};

    initProbabilityMap[nodeId] = 1;

    // call helper to iterate thrice
    return this.pprHelper(nodeId, initProbabilityMap, 3);
};
```

Since our control is defined to start from a fixed node, we are setting it the probability of 1. We will be iterating three times simply because we want to go only three levels out to get the suggestions. Level 1 is the target node, level 2 is the neighbors of the target node (that is, current friends) and then level 3 is the neighbors of neighbors (that is, friends of friends).

Now, we get to the fun part. We will recursively calculate the probability of us jumping on to each of the neighboring nodes, starting from the target node:

```
pprHelper(nodeId, currentProbabilitiesMap, iterationCount) {
    // iterations done
    if (iterationCount === 0) {

        // get root nodes neighbors
        var currentNeighbors = this.getNeighbors(nodeId);

        // omit neighbors and self node from calculated probabilities
        currentProbabilitiesMap = _.omit(currentProbabilitiesMap,
        currentNeighbors.concat(nodeId));

        // format data and sort by probability of final suggestions
        return _.chain(currentProbabilitiesMap)
            .map((val, key) => ({ name: key, score: val }))
            .orderBy('score', 'desc')
```

```
            .valueOf();

    } else {
        // Holds the updated set of probabilities for the next iteration
        var nextIterProbabilityMap = {};

        // set alpha
        var alpha = 0.5;

        // With probability alpha, we teleport to the start node again
        nextIterProbabilityMap[nodeId] = alpha;

        // extract nodes within current loop
        var parsedNodes = _.keys(currentProbabilitiesMap);

        // go to next degree nodes of each of the currently parsed nodes
        _.forEach(parsedNodes, (parsedId) => {

            // get current probability of each node
            var prob = currentProbabilitiesMap[parsedId];

            // get connected nodes
            var neighbors = this.getNeighbors(parsedId);


            // With probability 1 - alpha, we move to a connected node...
            // And at each node we distribute its current probability
            equally to
            // its neighbors

            var probToPropagate = (1 - alpha) * prob / neighbors.length;


            // spreading the probability equally to neighbors
            _.forEach(neighbors, (neighborId) => {
              nextIterProbabilityMap[neighborId] =
            (nextIterProbabilityMap[neighborId] || 0) + probToPropagate;
              });
        });

        // next iteration
        return this.pprHelper(nodeId, nextIterProbabilityMap, iterationCount
- 1);
    }
}

getNeighbors(nodeId) {
    return _.get(this.data, [nodeId, 'neighbors'], []);
```

}

That was not half as bad as you thought, right? Once we have the PPR algorithm ready to go, we can now import this class into our `suggestions` route and can use it to generate the recommendations for any input user, as shown in the following code snippet:

```
const express = require('express');
const router = express.Router();
const _ = require('lodash');
const PPR = require('../utils/ppr');

// sample set of users with friends extracted from some grapgh db
const users = .... // from previous example

....

// route
router.route('/:userId')
    .get(function(req, res) {
        var suggestions;

        // take user Id
        const userId = req.params.userId;

----->  // generate suggestions
----->  suggestions = new PPR(users).getSuggestions(userId);

        // return suggestions
        res.send(suggestions);
    });

module.exports = router;
```

Results and analysis

Now, to test this, let's start off our web server by running the `npm start` command from the root folder. Once your application starts, you will see the following message on your terminal:

```
Application listening on port 3000!
```

Once the message appears, you can either open Postman or anything else of your choice to make the API calls for suggestions:

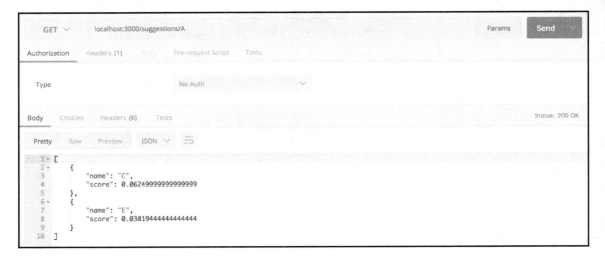

We can see that user C has received more score than user E. This is because we can see from the input dataset that the users A and C have more common friends than user A and E. This is why, as per our deduction earlier, the chances of our control landing on node C are higher than that of node E.

Also, the interesting thing to note is that the actual value of the score is immaterial here. You only need to look at the comparison of the scores to determine which one is more likely to happen. You can change alpha as you wish to decide how much probability each node is going to split between its neighbors, and that would ultimately change the score of each of the resultant nodes, for example, the results which shows the name and the score as we saw preceding are with the alpha value of 0.5; we will now change it to 0.33, that is, the parent node keeps one-third and splits the rest with the neighbors:

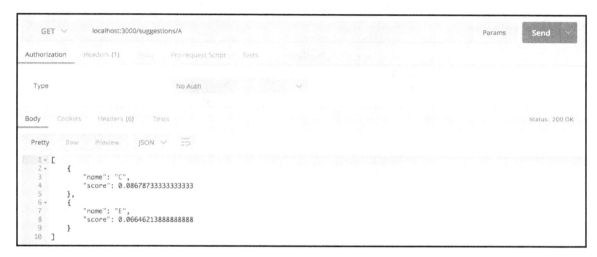

Few log statements are added before each recursive call for some additional clarity:

```
. . . . .

console.log(`End of Iteration ${ 4 - iterationCount} :
${JSON.stringify(nextIterProbabilityMap)}`);

// next iteration
return this.pprHelper(nodeId, nextIterProbabilityMap, iterationCount - 1);
```

The preceding log statements yield the following results:

```
/Users/kashyapmukkamala/.nvm/versions/node/v6.10.0/bin/node index.js
Application listening on port 3000!
End of Iteration 1 : {"A":0.33,"B":0.33499999999999996,"D":0.33499999999999996}
End of Iteration 2 : {"A":0.5170416666666666,"B":0.11055,"D":0.11055,"C":0.18704166666666663,"E":0.07481666666666666}
End of Iteration 3 : {"A":0.39172375,"B":0.24004518055555552,"D":0.21498159722222218,"C":0.08678733333333333,"E":0.06646213888888888}
```

From the preceding screenshot, you can note that at the end of the first iteration, the total probability of 1, which we assigned to target node A, has been split into three parts after our logic determined by BFS traversal that neighbors of node A are nodes B and D. Now, this became the input of iteration 2, where we repeated the process until the last iteration, at the end of which we remove the current target node A and its immediate neighbor nodes B and D (since they are already friends) and return the remaining, that is, nodes C and E.

Summary

In this chapter, we took some real-world challenges head-on and created some custom solutions based on the problem at hand. This is one of the most important takeaways from this chapter. Rarely would you find a scenario where an ideal solution is readily available. We took up one of the graph theories algorithms, known as BFS, and leveraged it to our advantage in generating the recommendations for our job portal and user suggestions. We also briefly discussed PageRank algorithm, which any developer should be familiar with. That brings the question of why and when to use one algorithm over the other. What are the pros and cons of choosing an algorithm? This will be the topic for our next chapter, where we will do an analysis of the different types of algorithms and where we can apply them.

6
Exploring Types of Algorithms

An algorithm in the computer science world is a set of instructions that takes finite space and time to execute. It starts at an initial state of the application and then performs a set of instructions step by step to achieve the end result.

Algorithms come in all shape and sizes, and all of them will fit the bill when you compare it with the overly generic definition of what an algorithm is. The big question is to decide which algorithm to use in which case and to make modifications to enhance its functionality based on the application's needs.

As I have shown in the use cases in previous chapters, most of the times, the algorithms that exist out there do not directly apply to the problems at hand. This is when a thorough understanding of the algorithm comes in handy. That is exactly what we will be doing in this chapter; we will take a look at a series of algorithms and then try to understand them better with the help of some examples.

In this chapter, we will discuss the following algorithms with some examples:

- Recursion
- Dijkstra
- Breadth First Search (BFS)
- Dynamic Programming
- Greedy Algorithm
- Branch And Bound

Let's set up a bare-bones Node.js project before we start looking at the use cases.

Creating a Node.js application

For this chapter, we will use a very simple and light Node.js application, which will be holding our example scripts. The main goal here is to be able to run each of the use cases individually and not have an entire web (client or server) application for each of them. This helps us to have a uniform base project.

1. The first step is to create your application's project folder. From the Terminal, run the following command:

```
mkdir <project-name>
```

2. Then, to initialize a Node.js project, run the init command in the root folder of the project. This will prompt a series of questions to generate the package.json file. You can fill out the answers you wish or just click on return to accept default values for the prompts:

```
cd <project-name>
npm init
```

3. Let's also install our beloved lodash to help us out with some of the trivial array and object manipulations and utilities:

```
npm install --save lodash
```

Use cases

Once your project is ready to go, we can now add the necessary scripts in the project's root and then run them independently.

Using recursion to serialize data

Recursion is a very popular **programming paradigm** in which a problem statement can be broken down into several smaller problems, which can be defined in terms of itself. Recursion is usually confused with **divide and concur**, in which the problem statement is broken into non-overlapping sub-problems which can be solved simultaneously.

In the following section, we will take a simple tree in which we have a root element followed by some child elements. We will be serializing this tree data, which can then be easily sent to the UI or persisted in the database.

Let's first create a folder called `recursion` within our project, which we created based on the preceding section. Then, we can create our `serializer.js` file within this folder, which will contain the class for serializing tree data.

Pseudocode

Let's formulate our algorithm in pseudo code before implementing the recursive serializer:

```
INITIALIZE response

FOR each node

    extract child nodes

    add current node info to serialized string

    IF childNodes exist

        repeat process for child nodes

    ELSE

        add ^ to indicate end of the level


IF rootnode

    return serialized string

ELSE

    add ^ to indicate child node of root
```

Serializing data

Now that we have the pseudo code in place, the code for serialization becomes quite simple, let us add the following to a file called `recursion.js` next to our serializer:

```
var _ = require('lodash');

class Recursion {
    constructor(tree) {
        this.tree = tree;
```

```
    }

    // serialize method which accepts list of nodes
    serialize(nodes) {
        // initialize response
        this.currentState = this.currentState || '';

        // loop over all nodes
        _.forEach(nodes, (node) => {

            // depth first traversal, extracting nodes at each level
            // traverse one level down
            var childNodes = this.tree[node];

            // add current node to list of serialized nodes
            this.currentState += ` ${node}`;

            // has child nodes
            if (childNodes) {

                // recursively repeat
                this.serialize(childNodes);
            } else {

                // mark as last node, traverse up
                this.currentState += ` ^`;
            }
        });

        // loop complete, traverse one level up
        // unless already at root otherwise return response
        if (!this.isRoot(nodes)) {
            this.currentState += ` ^`;
        } else {
            return this.currentState.trim();
        }
    }

    isRoot(nodes) {
        return _.isEqual(this.tree.root, nodes);
    }
}


module.exports = Recursion;
```

Note that in the preceding code we split the problem in terms of itself, that we determined what needs to be done for one level and then repeated the process for all the nodes **recursively.** Now, to consume this serialization method, create a `serialization.js` file and then add the following code to it:

```
var fs = require('fs');
var Recursion = require('./recursion');

// set up data
const tree = {
    root: ['A'],
    A: ['B', 'C', 'D'],
    B: ['E', 'F'],
    D: ['G', 'H', 'I', 'J'],
    F: ['K']
};

// initialize
var serializer = new Recursion(tree);

// serialize
var serializedData = serializer.serialize(tree.root);

console.log(serializedData);
```

When we run the preceding file with the `node recursion/serializer.js` command from the root of the project, we get the serialized response logged onto the console:

```
A B E ^ F K ^ ^ ^ C ^ D G ^ H ^ I ^ J ^ ^ ^
```

From the preceding response, you can note that the depth-first approach can be seen quite visibly based on our input dataset. B is a child of A, and E is a leaf child of B (indicated by the ^ symbol following E). Deserializing this serialized data using recursive is also a simple process, which you can try on your own.

Using Dijkstra to determine the shortest path

Until the preceding chapter, we explored only the simple ways of graph traversal, **Breadth First Search (BFS)** and **Depth First Search (DFS)**. We did discuss in brief in the preceding chapter about Dijkstra and how it can help us determine the path from node **A** to node **B** in a graph, provided the graph is directed with weighted edges.

In this example, we have just that. We have a graph of nodes (cities) and edges (approximate distance in miles), and we need to determine the fastest path for a user to reach a destination node from a given start node, provided other factors, such as speed, traffic, and weather, remain constant:

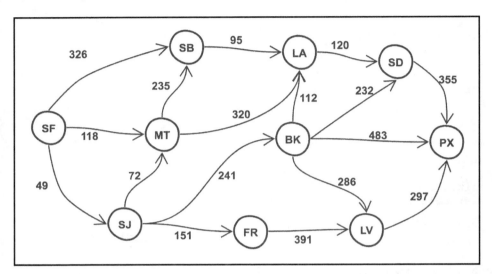

Our trip starts from **San Francisco (SF)** and ends in **Phoenix (PX)**. We have identified some intermediate cities in which the user can stop for rest or gas: **Monterey (MT)**, **San Jose (SJ)**, **Santa Barbara (SB)**, **Los Angeles (LA)**, **San Diego (SD)**, **Fresno (FR)**, **Bakersfield (BK)**, and **Las Vegas (LV)**. The distance to each of these cities is indicated by the weights that are associated with each of the edges between the cities.

Pseudo code

Let's take a look at the pseudo code for implementing Dijkstra's algorithm:

```
INITIALIZE Costs, Previous Paths, Visited Nodes

ADD each neighbor of start node to Previous Paths

GET cheapest node from start node and set as current node

WHILE node exists

    GET cost of current node from costs
```

```
GET neighbors of current node

FOREACH neighbor

    ADD cost of neighbor to current nodes cost as new cost

    IF cost of neighbor not recorded OR cost of
        neighbor is the lowest amongst all neighbors

        SET cost of neighbor as new cost

        SET the path of neighbor as current node


    MARK current node as visited

    GET cheapest node from start node and set as current node


INITIALIZE response

BACKTRACK path from end to start

RETURN distance and path
```

Implementing Dijkstra's algorithm

Let's break down the implementation of Dijkstra's algorithm based on the pseudo code described in the preceding section. The first step is to initialize all the variables. We will use one to track the costs of going through each node, one for tracking the path we are taking, and one more to track the already visited nodes to avoid recalculations:

```
var _ = require('lodash');

class Dijkstra {
    solve (graph, start, end) {

        // track costs of each node
        const costs = graph[start];

        // set end to infinite on 1st pass
        costs[end] = Infinity;

        // remember path from
        // which each node was visited
        const paths = {};
```

```
      // add path for the start nodes neighbors
      _.forEach(graph[start], (dist, city) => {
         // e.g. city SJ was visited from city SF
         paths[city] = start;
      });

      // track nodes that have already been visited nodes
      const visitedNodes = [];

      ....
```

Our `solve()` method here has initialized the `costs` with the `cost` of the start node, and then set the end nodes `cost` as `Infinity` as that is not calculated yet. This means that at the beginning, the `costs set` would contain exactly the same data as the nodes and edges, going out from the start node.

We also calculated the paths accordingly, for example, since we are starting with `SF` in our example, the nodes—`SJ`, `MT`, and `SB`—were all reached from node `SF`. Following code explains how we can extract the lowest cost at each node:

```
   ...

   // track nodes that have already been visited nodes
   const visitedNodes = [];

   // get current nodes cheapest neighbor
   let currentCheapestNode = this.getNextLowestCostUnvisitedNode(costs,
   visitedNodes);

   // while node exists
   while (currentCheapestNode) {

      // get cost of reaching current cheapest node
      let costToReachCurrentNode = costs[currentCheapestNode];

      // access neighbors of current cheapest node
      let neighbors = graph[currentCheapestNode];

      // loop over neighbors
      _.forEach(neighbors, (dist, neighbor) => {

         // generate new cost to reach each neighbor
         let newCost = costToReachCurrentNode + dist;

         // if not already added
         // or if it is lowest cost amongst the neighbors
         if (!costs[neighbor] || costs[neighbor] > newCost) {
```

```
            // add cost to list of costs
            costs[neighbor] = newCost;

            // add to paths
            paths[neighbor] = currentCheapestNode;

        }

    });

    // mark as visited
    visitedNodes.push(currentCheapestNode);

    // get cheapest node for next node
    currentCheapestNode = this.getNextLowestCostUnvisitedNode(costs,
visitedNodes);
}
```

    . . .

This is probably the most important part of the code; we are calculating the
currentCheapestNode based on the costs and the visitedNodes array, whose value in
the first iteration will be SJ, as we can see from our preceding diagram.

Once we have the first node, we can then access its neighbors and update the costs of
reaching these neighbors only if its costs are less than the current cost of the node. Also,
if the cost is lesser, it is only logical that we would like to pass through this node to get to
the end node, so we update the path to this neighbor as well. We then recursively repeat
this process after marking the visited nodes. At the end of all iterations, we will have the
updated costs of all the nodes and thus get the final cost of traveling to a node:

    . . . .

```
      // get cheapest node for next node
      currentCheapestNode =
      this.getNextLowestCostUnvisitedNode(costs, visitedNodes);
  }

  // generate response
  let finalPath = [];

  // recursively go to the start
  let previousNode = paths[end];

  while (previousNode) {
      finalPath.unshift(previousNode);
```

```
        previousNode = paths[previousNode];
    }

    // add end node at the end
    finalPath.push(end);

    // return response
    return {
        distance: costs[end],
        path: finalPath
    };
}

getNextLowestCostUnvisitedNode(costs, visitedNodes) {
    //extract the costs of all non visited nodes
    costs = _.omit(costs, visitedNodes);

    // return the node with minimum cost
    return _.minBy(_.keys(costs), (node) => {
        return costs[node];
    });
}
}

module.exports = Dijkstra;
```

Once all the nodes' costs are generated, we will simply backtrack the steps which were taken to reach the end node, and we can return the cost of the end node and the path taken to reach the end node. The Utility method to get the lowest cost unvisited node is added at the end.

Now, to consume this class, we can create a file called shortest-path.js under the dijkstra folder along with the dijkstra.js class that we just created:

```
var Dijkstra = require('./dijkstra');

const graph = {
    'SF': { 'SB': 326, 'MT': 118, 'SJ': 49 },
    'SJ': { 'MT': 72, 'FR': 151, 'BK': 241 },
    'MT': { 'SB': 235, 'LA': 320 },
    'SB': { 'LA': 95 },
    'LA': { 'SD': 120 },
    'SD': { 'PX': 355 },
    'FR': { 'LV': 391 },
    'BK': { 'LA': 112, 'SD': 232, 'PX': 483, 'LV': 286 },
    'LV': { 'PX': 297 },
    'PX': {}
```

```
};

console.log(new Dijkstra().solve(graph, 'SF', 'PX'));
```

Now, to run this file, simply run the following command:

node dijkstra/shortest-path.js

The preceding command logs the following code:

```
{ distance: 773, path: [ 'SF', 'SJ', 'BK', 'PX' ] }
```

This, when visualized based on the original illustration, would be something like as follows:

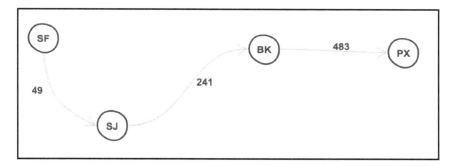

Using BFS to determine relationships

Okay, it's not what it sounds like. We are not heading down a romantic path where we ask each other the difficult question. We are, however, talking about a simple graph, for example, a family tree (yes, trees are forms of the graph). In this example, we will use BFS to determine the shortest path between two nodes, which can then establish the relationship between those two nodes.

Let's first set up our test data so that we have the input graph ready:

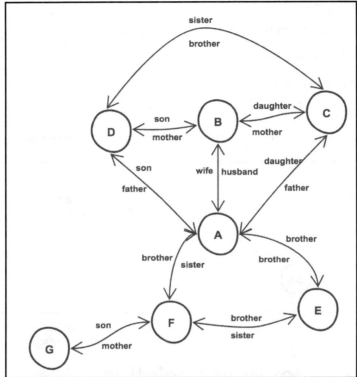

You can note from the preceding diagram that we have a small family in which nodes A, E, and F are siblings. A is married to B with nodes C and D as their children. Node G is a child of node F. Nothing complex or out of the ordinary here. We will use this data to determine the relationship between nodes C and G. You can surely look at the graph and tell it yourself, but that's not fun now, is it?

Let's now convert this into a format that our program can understand:

```
[
    {
        "name": "A",
        "connections": [
            {
                "name": "E",
                "relation": "Brother"
            },
```

```
          {
            "name": "F",
            "relation": "Sister"
          },
          {
            "name": "B",
            "relation": "Wife"
          },
          {
            "name": "D",
            "relation": "Son"
          },
          {
            "name": "C",
            "relation": "Daughter"
          }
        ]
      },
      {
        "name": "B",
        "connections": [
          {
            "name": "A",
            "relation": "Husband"
          },
          {
            "name": "D",
            "relation": "Son"
          },
          {
            "name": "C",
            "relation": "Daughter"
          }
        ]
      },
      {
        "name": "C",
        "connections": [
          {
            "name": "A",
            "relation": "Father"
          },
          {
            "name": "B",
            "relation": "Mother"
          },
          {
            "name": "D",
```

```
            "relation": "Brother"
          }
        ]
    },
    {
      "name": "D",
      "connections": [
        {
          "name": "A",
          "relation": "Father"
        },
        {
          "name": "B",
          "relation": "Mother"
        },
        {
          "name": "C",
          "relation": "Sister"
        }
      ]
    },
    {
      "name": "E",
      "connections": [
        {
          "name": "A",
          "relation": "Brother"
        },
        {
          "name": "F",
          "relation": "Sister"
        }
      ]
    },
    {
      "name": "F",
      "connections": [
        {
          "name": "E",
          "relation": "Brother"
        },
        {
          "name": "A",
          "relation": "Brother"
        },
        {
          "name": "G",
          "relation": "Son"
```

```
        }
      ]
    },
    {
      "name": "G",
      "connections": [
        {
          "name": "F",
          "relation": "Mother"
        }
      ]
    }
]
```

That got complex real quick, didn't it? This is a challenge with nodes where you want to establish a relationship (that is, labeled edges). Let's add this data to the `family.json` file and then take a look at the pseudo code for the BFS so that we can understand it better before implementing the same.

Pseudo code

The pseudo code for BFS is very similar to DFS, the main difference is that in BFS we iterate over all the connected nodes first before moving out to another level looking for our target node:

```
INITIALIZE paths, nodes to visit (queue), visited nodes

SET start node as visited

WHILE nodes to visit exist

    GET the next node to visit as current node from top of queue

    IF current node is target

        INITIALIZE result with target node

        WHILE path retrieval not at source

            EXTRACT how we got to this node

            PUSH to result

        FORMAT and return relationship
```

```
        ELSE

            LOOP over the entire graph

                IF node is connected to current node

                    SET its path as current node
                    MARK node as visited

                    PUSH it to queue for visiting breadth wise

        RETURN Null that is no result
```

Sounds very similar to the other example we worked on with DFS, doesn't it? That is because DFS and BFS are very similar in terms of how we approach the problem. The minor difference between the two is that we evaluate all connected nodes before spreading out one more level in BFS, whereas we select one of the connected nodes in case of DFS and then traverse it till the entire depth.

Implementing BFS

To implement the previously discussed pseudo code, we will first simplify our data a little bit. There are two ways to do this, as follows:

1. Create an adjacency matrix of the graph data that indicates the graph as a two-dimensional array of size *m x m*, which consists of 1s and 0s. *1s* indicates a connection between the *mrow* node with *mcolumn* and *0s* indicates no connection.
2. We simplify the dataset and only extract the nodes as a map in which the key is the node and the value is the list of nodes that it is connected to.

Although both approaches are fine ways of approaching the problem, the first option is usually preferred and is popular because the second option is of a higher code complexity because of all the overhead of sets and lists which come with it.

However, right now, we don't need to worry about code complexity as we want to get the simplest possible solution out there, so we will go with the second option.

First, we will simplify the input data so that we have the transformed input to pass into the BFS algorithm that we are going to create:

```
var _ = require('lodash');
var BFS = require('./bfs');
var familyNodes = require('./family.json');

// transform familyNodes into shorter format for simplified BFS
var transformedFamilyNodes = _.transform(familyNodes, (reduced,
currentNode) => {

        reduced[currentNode.name] = _.map(currentNode.relations, 'name');

        return reduced;
}, {});
```

This basically sets the `transformedFamilyNodes` to the structure, which is described earlier, and in our case, it looks as follows:

```
{
    A: [ 'E', 'F', 'B', 'D', 'C' ],
    B: [ 'A', 'D', 'C' ],
    C: [ 'A', 'B', 'D' ],
    D: [ 'A', 'B', 'C' ],
    E: [ 'A', 'F' ],
    F: [ 'E', 'A', 'G' ],
    G: [ 'F' ]
}
```

Then, we create the class for our BFS search and then add a method to implement the search functionality:

```
var _ = require('lodash');

class BFS {

    constructor(familyNodes) {
        this.familyNodes = familyNodes;
    }

    search (graph, startNode, targetNode) {
    }

}

module.exports = BFS;
```

We accept the list of the original family nodes in the constructor and then the modified graph within our search method, which we will iterate upon. Then, why would we need the original family nodes? Because once we extract the path from one node to another, we will need to establish the relationship between them, which is recorded on the original unprocessed family nodes.

We will move on to implement the `search()` method:

```
search (graph, startNode, targetNode) {
    // initialize the path to traverse
    var travelledPath = [];

    // mark the nodes that need to be visited breadthwise
    var nodesToVisit = [];

    // mark all visited nodes
    var visitedNodes = {};

    // current node being visited
    var currentNode;

    // add start node to the to be visited path
    nodesToVisit.push(startNode);

    // mark starting node as visited node
    visitedNodes[startNode] = true;

    // while there are more nodes to go
    while (nodesToVisit.length) {

        // get the first one in the list to visit
        currentNode = nodesToVisit.shift();

        // if it is the target
        if (_.isEqual(currentNode, targetNode)) {

            // add to result, backtrack steps based on path taken
            var result = [targetNode];

            // while target is not source
            while (!_.isEqual(targetNode, startNode)) {

                // extract how we got to this node
                targetNode = travelledPath[targetNode];

                // add it to result
                result.push(targetNode);
```

```
        }

        // extract the relationships between the edges and return
        // value
        return this.getRelationBetweenNodes(result.reverse());
    }

    // if result not found, set the next node to visit by traversing
    // breadth first
    _.forOwn(graph, (connections, name) => {

        // if not current node, is connected to current node
        // and not already visited
        if (!_.isEqual(name, currentNode)
            && _.includes(graph[name], currentNode)
            && !visitedNodes[name]) {

            // we will be visiting the new node from current node
            travelledPath[name] = currentNode;

            // set the visited flag
            visitedNodes[name] = true;

            // push to nodes to visit
            nodesToVisit.push(name);
        }
    });
    }

    // nothing found
    return null;
}
```

This was quick and painless. If you have noted, we are calling the getRelationBetweenNodes, which extracts the relations between the nodes based on the familyNodes, which are passed into the constructor once the path between two nodes is determined. This will extract the relationship of each node with the node that follows:

```
getRelationBetweenNodes(relationship) {
    // extract start and end from result
    var start = relationship.shift();
    var end = relationship.pop();

    // initialize loop variables
    var relation = '';
    var current = start;
    var next;
```

```
        var relationWithNext;

        // while end not found
        while (current != end) {
            // extract the current node and its relationships
            current = _.find(this.familyNodes, { name: current });

            // extract the next node, if nothing then set to end node
            next = relationship.shift() || end;

            // extract relationship between the current and the next node
            relationWithNext = _.find(current.relations, {name : next });

            // add it to the relation with proper grammar
            relation += `${relationWithNext.relation}${next === end ? '' :
            '\'s'} `;

            // set next to current for next iteration
            current = next;
        }

        // return result
        return `${start}'s ${relation}is ${end}`;
    }
```

Now that we have the class ready, we are ready to invoke this by calling node
bfs/relations.js:

```
var _ = require('lodash');
var BFS = require('./bfs');
var familyNodes = require('./family.json');

// transform familyNodes into shorter format for simplified BFS
var transformedFamilyNodes = _.transform(familyNodes, (reduced,
currentNode) => {

    reduced[currentNode.name] = _.map(currentNode.relations, 'name');

    return reduced;
}, {});

var relationship = new BFS(familyNodes).search(transformedFamilyNodes, 'C',
'G');

console.log(relationship);
```

The preceding code logs the following:

```
C's Father's Sister's Son is G
```

This can be represented visually as follows, based on the initial illustration:

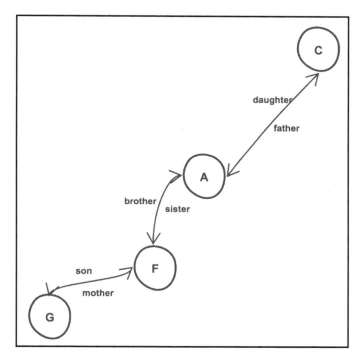

Using dynamic programming to build a financial planner

Dynamic programming (DP) is a very common and powerful approach to solve a certain class of problems. These problems present themselves in ways in which the main problem can be divided into sub-problems and the sub-problems can be broken down further into smaller problems, with some overlap in between.

DP is often confused with recursion because of their similarities. A DP problem is only a type of problem, whereas recursion is part of the solution to such problems. There are two main ways in which we can approach solving such problems:

- Break the problem down to sub-problems: If a sub-problem is solved already then return the saved solution, else solve and save the solution before returning it. This is also known as **memoization**. This is also known as a top-down approach.
- Break the problem to sub-problems: Start solving the smallest sub-problem and work up. This approach is known as **bottom-up** approach.

In this example, we have a series of expenses that a user has; we will need to provide the user with all the possible outcomes based on a total, which is set by the user. We want the users to be able to pick and choose what option they like, thus we will go with the bottom-up approach. First, let's break down the input data and then deduce the code from the pseudo code:

```
let expenses = [
    {
        type: 'rent',
        cost: 5
    },
    {
        type: 'food',
        cost: 3
    },
    {
        type: 'entertainment',
        cost: 2
    },
    {
        type: 'car and gas',
        cost: 2
    },
    {
        type: 'ski-trip',
        cost: 5
    }
];

let total = 10;
```

You can note from the preceding code that the sample input data has been normalized for simplicity and code efficiency. Once we have that setup, we can create our pseudo code to understand the algorithm.

Pseudo code

In this example, for this type of problem, we will be creating a two-dimensional array, where one dimension, (y), represents the values of the elements (that is, costs of each expense: 5, 3, 2, 2, and 5) and the other dimension, (x), represents the total cost incrementally (that is, 0 through 10). This is why we normalize our data in the first step—it helps us in terms of keeping our array small in terms of its dimensions.

Once we have the array, we will assign each of the array positions—arr[i][j]—as true if any of the 0 to i costs can create the j sum at any point, else it will be false:

```
CREATE empty 2d array with based on input data

IF expected total 0, any element can achieve this, so set [i][0] to true

IF cost of first row is less than total, set [0][cost] to true

LOOP over each row from the second row

    LOOP over each column

        IF current row cost is less than the current column total

            COPY from the row above, the value of the current column if
            it is true
                or else offset the column by current rows cost

        ELSE

            Copy value from the row above for the same column


IF last element of the array is empty

    No results found


generate_possible_outcomes()

FUNCTION generate_possible_outcomes
```

```
IF reached the end and sum is non 0
   ADD cost as an option and return options

IF reached the end and sum is 0

   return option

IF sum can be derived without current row cost

   generate_possible_outcomes() from the previous row

IF sum cannot be derived without current row

   ADD current row as an option
   generate_possible_outcomes() from the previous row
```

Note in the preceding code that the algorithm is quite straightforward; we just break down the problem into smaller sub-problems and try to answer the question for each sub-problem while working its way up to the bigger problem. Once we are done constructing the array, we start from the last cell of the array and then traverse up and add a cell to the path taken, based on whether the current cell is true or not. The recursive process is stopped once we reach the total of 0, that is, the first column.

Implementing the dynamic programming algorithm

Now that we understand the approach, let's first create the class for our algorithm and add the `analyze()` method, which will first create the 2D array before generating the algorithm.

When the class is initialized, we will construct our 2D array with all the values in it set to `false`. We will then use this 2D array and update some of the values within it based on our conditions, which we will discuss shortly:

```javascript
var _ = require('lodash');

class Planner {

    constructor(rows, cols) {
        // create a 2d array of rows x cols
        // all with value false
        this.planner = _.range(rows).map(() => {
            return _.range(cols + 1).map(()=> false);
        });
        // holds the response
        this.outcomes = [];
```

```
    }
}

module.exports = Planner;
```

Now, we can implement the analyze() method, which will set the appropriate values in each of the cells of the 2D array.

First, we will set the values of the first column, and then of the first row:

```
analyze(expenses, sum) {
    // get size of expenses
    const size = _.size(expenses);

    // if sum 0, result can be done with 0 elements so
    // set col 0 of all rows as true
    _.times(size, (i)=> {
        this.planner[i] = this.planner[i] || [];
        this.planner[i][0] = true;
    });

    // for the first row, if the first cost in the expenses
    // is less than the requested total, set its column value
    // to true
    if(expenses[0].cost <= sum) {
        this.planner[0][expenses[0].cost] = true;
    }
```

Although the first column is all true, a cell of the first row, on the other hand, is only true when the cost associated with that row is less than the sum, that is, we can build the requested sum with only one element. Next, we take the row and column that has been filled out and use that to build the rest of the array:

```
    // start from row #2 and loop over all other rows
    for(let i = 1; i < size; i++) {

        // take each column
        _.times(sum + 1, (j) => {

            // if the expenses cost for the current row
            // is less than or equal to the sum assigned to the
            // current column
            if (expenses[i].cost <= j) {

                // copy value from above row in the same column if true
                // else look at the value offset by the current rows cost
                this.planner[i][j] =  this.planner[i - 1][j]
```

```
                                      || this.planner[i - 1][j -
                                  expenses[i].cost];
              } else {
                  // copy value from above row in the same column
                  this.planner[i][j] =  this.planner[i - 1][j];
              }
          });
      }

      // no results found
      if (!this.planner[size - 1][sum]) {
          return [];
      }

      // generate the outcomes from the results found
      this.generateOutcomes(expenses, size - 1, sum, []);

      return this.outcomes;
  }
```

Next, we can implement the `generateOutcomes()` method, which will allow us to capture the possible paths recursively. When we list down our 2D array and take a look at what the generated array looks as follows:

```
COST
      [   0      1      2      3      4      5      6      7      8      9      10       SUM
  5   [ true, false, false, false, false, true,  false, false, false, false, false ],
  3   [ true, false, false, true,  false, true,  false, false, true,  false, false ],
  2   [ true, false, true,  true,  false, true,  false, true,  true,  false, true  ],
  2   [ true, false, true,  true,  true,  true,  false, true,  true,  true,  true  ],
  5   [ true, false, true,  true,  true,  true,  false, true,  true,  true,  true  ]
      ]
```

You can see in the preceding screenshot that the column 0 (i.e. sum 0) is all `true`, and for row 0 (cost 5), the only other column in which all the values are true is column 5 (i.e. sum 5).

Now, moving on to the next row, let's analyze the values one by one, for example, at that stage, the costs 5 and 3 (taken from the cost of the current row and the row above it) cannot add up to give a cost of 1 or 2 but it can give 3, 5, and 8, so only they are `true` and the rest are `false`.

Now, moving on to each of the next rows, we can try to import the value from the row above if it is true, if it is not then subtract the current row's cost from the column sum and check whether that column for the above row is true. This lets us determine whether the sum was determined by an earlier subset.

For example, in row 3 column 1, we just import from the parent row (remember that column 0 is always `true`). When we reach column 2, we see that the parent rows' col 2 is `false`, so we offset this columns sum (2) with the current rows cost (2) so we end up with row 2 column 0 which is `true`. Hence we assign a value of `true` to row 2 column 2, and then we continue this process for the next column till the end.

Once the entire array is constructed, we will need to start at the very end, which in this case, is `array[4][10]`, and recursively traverse up until we reach the sum of 0 or reach the top with a nonzero sum:

```
generateOutcomes(expenses, i, sum, p) {
    // reached the end and the sum is non zero
    if(i === 0 && sum !== 0 && this.planner[0][sum]) {
        p.push(expenses[i]);
        this.outcomes.push(_.cloneDeep(p));
        p = [];
        return;
    }

    // reached the end and the sum is zero
    // i.e. reached the origin
    if(i === 0 && sum === 0) {
        this.outcomes.push(_.cloneDeep(p));
        p = [];
        return;
    }

    // if the sum can be generated
    // even without the current value
    if(this.planner[i - 1][sum]) {
        this.generateOutcomes(expenses, i - 1, sum, _.cloneDeep(p));
    }

    // if the sum can be derived
    // only by including the the current value
    if(sum >= expenses[i].cost && this.planner[i - 1][sum -
expenses[i].cost]) {
        p.push(expenses[i]);
        this.generateOutcomes(expenses, i - 1, sum - expenses[i].cost,
        p);
    }
}
```

Now, this can be consumed in our planner to generate the list of options for our users to choose from:

```
var Planner = require('./dp');

let expenses = [
    {
        type: 'rent',
        cost: 5
    },
    {
        type: 'food',
        cost: 3
    },
    {
        type: 'entertainment',
        cost: 2
    },
    {
        type: 'car and gas',
        cost: 2
    },
    {
        type: 'ski-trip',
        cost: 5
    }
];
let total = 10;

var options = new Planner(expenses.length, total).analyze(expenses, total);

console.log(options);
```

Running the previous code logs the different combinations which fit our budget, resulting in:

```
[
    [ { type: 'entertainment', cost: 2 },
      { type: 'food', cost: 3 },
      { type: 'rent', cost: 5 }
    ],
    [ { type: 'car and gas', cost: 2 },
      { type: 'food', cost: 3 },
      { type: 'rent', cost: 5 }
    ],
    [ { type: 'ski-trip', cost: 5 },
      { type: 'rent', cost: 5 }
```

```
    ],
    [ { type: 'ski-trip', cost: 5 },
      { type: 'entertainment', cost: 2 },
      { type: 'food', cost: 3 }
    ],
    [ { type: 'ski-trip', cost: 5 },
      { type: 'car and gas', cost: 2 },
      { type: 'food', cost: 3 }
    ]
]
```

Using a greedy algorithm to build a travel itinerary

A greedy algorithm is one in which a problem is broken down into smaller sub-problems and a solution to each of these sub-problems is pieced together based on a locally optimized choice at each step. This means that, in case of weighted edge graphs, for example, the next node is picked on the basis of whatever provides the least cost to travel from the current node. This may not be the best path to take, but, in the case of greedy algorithms, getting a solution is the main goal rather than getting the perfect or the ideal solution.

In this use case, we have a set of cities along with the weight associated with traveling to each of these cities *(cost to travel/stay + enjoyment factor and so on)*. The objective is to figure out a way in which we want to travel and visit these cities so that the travel is complete and fun. Of course, for a given set of cities, you can travel to them in many possible ways, but that does not guarantee that the path is going to be optimized. To solve this problem, we will be using Kruskal's minimum spanning tree algorithm, which is a type of greedy algorithm that will generate the best possible solution for us. A spanning tree in a graph is one in which all the nodes are connected and there are no cycles between the nodes.

Let's assume that our input data is of the following format, which is the same as what we have seen earlier in the Dijkstra example, except that we are not defining any direction between the nodes, allowing us to travel from either direction:

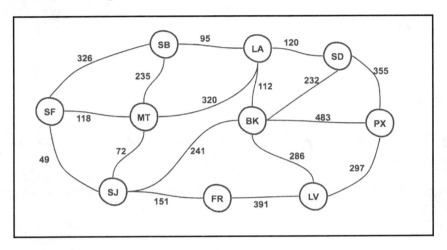

This data can be programmatically written as follows:

```
const graph = {
    'SF': { 'SB': 326, 'MT': 118, 'SJ': 49 },
    'SJ': { 'MT': 72, 'FR': 151, 'BK': 241 },
    'MT': { 'SB': 235, 'LA': 320 },
    'SB': { 'LA': 95 },
    'LA': { 'SD': 120 },
    'SD': { 'PX': 355 },
    'FR': { 'LV': 391 },
    'BK': { 'LA': 112, 'SD': 232, 'PX': 483, 'LV': 286 },
    'LV': { 'PX': 297 },
    'PX': {}
};
```

From this information, we can extract the unique edges, as follows:

```
[
    { from: 'SF', to: 'SB', weight: 326 },
    { from: 'SF', to: 'MT', weight: 118 },
    { from: 'SF', to: 'SJ', weight: 49 },
    { from: 'SJ', to: 'MT', weight: 72 },
    { from: 'SJ', to: 'FR', weight: 151 },
    { from: 'SJ', to: 'BK', weight: 241 },
    { from: 'MT', to: 'SB', weight: 235 },
    { from: 'MT', to: 'LA', weight: 320 },
```

```
  { from: 'SB', to: 'LA', weight: 95 },
  { from: 'LA', to: 'SD', weight: 120 },
  { from: 'SD', to: 'PX', weight: 355 },
  { from: 'FR', to: 'LV', weight: 391 },
  { from: 'BK', to: 'LA', weight: 112 },
  { from: 'BK', to: 'SD', weight: 232 },
  { from: 'BK', to: 'PX', weight: 483 },
  { from: 'BK', to: 'LV', weight: 286 },
  { from: 'LV', to: 'PX', weight: 297 }
]
```

Understanding spanning trees

Before we go ahead and implement the pseudo code and the code, let's take some time to understand what spanning trees are and how we can employ them to simplify the problems as stated previously.

A spanning tree within a graph is a series of edges that can connect all the nodes without any cycles within them. By saying that, it is obvious that there can be more than one spanning tree for any given graph. In terms of our example, it makes more sense now that we want to generate the **minimum spanning tree** (**MST**), that is, the spanning tree in which the combined edge weight is the minimum.

However, how do we generate the spanning tree and make sure that it has the minimum value? The solution, although not quite obvious, is quite simple. Let's explore the approach with the pseudo code.

Pseudo code

The problem at hand now has boiled down to the following—connect all the nodes of our graph with least weight edges and no cycles. To achieve this, first, we will need to isolate all our edges and sort by weight in an increasing order. Then, we employ a technique called union by rank to get the final list of the edges, which can be used to create the MST:

```
SORT all edges by weight in increasing order

DIVIDE all nodes into their own subsets whose parent is the node iteself

WHILE more edges are required

    EXTRACT the first edge from the list of edges

    FIND the parent nodes of the from and to nodes of that edge
```

```
    IF start and end nodes do not have same parent

        ADD edge to results

        GET parent of from node and to node

        IF parent nodes of from and to are the same rank

            SET one node as the parent of the other and increment rank
            of parent

        ELSE

            SET parent of element with lesser rank

    RETURN Results
```

In the `find()` method, we will perform a small optimization called path compression. Sounds fancy, but it really isn't. Let's say that we are at a node A whose parent is node B and its parent is node C. When we are trying to determine that, we only parse this entire path once, and for next time, we remember that the parent of node A is ultimately node C. The way we do it is also relatively easy—every time we traverse up the tree for a node, we will be updating its `parent` property:

```
FIND_PARENT(all_subsets, currentNode)

    IF parent of currentNode is NOT currentNode

        FIND_PARENT(all_subsets, currentNode.parent)

    RETURN currentNode.parent
```

Implementing a minimum spanning tree using a greedy algorithm

So far, we have the dataset up as described earlier. Now, we will generate the edges from that data and then pass it on to our spanning tree class to generate the MST. So let us add the following code to `greeds/travel.js`:

```
const _ = require('lodash');
const MST = require('./mst');

const graph = {
    'SF': { 'SB': 326, 'MT': 118, 'SJ': 49 },
```

```
        'SJ': { 'MT': 72, 'FR': 151, 'BK': 241 },
        'MT': { 'SB': 235, 'LA': 320 },
        'SB': { 'LA': 95 },
        'LA': { 'SD': 120 },
        'SD': { 'PX': 355 },
        'FR': { 'LV': 391 },
        'BK': { 'LA': 112, 'SD': 232, 'PX': 483, 'LV': 286 },
        'LV': { 'PX': 297 },
        'PX': {}
};

const edges= [];

_.forEach(graph, (values, node) => {
    _.forEach(values, (weight, city) => {
        edges.push({
            from: node,
            to: city,
            weight: weight
        });
    });
});

var mst = new MST(edges, _.keys(graph)).getNodes();

console.log(mst);
```

Our MST class can be added to `greedy/mst.js` which is as follows:

```
const _ = require('lodash');

class MST {

    constructor(edges, vertices) {
        this.edges = _.sortBy(edges, 'weight');
        this.vertices = vertices;
    }


    getNodes () {
        let result = [];

        // subsets to track the parents and ranks
        var subsets = {};

        // split each vertex into its own subset
        // with each of them initially pointing to themselves
        _.each(this.vertices, (val)=> {
```

```
            subsets[val] = {
                parent: val,
                rank: 0
            };
        });

        // loop over each until the size of the results
        // is 1 less than the number of vertices
        while(!_.isEqual(_.size(result), _.size(this.vertices) - 1)) {

            // get next edge
            var selectedEdge = this.edges.shift();

            // find parent of start and end nodes of selected edge
            var x = this.find(subsets, selectedEdge.from);
            var y = this.find(subsets, selectedEdge.to);

            // if the parents nodes are not the same then
            // the nodes belong to different subsets and can be merged
            if (!_.isEqual(x, y)) {

                // add to result
                result.push(selectedEdge);

                // push is resultant tree as new nodes
                this.union(subsets, x, y);
            }
        }

        return result;
    }

    // find parent with path compression
    find(subsets, i) {
        let subset = subsets[i];

        // until the parent is not itself, keep updating the
        // parent of the current node
        if (subset.parent != i) {
            subset.parent = this.find(subsets, subset.parent);
        }

        return subset.parent;
    }

    // union by rank
    union(subsets, x, y) {
        // get the root nodes of each of the nodes
```

```
    let xRoot  = this.find(subsets, x);

    let yRoot  = this.find(subsets, y);

    // ranks equal so it doesnt matter which is the parent of which
    node
    if (_.isEqual(subsets[xRoot].rank, subsets[yRoot].rank)) {

        subsets[yRoot].parent = xRoot;

        subsets[xRoot].rank++;

    } else {
        // compare ranks and set parent of the subset
        if(subsets[xRoot].rank < subsets[yRoot].rank) {

            subsets[xRoot].parent = yRoot;
        } else {

            subsets[yRoot].parent = xRoot;
        }
    }
  }


}

module.exports = MST;
```

Running the preceding code would log the edges, which will be as follows:

```
[ { from: 'SF', to: 'SJ', weight: 49 },
  { from: 'SJ', to: 'MT', weight: 72 },
  { from: 'SB', to: 'LA', weight: 95 },
  { from: 'BK', to: 'LA', weight: 112 },
  { from: 'LA', to: 'SD', weight: 120 },
  { from: 'SJ', to: 'FR', weight: 151 },
  { from: 'MT', to: 'SB', weight: 235 },
  { from: 'BK', to: 'LV', weight: 286 },
  { from: 'LV', to: 'PX', weight: 297 } ]
```

Once connected, these paths will look as follows:

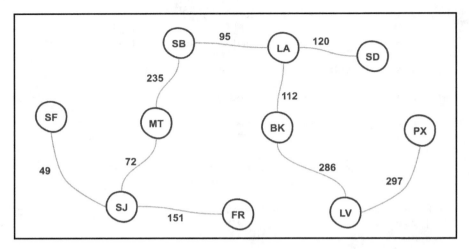

Using branch and bound algorithm to create a custom shopping list

The branch and bound algorithm are applied to a set of problems, which involves combinational optimization. What that means is that we can have a problem at hand that does not necessarily have one correct solution, but with the information that we have, we will need to generate the best possible solution out of the finite yet very large number of available solutions.

We will be using the branch and bound algorithm to optimize and solve a particular class of dynamic programming problems known as the 0/1 knapsack problem. In this case, consider that we have a shopping list in which we have a list of items, their cost in dollars, and their importance (value) to you on a scale of 0 to 10. For example, consider the following sample list:

```
const list = [
  {
    name: 'vegetables',
    value: 12,
    cost: 4
  },
  {
    name: 'candy',
    value: 1,
```

```
        cost: 1
    },
    {
        name: 'magazines',
        value: 4,
        cost: 2
    },
    {
        name: 'dvd',
        value: 6,
        cost: 2
    },
    {
        name: 'earphones',
        value: 6,
        cost: 3
    },
    {
        name: 'shoes',
        value: 4,
        cost: 2
    },
    {
        name: 'supplies',
        value: 9,
        cost: 3
    }
];
```

Given the list, we now need to find the best possible combination to maximize the value, given a fixed budget (for example, $10). The algorithm is called 0/1 knapsack because the decision that you can take is only a binary, that is, either take an item or drop it.

Now, let's try to understand what the problem statement is from a mathematical standpoint. We want to maximize the value while staying within our budget, so if we assume that we have e_1, e_2, e_3 and so on up to e_n elements, and know that each of these elements can either be picked (which will assign it a value of 1) or not picked (which will assign it a value of 0), to determine the total value, we can formulate it as follows:

$$\sum_{0}^{n} eivi$$

While we try to keep the value maximized, we also want to keep the total cost less than the budget:

$$\sum_{0}^{n} eici < Total$$

Okay, great, now we know the problem, but what can be the solution for this? Since we know that the value is always going to be either 0 or 1, we can create a binary tree to represent the state space of our solution and then layout a branch for each possibility at every node; for example in our case, we will have 2^n possibilities ($n = 7$), which is a total of 128. Now, going through each of the 128 possibilities does not sound very optimal, and we can note that this number is going to increase exponentially.

Understanding branch and bound algorithm

Before writing the pseudo code, let's break down the solution for a better understanding. What we want to do is to create a binary tree, and at each level of the tree we want to assign the cost to get to the node, the value of the node and the upper bound of the cost that it takes to reach to that node.

However, how do we calculate the upper bound of the tree? To determine that, let's first break our problem down into smaller parts:

```
const costs = [4, 1, 2, 2, 3, 2, 3];
const value = [12, 1, 4, 6, 6, 4, 9];
const v2c = [12/4, 1/1, 4/2, 6/2, 6/3, 4/2, 9/3];
const maxCost = 10
```

Once we have that, we will rearrange our elements in the decreasing order of our value to cost ratio because we want to pick the elements with the highest value for the least cost:

```
const costs = [4, 2, 3, 3, 2, 2, 1];
const value = [12, 6, 9, 6, 4, 4, 1];
const v2c = [3, 3, 3, 2, 2, 2, 1];
const maxCost = 10;
```

To determine the upper bound, we will now use a greedy algorithm (elements arranged in a decreasing order) in which we will allow fractional values to get the highest possible upper bound.

So, let's pick the obvious first element, which has a value of 12 and cost of 4, so the total upper bound of value at this step is 12 and the total cost is 4, which is less than the maximum, that is, 10. Then, we move on to the next element, where the upper bound now becomes *12+6=18* and the cost is *4+2 = 6* , which is still less than 10. Then, we pick the next, which brings the upper bound of the value to *18+9=27* and the cost to *6+3=9*. If we take the next element with a cost of 3, we will go over the maximum cost, so we will take it fractionally, that is, *(remaining cost/cost of the item) * value of the item which would be equal to (1/3)*6*, which is 2. So, the upper bound of the root element is *27+2 = 29*.

So, we can now say that under the given constraints, such as the cost and value, the upper bound value which we can get is 29. Now that we have the upper bound on the value, we can create a root element for our binary tree with this upper bound value and a cost and value of 0 each.

Once the root nodes maximum upper bound is calculated, we can repeat this process recursively for the subsequent nodes starting from the first node. At each level, we will update the cost, value, and upper bound in such a way that it reflects what the values would be when a node is picked versus when it is not picked:

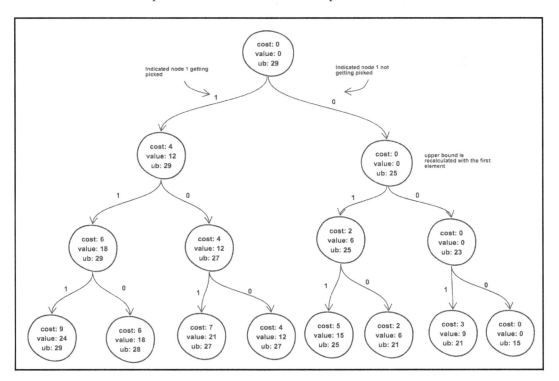

In the preceding image, you can note that we have built the state space tree for a few levels, which show what the state of each of the nodes would be when the branch is taken and also when it is not taken. As you can see, few of the branches are below the maximum upper bound of **27** (which we calculated earlier), whereas one of the branches goes over **27**, so we can remove that branch from further consideration. Now, at each of these steps, our main goal is to keep traversing the state space while increasing the value accumulated and staying below or equal to the upper bound. Any branch that deviates too far or exceeds from the upper bound can be safely removed from consideration.

Implementing branch and bound algorithm

So far, we have discussed how we can construct the state space tree step by step for each of the elements that are available, but that is not necessary, we only need to add the nodes selectively based on our bounds and the maximum cost that has been set.

So, what does that mean for us in implementation? We will take nodes one by one, consider what would happen if we include it or if we do not, and then add it to the queue for further processing if it falls under the conditions (bounds) that are set by us (maximum overall cost and the maximum upper bound of each branch).

Since we already have a list of items with us, we will first do some transformations to make the rest of the algorithm simpler:

```
const _ = require('lodash');

class BranchAndBound {

    constructor(list, maxCost) {
        // sort the costs in descending order for greedy calculation of
        upper bound
        var sortedList = _.orderBy(list,
                    (option) => option.value/option.cost,
                    'desc');

        // original list
        this.list = list;

        // max allowed cost
        this.maxCost = maxCost;

        // all costs
        this.costs = _.map(sortedList, 'cost');

        // all values
```

```
        this.values = _.map(sortedList, 'value');
    }
}

module.exports = BranchAndBound;
```

Once we have the costs and the values sorted and extracted, we can then implement the algorithm to calculate the maximum value at each with, and without, the current node:

```
const _ = require('lodash');

class BranchAndBound {

    constructor(list, maxCost) {
        // sort the costs in descending order for greedy calculation of
        // upper bound
        var sortedList = _.orderBy(list,
                        (option) => option.value/option.cost,
                        'desc');

        // original list
        this.list = list;

        // max allowed cost
        this.maxCost = maxCost;

        // all costs
        this.costs = _.map(sortedList, 'cost');

        // all values
        this.values = _.map(sortedList, 'value');
    }

    calculate() {
        // size of the input data set
        var size = _.size(this.values);

        // create a queue for processing nodes
        var queue = [];

        // add dummy root node
        queue.push({
            depth: -1,
            value: 0,
            cost: 0,
            upperBound: 0
        });
```

```
// initialize result
var maxValue = 0;

// initialize path to the result
var finalIncludedItems = [];

// while queue is not empty
// i.e leaf node not found
while(!_.isEmpty(queue)) {

    // initialize next node
    var nextNode = {};

    // get selected node from queue
    var currentNode = queue.shift();

    // if leaf node, no need to check for child nodes
    if (currentNode.depth !== size - 1) {

        // increment depth of the node
        nextNode.depth = currentNode.depth + 1;

        /*
         *
         *   We need to calculate the cost and value when the next
             item
         *   is included and when it is not
         *
         *
         *   First we check for when it is included
         */

        // increment cost of the next node by adding current nodes
        cost to it
        // adding current nodes cost is indicator that it is
        included
        nextNode.cost =  currentNode.cost +
        this.costs[nextNode.depth];

        // increment value of the next node similar to cost
        nextNode.value =  currentNode.value +
        this.values[nextNode.depth];

        // if cost of next node is below the max and the value
        provided
        // by including it is more than the currently accrued value
        // i.e. bounds and constrains satisfied
        if (nextNode.cost <= this.maxCost && nextNode.value >
```

```
maxValue) {

    // add node to results
    finalIncludedItems.push(nextNode.depth);

    // update maxValue accrued so far
    maxValue = nextNode.value;
}

// calculate the upper bound value that can be
// generated from the new node
nextNode.upperBound = this.upperBound(nextNode, size,
                    this.maxCost, this.costs, this.values);

// if the node is still below the upper bound
if (nextNode.upperBound > maxValue) {

    // add to queue for further consideration
    queue.push(_.cloneDeep(nextNode));
}

/*
 *   Then we check for when the node is not included
 */

// copy over cost and value from previous state
nextNode.cost = currentNode.cost;
nextNode.value = currentNode.value;

// recalculate upper bound
nextNode.upperBound = this.upperBound(nextNode, size,
                    this.maxCost, this.costs, this.values);

// if max value is still not exceeded,
// add to queue for processing later
if (nextNode.upperBound > maxValue) {

    // add to queue for further consideration
    queue.push(_.cloneDeep(nextNode));
}
        }
    }

// return results
return { val: maxValue, items: _.pullAt(this.list,
finalIncludedItems) };
}
```

```
upperBound(node, size, maxCost, costs, values) {
    // if nodes cost is over the max allowed cost
    if (node.cost > maxCost) {
        return 0;
    }

    // value of current node
    var valueBound = node.value;

    // increase depth
    var nextDepth = node.depth + 1;

    // init variable for cost calculation
    // starting from current node
    var totCost = node.cost;

    // traverse down the upcoming branch of the tree to see what
    // cost would be at the leaf node
    while ((nextDepth < size) && (totCost + costs[nextDepth] <=
    maxCost)) {
        totCost     += costs[nextDepth];
        valueBound += values[nextDepth];
        nextDepth++;
    }

    // allow fractional value calculations
    // for the last node
    if (nextDepth < size) {
        valueBound += (maxCost - totCost) * values[nextDepth] /
        costs[nextDepth];
    }

    // return final value at leaf node
    return valueBound;
    }
}

module.exports = BranchAndBound;
```

On running the same algorithm, we get the results with the maximum value returned to us:

```
const _ = require('lodash');
const BnB = require('./bnb');

const list = [
    {
        name: 'vegetables',
        value: 12,
```

```
        cost: 4
    },
    {
        name: 'candy',
        value: 1,
        cost: 1
    },
    {
        name: 'magazines',
        value: 4,
        cost: 2
    },
    {
        name: 'dvd',
        value: 6,
        cost: 2
    },
    {
        name: 'earphones',
        value: 6,
        cost: 3
    },
    {
        name: 'shoes',
        value: 4,
        cost: 2
    },
    {
        name: 'supplies',
        value: 9,
        cost: 3
    }
];

const budget = 10;

var result = new BnB(list, budget).calculate();

console.log(result);
```

This logs the following:

```
{
  val: 28,
  items:[
      { name: 'vegetables', value: 12, cost: 4 },
      { name: 'candy', value: 1, cost: 1 },
      { name: 'magazines', value: 4, cost: 2 },
      { name: 'supplies', value: 9, cost: 3 }
  ]
}
```

When not to use brute-force algorithm

Brute-force algorithm is a type of problem-solving technique in which every possible solution to a particular problem is explored before either selecting or rejecting one of the solutions as the final solution to the problem.

When posed with a challenge, the most natural reaction is to brute-force the solution or try to brute-force it first and then optimize it later. However, is that really the best way to approach such problems? Are there better ways of doing things?

The answer is most definitely yes, as we have seen very well in the entire chapter so far. brute-force is not the solution until it is the only solution. Sometimes, we may feel that we are creating a custom algorithm to find the solution to our given problem, but we need to ask ourselves if we are really going through all the possible solutions to the problem, if we are, then that's brute-force again.

Unfortunately, brute-force is not one fixed algorithm for us to detect it. The approach keeps changing with the problem statements, hence the need to see if we are trying to generate all solutions and avoid doing that.

However, you may ask, how do I know when to brute-force a problem and when should I try to find an optimal solution? How do I know a more optimal solution or algorithm exists for such a problem?

There is no quick and dirty way to tell if there are easier solutions than brute-force to calculate any solutions. For example, a problem can be solved in a brute-force manner, take any of the examples in this chapter, for instance. We can come up with a list of all possibilities (however hard it may be to generate this list, as a large number of them may exist) and then shortlist the ones that we deem as solutions.

In our example to generate the shortest path, we used Dijkstra's algorithm to use the cost associated with traveling to each city. A brute-force solution of this would be to calculate all the paths available in the graph from start to end nodes and then calculate the cost of each of the paths and then ultimately select the path with the lowest cost.

Knowing about the problem statement can greatly help with reducing the complexity of problems and also help us avoid brute-force solutions.

Brute-force Fibonacci generator

Let's take a Fibonacci generator, for example, and brute-force the generation of some numbers:

```
var _ = require('lodash');

var count = 10;

bruteForceFibonacci(count);

function bruteForceFibonacci(count) {
    var prev = 0;
    var next = 1;
    var res = '';

    res += prev;
    res += ',' + next;

    _.times(count, ()=> {
        var tmp = next;
        next = prev + next;
        prev = tmp;

        res += ',' + next;
    });

    console.log(res);
}
```

Here, we can see that we are not applying any domain knowledge; we simply take the two previous numbers from the series and add them. This is a fine way of doing it, but we can see that there are some improvements to be made here.

Recursive Fibonacci generator

We can use recursion to generate Fibonacci series as follows:

```
function recursiveFibonacci(num) {
    if (num == 0) {
        return 0;
    } else if (num == 1 || num == 2) {
        return 1;
    } else {
        return recursiveFibonacci(num - 1) + recursiveFibonacci(num - 2);
    }
}
```

You can see that we apply the same concept as earlier, that the next number is a summation of the two previous numbers of the Fibonacci series numbers. However, we are relying on recursion to recalculate all the old values as and when a new value is demanded.

Memoized Fibonacci generator

We can further enhance the generator using memoization, which is a technique of calculating a value only once and remembering it for later:

```
function memoizedFibonacci(num) {
    if (num == 0) {
        memory[num] = 0;
        return 0;
    } else if (num == 1 || num == 2) {
        memory[num] = 1;
        return 1;
    } else {
        if (!memory[num]) {
            memory[num] = memoizedFibonacci(num - 1) +
            memoizedFibonacci(num - 2);
        }

        return memory[num];
    }
}
```

Here, we are relying on an in-memory variable called `memory` to store and retrieve the previously calculated value of the Fibonacci number within the series, hence avoiding a series of duplicate calculations.

If you log the time taken for each of these methods, you can see that as the size of the input number increases, the performance does go down significantly for the recursive approach. Just because an algorithm is brute-force, that does not mean it is the worst/slowest/costliest. However, with a simple change to recursion(memoization), you can see that it is again faster than the brute-force technique.

When trying to code the solution for any problem, the biggest help is to reduce unnecessary space and time complexity.

Summary

In this chapter, we covered some of the important types of algorithms and implemented them for some example use cases. We also discussed various algorithmic optimization techniques, such as memoization and backtracking.

In the next chapter, we will discuss some of the sorting techniques and apply them to solve some examples.

7
Sorting and Its Applications

Sorting is a very common algorithm that we use to rearrange a list of numbers or objects in an ascending or descending order. A more technical definition of sorting is as follows:

> *In computer science, a sorting algorithm is an algorithm that puts elements of a list in a certain order.*

Now, let's assume that you have a list of n items, and you want to sort them. You take all the n items and determine all the possible sequences in which you can place these items, which, in this case, would be n! in total. We now need to determine which of these n! series does not have any inverted pairs to find out the sorted list. An inverted pair is defined as a pair of elements whose position in the list is represented by i, j where i < j, but the values $x_i > x_j$.

Of course, the preceding method is tedious and requires some heavy computation. In this chapter we will be discussing the following topics:

- Types of sorting algorithms
- Creating an API for a book management system (such as a library)
- Insertionsort Algorithm to sort the book data
- Mergesort Algorithm to sort the book data
- Quicksort Algorithm to sort the book data
- Performance Comparision of the different sorting algorithms

Let's take a look at some of the more optimal types of sorting as listed above, which can be employed in various scenarios.

Types of sorting algorithms

We all know that there are different types of sorting algorithms, and most of us would have heard of the names of these different types of algorithms at various times in our programming careers. The big difference between sorting algorithms and data structures is that the former always has the same goal, irrespective of which type of algorithm is used. That makes it very easy and important for us to compare the different sorting algorithms on various fronts, which in most of the cases boils down to speed and memory usage. We need to make this determination before we pick a particular sorting algorithm based on the type of the data that we have at hand.

Keeping the above in mind, we will compare and contrast the following three different types of algorithms:

- Insertionsort
- Mergesort
- Quicksort

Mergesort and Quicksort are the algorithms that v8 engine uses internally to sort the data; when the dataset size is too small (<10) the Mergesort is employed, else quicksort. Insertionsort, on the other hand, is an algorithm which is much simpler to implement.

However, before we jump into the implementation of each of these sorting algorithms, let's take a quick look at the use case and then set up the prerequisites for the same.

Use cases of different sorting algorithms

In order to test the different sorting algorithms, we will create a small express server, which will contain one endpoint to get a list of all books sorted by the number of pages in each of the books. In this example, we will start with an unordered list of books from a JSON file, which will serve as our data store.

In production applications, the sorting should be deferred to your database query and should not be done as a part of the application logic to avoid pain and confusion when dealing with scenarios such as filtering and paginated requests.

Creating an Express server

The first thing that we do to set up our project is to create the directory in which we want to write our application; to do so, run the following command in the terminal:

```
mkdir sorting
```

Once created, step into the directory by running cd and then run the npm initialization command to set it up as a Node.js project:

```
cd sorting
npm init
```

This will ask you a series of questions, which you can answer or leave empty for default answers, either of which is fine. Once your project is initialized, add the following npm package as we have done in previous chapters to help us set up the express server:

```
npm install express --save
```

Once added, we are now ready to create our server. Add the following code to a new file at the root of the project and call it index.js:

```
var express = require('express');
var app = express();

app.get('/', function (req, res) {
    res.status(200).send('OK!')
});

app.listen(3000, function () {
    console.log('Chat Application listening on port 3000!')
});
```

We have set up a single endpoint that returns OK and our server is running on port 3000. Let's also add a shortcut in scripts of our package.json file to start the application easily:

```
...
"scripts": {
  "start": "node index.js",
  "test": "echo \"Error: no test specified\" && exit 1"
},
...
```

Now, to test these changes, run npm start from your root folder and open localhost:3000 in your browser. You should note an OK! message on the screen as defined by our route in the index.js file.

Mocking library books data

Now, let's create the mock data of our library books, which we want to sort and return when the users request the list of books. In this chapter, we will focus on sorting the library books by the number of pages in each book, so we can add only the page count and the ID of the book for simplicity, as shown in the following code:

```
[
{"id":"dfa6cccd-d78b-4ea0-b447-abe7d6440180","pages":1133},
{"id":"0a2b0a9e-5b3d-4072-ad23-92afcc335c11","pages":708},
{"id":"e1a58d73-3bd2-4a3a-9f29-6cfb9f7a0007","pages":726},
{"id":"5edf9d36-9b5d-4d1f-9a5a-837ad9b73fe9","pages":1731},
...
]
```

We want to test the performance of each of these algorithms, so let's add 5,000 of these books to ensure that we have enough data to test the performance. Also, we will add these page counts randomly between 300 and 2,000 pages, and since we have a total of 5,000 books, there will be an obvious duplication of page sizes across different books.

The following is a sample script that you can use to generate this data if you want to use this script; ensure that you install the `uuid` npm module:

```
npm install uuid --save
```

Also, create a file at the root of the project called `generator.js` and add the following code:

```
const fs = require('fs');
const uuid = require('uuid');
const books = [];

for(var i = 0; i < 5000; i++) {
    books.push({
        "id": uuid.v4(),
        "pages": Math.floor(Math.random() * (2000 - 300 + 1) + 300)
    })
}

fs.writeFile('books.json', JSON.stringify(books), (err) => {});
```

Now, to run it, run the `node generator.js` command from the root, which will generate the `books.json` file with the data similar to the records shown in the preceding code.

Insertionsort API

Now, let's create an endpoint that uses Insertionsort to sort and return our data based on the page count.

What is Insertionsort

Insertionsort, as the name suggests, is a type of sort in which we extract elements from the input dataset one by one and then insert them in the sorted result dataset after determining where the element should be placed.

We can straight away determine that this approach will require an extra set (of the same size as the input) to hold the results. So, if we have a Set of 10 elements as the input, we will need another Set for the output whose size would be 10 as well. We can switch around this approach a little bit so that our sorting happens in-memory. Performing an action in-memory means that we will not request for any more memory (by creating extra sets of the same size as the input).

Pseudo code

Let's quickly chalk up the pseudo code for Insertionsort:

```
LOOP over all data excluding first entry (i = 1)

    INITIALIZE variable j = i - 1

    COPY data at index i

    WHILE all previous values are less than current

        COPY previous value to next

        DECREMENT j

    ADD current data to new position

RETURN sorted data
```

Implementing Insertionsort API

Based on the preceding pseudo-code described, implementing Insertionsort is very easy. Let's first create a folder called `sort` and then create a file called `insertion.js` in which we will add our insertion class, as shown in the following code:

```
class Insertion {
    sort(data) {
        // loop over all the entries excluding the first record
        for (var i = 1; i< data.length; ++i) {

            // take each entry
            var current = data[i];

            // previous entry
            var j = i-1;

            // until beginning or until previous data is lesser than
            current
            while (j >= 0 && data[j].pages < current.pages) {

                // shift entries to right
                data[j + 1] = data[j];

                // decrement position for next iteration
                j = j - 1;
            }

            // push current data to new position
            data[j+1] = current;
        }

        // return all sorted data
        return data;
    }
}

module.exports = Insertion;
```

As discussed in the pseudo code and the actual implementation, we will take each value and compare it with values before it, which does not sound like a very good thing to do when you have 5,000 items in a random order; and that is true, Insertionsort is a preferred choice only when the dataset is almost sorted and there are a few inverted pairs in the entire dataset.

One way to improve this functionality is by changing the way we determine the position at which we want to insert in the sorted list. Instead of comparing it with all the previous values, we can instead perform a binary search to determine where the data should be moved to in the sorted list. So, by slightly modifying the preceding code, we get the following:

```
class Insertion {

    sort(data) {
        // loop over all the entries
        for (var i = 1; i < data.length; ++i) {

            // take each entry
            var current = data[i];

            // previous entry
            var j = i - 1;

            // find location where selected sould be inseretd
            var index = this.binarySearch(data, current, 0, j);

            // shift all elements until new position
            while (j >= index) {
                // shift entries to right
                data[j + 1] = data[j];

                // decrement position for next iteration
                j = j - 1;
            }

            // push current data to new position
            data[j + 1] = current;
        }

        // return all sorted data
        return data;
    }

    binarySearch(data, current, lowPos, highPos) {
        // get middle position
        var midPos = Math.floor((lowPos + highPos) / 2);

        // if high < low return low position;
        // happens at the beginning of the data set
        if (highPos <= lowPos) {
            // invert condition to reverse sorting
            return (current.pages < data[lowPos].pages) ? (lowPos + 1):
```

```
            lowPos;
        }

        // if equal, give next available position
        if(current.pages === data[midPos].pages) {
            return midPos + 1;
        }

        // if current page count is less than mid position page count,
        // reevaluate for left half of selected range
        // invert condition and exchange return statements to reverse
        sorting
        if(current.pages > data[midPos].pages) {
            return this.binarySearch(data, current, lowPos, midPos - 1);
        }

        // evaluate for right half of selected range
        return this.binarySearch(data, current, midPos + 1, highPos);
    }
}

module.exports = Insertion;
```

Once implemented, we will now need to define the route for using this sort on our dataset. To do so, first, we will import the JSON data, which we earlier created, and then use that in our endpoint, which we specifically create to sort the data using Insertionsort:

```
var express = require('express');
var app = express();
var data = require('./books.json');
var Insertion = require('./sort/insertion');

app.get('/', function (req, res) {
    res.status(200).send('OK!')
});


app.get('/insertion', function (req, res) {
    res.status(200).send(new Insertion().sort(data));
});


app.listen(3000, function () {
    console.log('Chat Application listening on port 3000!')
});
```

Now, we can restart our server and try to hit the endpoint at `localhost:3000/insertion` either from the browser or postman, as shown in the following screenshot, to see the response containing sorted data:

Mergesort API

Now, let's create the endpoint, which uses Mergesort to sort and return our data based on the page count.

What is Mergesort

Mergesort is a type of divide and conquer sorting algorithm in which the entire dataset is first divided into subsets of one element each—these subsets are then joined and sorted repeatedly until we get one sorted set.

This algorithm uses both recursion and divide and conquer methods. Let's take a look at the pseudo code for such an implementation.

Pseudo code

Based on what we have known so far about the mergesort, we can come up with the pseudo code for the implementation, as follows:

```
MERGE_SORT(array)
    INITIALIZE middle, left_half, right_half

    RETURN MERGE(MERGE_SORT(left_half), MERGE_SORT(right_half))

MERGE(left, right)

    INITIALIZE response

    WHILE left and right exist

        IF left[0] < right[0]

            INSERT left[0] in result

        ELSE

            INSERT right[0] in result

    RETURN result concatenated with remainder of left and right
```

Note in the preceding code, we first recursively divide the input dataset, then sort and combine the dataset back. Now, let's implement this sorting algorithm.

Implementing Mergesort API

Let's now create our Mergesort class alongside the Insertionsort class, which we earlier created, and call it merge.js:

```
class Merge {
    sort(data) {
        // when divided to single elements
        if(data.length === 1) {
            return data;
        }
}
```

```
    // get middle index
    const middle = Math.floor(data.length / 2);

    // left half
    const left = data.slice(0, middle);

    // right half
    const right = data.slice(middle);

    // sort and merge
    return this.merge(this.sort(left), this.sort(right));
  }
  merge(left, right) {
    // initialize result
    const result = [];

    // while data
    while(left.length && right.length) {

      // sort and add to result
      // change to invert sorting
      if(left[0].pages > right[0].pages) {
        result.push(left.shift());
      } else {
        result.push(right.shift());
      }
    }

    // concat remaining elements with result
    return result.concat(left, right);
  }
}


module.exports = Merge;
```

Once we have the class, we can now add a new endpoint to use this class:

```
var express = require('express');
var app = express();
var data = require('./books.json');
var Insertion = require('./sort/insertion');
var Merge = require('./sort/merge');

app.get('/', function (req, res) {
   res.status(200).send('OK!')
});
```

```
app.get('/insertion', function (req, res) {
    res.status(200).send(new Insertion().sort(data));
});


app.get('/merge', function (req, res) {
    res.status(200).send(new Merge().sort(data));
});


app.listen(3000, function () {
    console.log('Chat Application listening on port 3000!')
});
```

Now, restart your server and test the changes made:

Quicksort API

Similar to Mergesort, Quicksort is also a type of divide and conquer algorithm. In this section, we will create the endpoint that will use this algorithm to sort and return our dataset.

What is Quicksort

Quicksort divides the set into two smaller subsets of low and high values based on a preselected pivot value, and these smaller subsets are then recursively sorted.

The selection of the pivot values can be done in several ways, and it is the most important aspect of the algorithm. One way is to simply pick the first, last, or the median values from the set. Then, there are custom partition schemes, such as Lomuto or Hoare (which we will use later in this chapter), which can be used to achieve the same. We will explore a couple of these implementations in this section.

Let's take a look at the pseudo code for this implementation.

Pseudo code

The pseudo code for quicksort is very obvious based on what we have discussed so far:

```
QUICKSORT(Set, lo, high)

    GET pivot

    GENERATE Left, Right partitions

    QUICKSORT(SET, lo, Left - 1)

    QUICKSORT(SET, Right + 1, high)
```

As you can note in the preceding code, the algorithm is not very complex once we abstract out the logic to get the pivot.

Implementing the Quicksort API

First, let's create the Quicksort class, which will sort the elements based on the pivot as the first element in the set passed. Let's create a file called quick.js under the sort folder:

```
class Quick {

    simpleSort(data) {

        // if only one element exists
        if(data.length < 2) {
            return data;
        }
```

```
    // first data point is the pivot
    const pivot = data[0];

    // initialize low and high values
    const low = [];
    const high = [];

    // compare against pivot and add to
    // low or high values
    for(var i = 1; i < data.length; i++) {

        // interchange condition to reverse sorting
        if(data[i].pages > pivot.pages) {
            low.push(data[i]);
        } else {
            high.push(data[i]);
        }
    }

    // recursively sort and concat the
    // low values, pivot and high values
    return this.simpleSort(low)
        .concat(pivot, this.simpleSort(high));
    }

}


module.exports = Quick;
```

That was straightforward, now, let's quickly add the endpoint to access this algorithm to sort our books and return them to the requested user:

```
var express = require('express');
var app = express();
var data = require('./books.json');
var Insertion = require('./sort/insertion');
var Merge = require('./sort/merge');
var Quick = require('./sort/quick');


....


app.get('/quick', function (req, res) {
    res.status(200).send(new Quick().simpleSort(data));
});
```

```
app.listen(3000, function () {
    console.log('Chat Application listening on port 3000!')
});
```

Also, now, restart the server to access the new endpoint that is created. We can see here that the approach is not ideal as it is requesting additional memory to contain the low and the high values compared to the pivot.

So, instead, we can use the previously discussed Lomuto or Hoare Partition Schemes to perform this operation in memory and reduce the memory costs.

Lomuto Partition Scheme

The Lomuto Partition Scheme is very similar to the simple sort function that we implemented earlier. The difference is that once we select the last element as the pivot, we need to keep adjusting its position by sorting and swapping the elements in memory, as shown in the following code:

```
partitionLomuto(data, low, high) {

    // Take pivot as the high value
    var pivot = high;

    // initialize loop pointer variable
    var i = low;

    // loop over all values except the last (pivot)
    for(var j = low; j < high - 1; j++) {

        // if value greater than pivot
        if (data[j].pages >= data[pivot].pages) {

            // swap data
            this.swap(data, i , j);

            // increment pointer
            i++;
        }
    }

    // final swap to place pivot at correct
    // position by swapping
    this.swap(data, i, j);

    // return pivot position
    return i;
```

```
}
```

For example, let's consider the following data:

```
[{pages: 20}, {pages: 10}, {pages: 1}, {pages: 5}, {pages: 3}]
```

When we call our partition with this dataset, our pivot is first the last element 3 (indicating `pages: 3`), the low value is 0 (so is our pointer) and high value is 4 (the index of the last element).

Now, in the first iteration, we see that the value of the jth element is greater than the pivot, so we swap the jth value with the low current pointer position; since both of them are the same, nothing happens on the swap, but we do increment the pointer. So, the dataset remains the same:

```
20, 10, 1, 5, 3
pointer: 1
```

In the next iteration, the same thing happens:

```
20, 10, 1, 5, \3
pointer: 2
```

In the third iteration, the value is smaller, so nothing happens and the loop continues:

```
20, 10, 1, 5, 3
pointer: 2
```

In the fourth iteration, the value (5) is greater than the pivot value, so the values swap and the pointer increments:

```
20, 10, 5, 1, 3
pointer: 3
```

Now, the control breaks out of the `for` loop, and we finally place our data in the correct position by swapping for the pivot one last time, which gives us the following:

```
20, 10, 5, 3, 1
```

After this, we can return the position of the pointer, which is nothing but the new position of the pivot. In this example, the data is sorted in the first iteration, but there can, and will, be scenarios where such is not the case, hence we repeat the process recursively for the subsets to the left and right of the pivot position.

Hoare Partition Scheme

Hoare Partition Scheme, on the other hand, takes a pivot value from the middle of the dataset and then starts parsing the values from the low and high end to determine the actual position of the pivot; this results in fewer number of operations as compared to the Lomuto Scheme:

```
partitionHoare(data, low, high) {
    // determine mid point
    var pivot = Math.floor((low + high) / 2 );

    // while both ends do not converge
    while(low <= high) {

        // increment low index until condition matches
        while(data[low].pages > data[pivot].pages) {
            low++;
        }

        // decrement high index until condition matches
        while(data[high] && (data[high].pages < data[pivot].pages)) {
            high--;
        }

        // if not converged, swap and increment/decrement indices
        if (low <= high) {
            this.swap(data, low, high);
            low++;
            high--;
        }
    }

    // return the smaller value
    return low;
}
```

Now, we can put this all together into our Quick class and update our API to use the newly created method, as shown in the following code:

```
class Quick {

    simpleSort(data) {
        ...
    }

    // sort class, default the values of high, low and sort
    sort(data, low = 0, high = data.length - 1, sort = 'hoare') {
```

```
// get the pivot
var pivot =  (sort === 'hoare') ? this.partitionHoare(data, low,
high)
            : this.partitionLomuto(data, low, high);

// sort values lesser than pivot position recursively
if(low < pivot - 1) {
   this.sort(data, low, pivot - 1);
}

// sort values greater than pivot position recursively
if(high > pivot) {
   this.sort(data, pivot, high);
}

// return sorted data
return data;
}

// Hoare Partition Scheme
partitionHoare(data, low, high) {
    ...
}

// Lomuto Partition Scheme
partitionLomuto(data, low, high) {
    ...
}

// swap data at two indices
swap(data, i, j) {
   var temp = data[i];
   data[i] = data[j];
   data[j] = temp;
}

}


module.exports = Quick;
```

When we update our API call signature, we get the following in our `index.js` file:

```
app.get('/quick', function (req, res) {
   res.status(200).send(new Quick().sort(data));
});
```

On restarting the server and accessing the endpoint, we get the following result:

We can see from the preceding screenshot that the quicksort is marginally faster than the Mergesort for the given dataset.

Performance comparison

Now that we have a few sorting algorithms listed and implemented, let's quickly take a look at their performance. We briefly talked about some performance enhancements while we were implementing these algorithms; we will try to quantify this performance enhancement.

To do so, we will first install the node module called benchmark to create our test suite:

```
npm install benchmark --save
```

Once we have installed the benchmark framework, we can add our tests to a file called benchmark.js at the root of the project, which will run the different sorting algorithms described in the preceding section:

```
var Benchmark = require('benchmark');
var suite = new Benchmark.Suite();
var Insertion = require('./sort/insertion');
var Merge = require('./sort/merge');
var Quick = require('./sort/quick');
var data = require('./books.json');

suite
   .add('Binary Insertionsort', function(){
      new Insertion().sort(data);
   })
   .add('Mergesort', function(){
      new Merge().sort(data);
   })
   .add('Quicksort -> Simple', function(){
      new Quick().simpleSort(data);
   })
   .add('Quicksort -> Lomuto', function(){
      new Quick().sort(data, undefined, undefined, 'lomuto');
   })
   .add('Quicksort -> Hoare', function(){
      new Quick().sort(data);
   })
   .on('cycle', function(e) {
      console.log(`${e.target}`);
   })
   .on('complete', function() {
      console.log(`Fastest is ${this.filter('fastest').map('name')}`);
   })
   .run({ 'async': true });
```

Let's now update the scripts tag of our package.json file to update and run the tests:

```
...

"scripts": {
  "start": "node index.js",
  "test": "node benchmark.js"
},

...
```

To see the changes, run the `npm run test` command from the root of the project, and we will see something similar in the terminal:

```
Binary Insertionsort x 1,366 ops/sec ±1.54% (81 runs sampled)
Mergesort x 199 ops/sec ±1.34% (78 runs sampled)
Quicksort -> Simple x 2.33 ops/sec ±7.88% (10 runs sampled)
Quicksort -> Lomuto x 2,685 ops/sec ±0.66% (86 runs sampled)
Quicksort -> Hoare x 2,932 ops/sec ±0.67% (88 runs sampled)
Fastest is Quicksort -> Hoare
```

Summary

Sorting is something that we use frequently. It is important to know how sorting algorithms work and how we can use these based on the type of dataset. We made some critical changes from the base approach to ensure that we are optimizing our algorithms and finished off with some statistics on how efficiently these algorithms perform when compared side by side. However, of course, one might think about whether performance tests are necessary to check whether an algorithm is better than another. We will be discussing that in our next chapters.

8

Big O Notation, Space, and Time Complexity

In the previous chapters, we have often spoken about optimizing our code/algorithms and have briefly used the terms space and time complexity and how we want to reduce them. As the name suggests, it is the complexity of the code that we want to keep to a minimum, but what does that entail? What are the different levels of this said complexity? How do we calculate the space and time complexity of an algorithm? These are the questions that we will address in this chapter while discussing the following topics:

- Varying degrees of time complexity
- Space complexity and Auxiliary space

Terminology

The terminology used when discussing the space and time complexity of an algorithm is something that one, as a developer, will come across very often. Popular terms such as **Big-O**, also known as **O (something)**, and some not-so-popular terms such as **Omega (something)** or **Theta (something)** are often used to describe the complexity of an algorithm. The O actually stands for Order, which represents the order of the function.

Let's first talk only about the time complexity of an algorithm. This basically boils down to us trying to figure out how long it will take for a system to execute our algorithm for a given dataset (D). We can technically run this algorithm on the said system and log its performance, but since not all systems are the same (for example, OS, number of processors, and read write speeds), we can't necessarily expect the result to truly represent the average time it would take to execute our algorithm for our dataset, D. At the same time, we would also need to know how our algorithm performs with the changing size of our dataset, D. Does it take the same time for 10 elements and 1000 elements? Or does the time taken increase exponentially?

With all the above, how do we clearly understand the complexity of an algorithm? We do this by breaking down an algorithm into a set of basic operations and then combine them to get the overall number/complexity of each operation. This truly defines the time complexity of an algorithm as the rate of growth of time with the size of the input dataset, D.

Now, to calculate the time complexity in abstract terms, let's assume that we have a machine that takes one unit of time to perform some basic operations such as read, write, assignments, arithmetic, and logical calculations.

With that said, let's take a simple function that returns the square of a given number:

```
function square(num) {
    return num*num;
}
```

We have defined our machine, which consumes one unit of time, to perform the multiplication and another 1 unit to return the result. Irrespective of the input, our algorithm always takes only 2 units of time, and since this is not changing, it is referred to as a constant time algorithm. It does not matter that the constant time taken here is k units of time. We can represent all the similar functions, which take a constant time to execute as a set of functions O(1) or big-O(1).

Let's take another example in which we loop over a list of size n and multiply each of the elements by a factor:

```
function double(array) {
    for(var i = 0; i <  array.length; i++) {
        array[i] *= 2;
    }

    return array;
}
```

To calculate the time complexity of this function, we will need to first calculate the cost to execute each statement in this function.

The first statement executes *n + 1* times before it breaks out of it, and each time it is performed, it costs 1 unit to increment and 1 unit to make the comparison check among other things. In other words, we can assume that it costs us C_1 units of time in each iteration, so the total cost is $C_1*(n+1)$ for the following line of code:

```
for(var i = 0; i <  array.length; i++) {
```

In the next statement, we will multiply the value in the array at a given index by a factor of 2. Since this is within the loop, this statement is executed n times, and each time it does, let's assume it costs us C_2 units. So, the total cost of execution of this line would be $C_2* n$:

```
array[i]  *= 2;
```

Then, we finally have the return statement, which also takes a constant amount of time—C_3—to return the final array to the caller. Putting all these costs together, we have the total cost of the method as follows:

```
T_double  = C₁*(n + 1) + C₂* n + C₃;
          = C₅ * n + C₄ // where C₄ = C₃ + C₁ and C₅ = C₁ + C₂
```

We can see that, in this case, the cost of the method is directly proportional to the size of the input array, N. Thus, this set of functions can be represented by O(n), indicating that they are directly proportional to the input size.

However, before we jump to more examples, let's first take a look at how we will represent the complexity without all the calculations.

Asymptotic Notations

Asymptotic Notations come in handy when we want to derive and compare the time complexity of two or more algorithms. What Asymptotic Notations mean is that, once we have the time complexity of an algorithm calculated, we are simply going to start replacing *n* (the size of the input of our algorithm) with a very large number (tending toward infinity) and then get rid of the constant from the equation. Doing this would leave us with the only factors that truly affect our execution time.

Let's take the same example as we did in the preceding section:

```
T_double = C₁*(n + 1) + C₂* n + C₃;
         = C₅ * n + C₄ // where C₄ = C₃ + C₁ and C₅ = C₁ + C₂
```

When we apply the rules we just described relating to Asymptotic Notations, that is, *n ->
Infinity*, we can quickly see that the effects of C_4 are rather insignificant and can be dropped.
We can also say the same for the multiplication factor C_5. What we are left with is that this
time, T_{double}, is directly proportional to the size of the input array (n) and thus we were able
to denote this with the O(n) notation since the size n is the only variable that matters in this
case.

There are three main types of Asymptotic Notations, which can be used to classify the
running time of an algorithm:

- **Big-O**: Represents the upper bound of the rate of growth of runtime
- **Omega**: Represents the lower bound of the rate of growth of runtime
- **Theta**: Represents the tight bound of the rate of growth of runtime

Big-O notation

Let's assume that we have a f(n) method, which we want to represent with a time
complexity function (that is, a Set) g(n):

f(n) is O(g(n)) if, and only if, there exists constants c and n_0, where f(n) <= cg(n) and
where the input size n >= n_0.

Now, let's try to apply this to our previous example:

```
f(n) = T_double = C₅ * n + C₄
f(n) = T_double = 4n + 1 // cause C₅ and C₄ can be any constants
```

For this example, we denoted it with the set O(n), that is, g(n) = n.

For our time complexity assertion to hold, we will need to satisfy the following condition:

```
4n + 1 <= c * n , where n >= n₀
```

This equation is satisfied for values $c = 5$ and $n_0 = 1$. Also, since the definition is met, we can safely say that the $f(n)$ function is big-$O(g(n))$, that is, $O(g(n))$ or, in this case, $O(n)$. We can also see this when plotted on a graph, as shown in the following diagram; after the value of $n = 1$, we can see that the value of $c * g(n)$ is always greater than $f(n)$ asymptotically. Take a look at the following diagram:

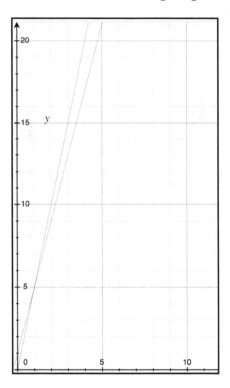

Omega notation

Similar to the Big O notation discussed earlier, Omega notation denotes the lower bound rate of growth of the runtime of an algorithm. So, if we have a $f(n)$ method, which we want to represent with a time complexity function (that is, a Set) $g(n)$, then Omega notation can be defined as the following:

$f(n)$ is $O(g(n))$ if and only if there exists constants c and n_0 where $f(n) >= cg(n)$ where the input size $n >= n_0$.

Taking the same preceding example, we have $f(n) = 4n + 1$ and then $g(n) = n$. We will need to validate the existence of c and n_0 such that the preceding condition holds, as shown in the following snippet:

```
4n + 1 >= c * n , where n >= n₀
```

We can see that this condition holds for $c = 4$ and $n_0 = 0$. Thus, we can say that our function $f(n)$ is $\Omega(n)$. We can plot this as well on a chart and take a look at how it represents our function f(n) and its upper and lower bounds:

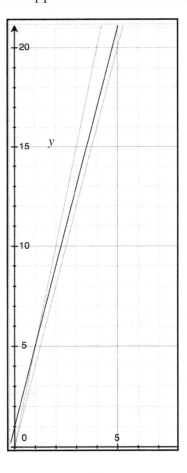

From the preceding diagram, we can see that our function—f(n)—(in black) lies in between our asymptotic upper and lower bounds (in gray). The *x*-axis indicates the value of the size (*n*).

Theta Notation

Having calculated the upper and lower bound rates of growth of our function f(n), we can now determine the tight bound or theta of our function f(n) as well. So, if we have a f(n) method, which we want to represent with a time complexity function (also known as a set) g(n), then the tight bound of a function can be defined as follows:

f(n) is O(g(n)) if , and only if , there exists constants c and n_0, where $c_1 g(n) <= f(n) <= c_2 g(n)$ where the input size n >= n_0

The preceding operation, from the previous two sections, is already calculated for our function, that is, f(n) = 4n + 1: the value of c_1 = 4 , c_2 = 5, and n_0 = 1.

This provides us with the tight bound of our function f(n) and, since the function always lies within the tight bound after n = 1, we can safely say that our function f(n) has a tightly bound rate of growth as θ(n).

Recap

Let's quickly take a look at what we discussed the different types of notations before moving on to the next topic:

- O means that the growth rate of f(n) is asymptotically less than or equal to the growth rate of *g(n)*
- Ω means that the growth rate of f(n) is asymptotically greater than or equal to the growth rate of *g(n)*
- θ means that the growth rate of f(n) is asymptotically equal to the growth rate of g(n)

Examples of time complexity

Let's now examine some examples of time complexity calculations, since in 99% of the cases we need to know the maximum time a function might take to execute; we will be mostly analyzing the worst case time complexity, that is, the upper bound of the rate of growth based on the input of a function.

Constant time

A constant time function is one which takes the same amount of time to execute, irrespective of the size of the input that is passed into the function:

```
function square(num) {
    return num*num;
}
```

The preceding code snippet is an example of a constant time function and is denoted by $O(1)$. Constant time algorithms are the most sought out algorithms for obvious reasons, such as them running in a constant time, irrespective of the size of the input.

Logarithmic time

A Logarithmic time function is one in which the time of execution is proportional to the logarithm of the input size. Consider the following example:

```
for(var i = 1; i < N; i *= 2) {
    // O(1) operations
}
```

We can see that in any given iteration, the value of $i = 2^i$, so in the nth iteration, the value of $i = 2^n$. Also, we know that the value of i is always less than the size of the loop itself (N). From that, we can deduce the following result:

```
2ⁿ < N
```

```
log(2ⁿ) < log(N)
```

```
n < log(N)
```

From the preceding code, we can see that the number of iterations would always be less than the log on the input size. Hence, the worst-case time complexity of such an algorithm would be `O(log(n))`.

Let's consider another example, where we halve the value of `i` for the next iteration:

```
for(var i = N; i >= 1; i /= 2) {
    // O(1) operations
}
```

Here, the value of `i` in the nth iteration will be $N/2^n$, and we know that the loop ends with the value of 1. So, for our loop to stop, the value of `i` needs to be <= 1; now, by combining those two conditions, we get the following:

```
N/2ⁿ  <= 1
```

```
N  <=  2ⁿ
```

```
Log(N)  <= n
```

We can again come to a similar conclusion as our first example, that the number of iterations will always be less than the log value of the input size or value.

One thing to notice is that this is not limited to the doubling or halving phenomenon only. This can be applied to any algorithm in which the number of the steps are being cut down by a factor, k. The worst case time complexity of such algorithms would be $O(log_k(N))$, and, in our preceding examples, k happens to be 2.

Logarithmic Time complexity algorithms are the next favorites since they consume time logarithmically. Even if the size of the input doubles, the running time of the algorithm only increases by a small number additively (which is the definition of a logarithm).

Linear time

Let's now discuss one of the most common time complexities, the linear time. As one can guess, linear time complexity of a method indicates that the method takes linear time to execute:

```
for(var i = 0; i < N; i += c) {
    // O(1) operations
}
```

This is a very basic `for` loop, within which we are performing some constant time operations. As the size of N increases, the number of the times the loop gets executed also increases.

As you can see, the value of `i` in each iteration is incremented by a constant, `c`, and not by 1. This is because it does not matter what the increments are, as long as they are linear.

In the first iteration, the value of `i = 0`; in the second iteration, the value of `i = c`, then its `c + c = 2c` in the third iteration, and `3c` in the fourth iteration, and so on. So, in the nth iteration, we have the value of `i = c(n-1)`, which asymptotically is `O(n)`.

Depending on what your use case is, linear time complexity may, or may not, be good. This is kind of the gray area, which you may sometimes want to let go if you are unsure of whether further optimization is necessary or not.

Quadratic time

With quadratic time algorithms, we have now entered the dark side of the time complexity. As the name suggests, the size of the input quadratically affects the running time of the algorithm. One common example is nested loops:

```
for (int i = 0; i <n; i += c) {
    for (int j = 0; j < n; j += c) {
        // some O(1) expressions
    }
}
```

As you can see from the preceding example, for `i = 0`, the inner loop runs *n* times, and the same for `i = 1`, and `i = 2`, and so on. The inner loop always runs n times and is not dependent on the value of n, thus making the algorithms time complexity `O(n²)`.

Polynomial time

Polynomial time complexity is the running time complexity of algorithms, which runs to the order of n^k. Quadratic time algorithms are certain types of polynomial time algorithms where `k = 2`. A very simple example of such an algorithm would be as follows:

```
for (int i = 0; i <n; i += c) {
    for (int j = 0; j < n; j += c) {
        for (int k = 0; k < n; k += c) {
            // some O(1) expressions
```

```
        }
    }
}
```

As you can see, this example is just an extension of the example in the quadratic time section. The worst case complexity of this case is $O(n^3)$.

Polynomial time complexity classes

Now that we have started this conversation, most of the time complexity types that we have discussed here so far are of the $O(n^k)$ type, for example, it is a constant time complexity for $n = 1$, whereas it is quadratic complexity for $k = 2$.

The concept of polynomial time complexity leads us into a class of problems, which are defined based on the complexity of their solutions. The following are the types of classes:

- **P**: Any problem that can be solved in polynomial time $O(n^k)$.
- **NP**: Any problem that can be verified in polynomial time. There can exist problems (such as sudoku solving) that can be solved in non-deterministic polynomial time. If the solution to these problems can be verified in polynomial time, then the problem is classified as an NP-class problem. NP-class problems are a superset of the P-class problems.
- **NP-Complete**: Any NP problem that can be reduced as a function of another NP problem in polynomial time can be classified as an NP-Complete problem. This means that if we know the solution to a certain **NP** problem, then a solution to another NP problem can be derived in polynomial time.
- **NP-Hard**: A problem can be classified as an NP-Hard problem (H) if there exists an **NP-Complete** problem (C) that can be reduced to H in polynomial time.

In a majority of the real-world scenarios, we will encounter a lot of P and NP problems, a classic example of NP-class problem is Traveling Salesman, where a salesman wants to visit n number of cities to start and end his trip from his house. With a limited amount of gasoline and an upper limit on the total miles that can be driven, can the salesman visit all the cities without running out of gas?

Recursion and additive complexity

Until now, we have seen some examples that are pretty straightforward: they all have a single loop or nested loops. However, a lot of times, there will be scenarios in which we will have to handle multiple loops/function calls/branches originating from the same algorithm. Let us see an example of how we can calculate the complexity in that case?

1. When we have subsequent loops/function calls, we will need to calculate the individual complexity of each step and then add them to get the overall complexity, as follows:

```
function xyz() {
    abc(); // O(n) operation

    pqr(); // O(log(n)) operation

}
```

The collective complexity of this code would be the summation of the complexity of both the sections. So, in this case, the overall complexity would be `O(n + log n)`, which asymptotically will be `O(n)`.

2. When we have branches in our function with varying time complexity, depending on what type of runtime complexity we are talking about, we will need to pick the correct choice:

```
function xyz() {
    if (someCondition) {
        abc(); // O(n) operation

    } else {

        pqr(); // O(log(n)) operation

    }

}
```

In this case, the worst case complexity will be decided by whatever is worst of the two branches, which would be `O(n)`, but the best case complexity would be `O(log(n))`.

3. Recursive algorithms are a little tricky compared to their non-recursive counterparts, since not only do we need to determine what the complexity of our algorithm is, we also need to keep in mind how many times recursion would get triggered because that would contribute toward the overall complexity of the algorithm as shown in the following code snippet:

```
function rec1(array) {
    // O(1) operations

    if (array.length === 0) return;

    array.pop();

    return rec1(array);
}
```

Although our method only performs some O(1) operations, it constantly changes the input and calls itself until the size of the input array is zero. So, our method ends up executing n times, making the overall time complexity of O(n).

Space complexity and Auxiliary space

Space complexity and Auxiliary space are two of the most often confused and interchangeably used terms when talking about the space complexity of a certain algorithm:

- **Auxiliary Space:** The extra space that is taken by an algorithm temporarily to finish its work
- **Space Complexity:** Space complexity is the total space taken by the algorithm with respect to the input size plus the auxiliary space that the algorithm uses.

When we try to compare two algorithms, we usually have a similar type of input, that is, the size of the input can be disregarded and thus what we do end up comparing is the auxiliary space of the algorithms. It's not a big deal to use either of the terms, as long as we understand the distinction between the two and use them correctly.

If we were using a low-level language such as C, then we can break down the memory required/consumed based on the data type, for example, 2 bytes to store an integer, 4 bytes to store floating point, and so on. However, since we are working with JavaScript, which is a high-level language, this is not as so straightforward, as we do not make a distinction between different data types explicitly.

Examples of Space complexity

When it comes to space complexity of an algorithm, we have types similar to that of the time complexity, such as constant space `S(1)` and linear space `S(N)`. Let's take a look at some of the examples in the following section.

Constant space

A constant space algorithm is one in which the space consumed by an algorithm does not change by the size of the input or the algorithms input parameters in any way.

At this point, I would like to reiterate that when we talk about the space complexity of an algorithm we are talking about the auxiliary space that is consumed by the algorithm. This implies that even if our array is of size *n*, the auxiliary (or the extra) space that is consumed by our algorithm will remain constant, as shown in the following code snippet:

```
function firstElement(arr) {
    return arr[0];
}
```

We can see here that the `firstElement` method does not take any more space, irrespective of what the input is. Hence, we can denote this as space complexity `S(1)`.

Linear space

A linear space algorithm is one in which the amount of space taken by an algorithm is directly proportional to the size of the input, for example, algorithms that loop over an array and push values to a new array before returning them:

```
function redundant(array) {
    var result = [];

    for(var i = 0, i < array.size; i++) {
        result.push(array[i]);
    }

    return result;
}
```

As you can see, although redundant, we are creating a new array and pushing all the values into that array, which will use up the same space as that of the input array. Consider the situation in which you have a condition before the `push`, as shown in the following code:

```
function notRedundant(array) {
    var result = [];

    for(var i = 0, i < array.size; i++) {
        if (someCondition) {
            result.push(array[i]);
        }
    }

    return result;
}
```

In the worst case, the `someCondition` flag is always true, and we end up with the result that is again of the same size as that of the input. Thus, we can assert that the space complexity of the preceding method is `S(n)`.

Summary

In this chapter, we scratched the surface of a beast known as computational complexity. There is a lot more to computational complexity than we discussed in this chapter. However, the topics and examples discussed in this chapter are the ones that most of us face in our day-to-day work. There are more advanced topics in space complexity, such as LSPACE, which is a class of problems that can be solved in logarithmic space and NLSPACE, which is the amount of space but using a non-deterministic Turing machine. The main goal of this chapter is to ensure that we understand how the complexity of our algorithms is calculated and how it affects the overall output. In the next chapter, we will be discussing what kind of micro-optimizations we can make to our applications, and understand the internals of how browsers (mostly Chrome) work and how we can leverage them to better our applications.

9
Micro-Optimizations and Memory Management

In this chapter, we will cover some of the basic concepts of HTML, CSS, JavaScript, and the browser in which we expect all of these to run in union. We always have, and always will, code in a certain style, which is natural. However, how did we develop this style? Is it good or can it get better? How do we get to decide what we should and should not ask others to follow? These are some of the questions that we will try and answer in this chapter.

In this chapter, we will discuss the following:

- Importance of best practices and take a look at some of the examples.
- Exploring different kinds of HTML, CSS, and JavaScript optimizations
- Delve into the internal working of some of the features of Chrome.

Best practices

Best practices is a relative term for obvious reasons. What is considered best is rather dependent on the team in which you work and what version of JavaScript you work with. In this section, we will try to cast a wide net over some of these best practices, and get an understanding of what some of the practices look like so that we can adapt and use them as well.

Best practices for HTML

Let's approach this section top-down and address the best practices for each of the sections within an HTML file.

Declaring the correct DOCTYPE

Have you ever wondered why we have `<!DOCTYPE html>` at the top of our page? We can clearly leave it out, and still the page seems to work. Then, why exactly do we need this? The answer is **avoiding backward compatibility**—if we do not specify the DOCTYPE, the browser that is interpreting and rendering our HTML goes into quirks mode, which is a technique to support really old websites that were built with outdated versions and markups of HTML, CSS, and JS. Quirks mode emulates a lot of bugs that existed in the older versions of the browsers, and we do not want to deal with those.

Adding the correct meta-information to the page

Any web page, when rendered, needs some meta-information. Although this information does not get rendered on the page, it's critical to render the page correctly. The following are some of the good practices for adding the meta-information:

- Adding the right `lang` attribute to your `html` tag to comply with w3c's internationalization standards:

    ```
    <html lang="en-US">
    ```

- Declaring the correct `charset` to support special characters on your web page:

    ```
    <meta charset="UTF-8">
    ```

- Add the correct `title` and `description` tags to support search engine optimization:

    ```
    <title>This is the page title</title>

    <meta name="description" content="This is an example description.">
    ```

- Add the appropriate `base` URL to avoid providing absolute URLs everywhere:

```
<base href="http://www.mywebsite.com" />
...
...
<img src="/cats.png" /> // relative to base
```

Dropping unnecessary attributes

This might seem obvious, but is still largely used. When we add a `link` tag to download a `stylesheet`, our browser already knows that it is a `stylesheet`. There is no reason to specify the type of that link:

```
<link rel="stylesheet" href="somestyles.css" type="text/css" />
```

Making your app mobile ready

Have you ever seen one of those websites that look exactly the same on desktop and mobile and wonder why they would build it like that? In the new age of web development, why would someone not leverage the responsiveness provided by the latest HTML and CSS versions? This could happen to anyone; we have all the right breakpoints defined and are using media queries as expected, but nothing happens. This is usually because we forgot to include the `viewport`, the `meta` tag; including the `meta` tag for `viewport` fixes all our problems:

```
<meta name="viewport" content="width=device-width, initial-scale=1">
```

The `viewport` is basically the total viewable area for a user, which will be smaller in a mobile and larger in a desktop; the `meta` tag defines how the browser should render the website, based on the size of the `viewport`.

Loading style sheets in the <head>

This is a matter of preference and choice. Can we load the style sheets at the end of the page load? Sure we can, but we want to avoid it so that our users do not see unstyled page flashing before it picks up the correct styles. Our browsers, when provided with CSS and HTML, create a **CSS Object Model** (**CSSOM**) and **Document Object Model** (**DOM**). When a DOM is being constructed, the browser looks up the CSSOM to check whether there are any styles corresponding to that node of the DOM. Hence, we want to make sure that the CSSOM is constructed and ready for the DOM to render.

An alternative is to load only the basic styles first in the head tag of the page, and the rest of the styles can be requested at the end of the body. That means our page can be rendered a little faster, but it is worth noting that this may not be worth the effort sometimes, depending on your application size and use case.

Avoiding inline styles

Using inline styles by providing them directly on the element in an HTML file is bad for multiple reasons:

- We cannot reuse the styles applied to one element
- Our HTML is flooded with CSS, making it very noisy
- We cannot leverage pseudo elements, such as `before` and `after`

Using semantic markup

With HTML5, we no longer have to worry about using a `<div>` tag for everything. We have been gifted with a more robust set of semantic tags, which help us construct our templates in a more meaningful fashion:

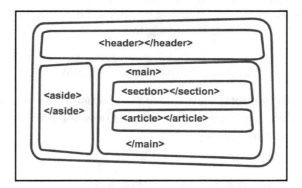

 A point worth noting is that these new tags only provide meaning to our template but no styling. If we want it to look a certain way, we will need to style the elements as we want them to look. Also, the new HTML5 tags are not available in browsers older than IE9, so we need to prepare for fallbacks such as HTML5shiv.

Using Accessible Rich Internet Applications (ARIA) attributes

Whenever we are developing a web application, we will need to ensure that our applications are compatible with screen readers to support users with disabilities:

```
<div id="elem" aria-live="assertive" role="alert" aria-hidden="false"> An
error occurred </div>
```

This information does not collide with any of the existing information on the screen, and it enables the screen readers to pick up and process this information. Of course, all of this is possible only if the HTML renderer supports ARIA, which is available in all the latest browsers.

Loading scripts at the end

The heart of any application lives in the JavaScript files that are defined by the developers. Hence, we will need to pay extra attention while we try to load and execute these files, which can be significantly larger than that of their counterpart HTML and CSS files. When we try to load external JS files using a script tag, the browser first downloads them and then executes them (after parsing and compiling). We will need to make sure that our application is loaded and executed at the right time. What that means for us is that if our application logic is reliant on the DOM, we need to ensure that the DOM is rendered before the script is executed. This makes it a pretty good reason for us to load the scripts at the end of the body tag within our application.

Even if we do not rely on the DOM in our JavaScript, we would still want to load our scripts at the end because the script tags are render blocking by default, that is, if your browser encounters your script tag in the head (for example), it begins to download and execute the JS files and does not render the rest of the page until the execution is complete. Also, if we have too many JS files, then the page appears to have hung and does not render the UI completely to our end user until all the JS files have been downloaded and executed successfully.

There is one workaround if you still want to add the script tags along with the link tag to download the style sheets. You can add the defer or async attribute to the script tag. Defer lets you download the file parallel to the DOM rendering and executes the script once the render is complete. The async downloads the file parallel to the DOM render and pauses rendering for execution and then resumes after execution. Use them wisely.

CSS best practices

The list of CSS best practices is not as long as that of HTML. Also, a lot of potential issues can be subsided significantly by the use of a preprocessing language, such as **Sassy CSS** (**SCSS**). Let's assume that you cannot use SCSS for some reason and discuss good and bad of plain old CSS.

Avoiding inline styles

This is important enough to be part of both HTML's and CSS's best practices. Just do not do apply inline styles.

Do not use !important

Easy to say, hard to do. Using `!important` is one of the easiest workarounds available to make your styles apply to an element. However, this comes at a price of its own. CSS or Cascading Style Sheets rely on the fact that the styles will be cascaded based on the priority of the application (ID, class, and element tag) or the order in which they appear. Using `!important` messes that up, and if you have multiple CSS files, then it becomes a big mess to correct. It's better to avoid such a practice and do it the right way from the get-go.

Arranging styles within a class alphabetically

This does not sound like a big deal, does it? Well, if all you have is one CSS file with a couple of classes, then maybe it is okay. However, when you have big files with a complex hierarchy, the last thing you want is to commit a small mistake which costs you a lot of time. Take a look at the following example:

```css
.my-class {
    background-image: url('some-image.jpg');
    background-position: 0 100px;
    background-repeat: no-repeat;
    height: 500px;
    width: 500px;
    ...
    ...
    margin: 20px;
    padding: 10px;
    background: red;
}
```

Note in the preceding code that we added conflicting styles for the background property of the element, and now when rendered, it is all red. This could have been easily caught, but because of the ordering of the properties within the class, it got lost.

Defining the media queries in an ascending order

Defining media queries is another area which gets confusing as the size of the application grows. When defining the media queries, always define them in an increasing order so that you can isolate your styles and leave an open upper bound, as follows:

```
...

Mobile specific styles

...


// if screen size is greater than a small mobile phone
@media only screen and (min-width : 320px) {
    // overrides which apply
}

// if screen size is greater than a small mobile phone in portrait mode
// or if screen size is that of a tablet
@media only screen and (min-width : 480px) {
    // overrides that apply
  }

// if screen size is greater than a tablet
@media only screen and (min-width : 768px) {
    // overrides that apply
}

// large screens
@media only screen and (min-width : 992px) { ... }

// extra large screens and everything above it
@media only screen and (min-width : 1200px) { ... }
```

Note in the preceding code that we have left the last media query to apply for all screens that are 1200px and more in size, which would cover monitors, TVs, and so on. This would not have worked well if we were doing it the other way, in which we set the styles based on the max-width of the screen size. What would happen if we open it on a projector? It will certainly not work like you hoped it would.

Best practices for JavaScript

There is no start and end to this topic. There are a lot of opinions regarding how things should be done in JavaScript, and it turns out that most of them are correct (depending on your background, experience, and use case). Let's take a look at some of the most commonly discussed best practices for JavaScript (ES5).

Avoiding polluting the global scope

Do not add properties or methods to the global scope. These will bloat your window object and make your page slow and stuttery. Instead, always create a variable within a method, which will be taken care of when the method is destroyed.

Using 'use strict'

It's a one-line change, which can go a long way when it comes to catching code smells and any code irregularities, such as deleting a variable. The `use strict` clause throws an error when an illegal action is performed at the runtime, so it doesn't necessarily prevent our app from breaking, but we can catch and fix issues before they are deployed.

Strict checking (== vs ===)

JavaScript can be a fairly tricky language when coming to typecasting or type conversions. The fact that there are no data types does not make this any simpler. Using a == forces an implicit typecasting as compared to ===. So, it is advisable to always use === unless you want 12== 12 to be true.

For more details on understanding why it works the way it does, refer to the Abstract Equality Comparison Algorithm, found at `https://www.ecma-international.org/ecma-262/5.1/#sec-11.9.3`.

Using ternary operators and Boolean || or &&

It is always suggested to keep your code readable but, when warranted, use the ternary operators to make your code concise and readable:

```
if(cond1) {
    var1 = val1;
} else {
    var1 = val2
```

```
}

if(cond2) {
    var2 = val3;
} else {
    var2 = val4
}
```

For example, the preceding code can be condensed as follows:

```
var1 = cond1 ? val1 : val2;
var2 = cond2 ? val3 : val4;
```

Setting default values can also be achieved easily as follows:

```
var1 = ifThisVarIsFalsy || setThisValue;
var2 = ifThisVarIsTruthy && setThisValue;
```

Modularization of code

When we create a script, it is obvious that we want it to do multiple things, for example, if we have a login page, the script for the login page should handle login (obviously), reset a password, and signup. All of these operations would require the email validation. Keeping validation part of each of these operations in its own method is known as Modularization. It helps us keep our methods small, readable, and makes unit testing a lot easier.

Avoiding pyramid of doom

Pyramid of doom is a classic scenario where we have tons of nesting or branching. This makes the code overly complex and the unit testing a very complex job:

```
promise1()
    .then((resp) => {
        promise2(resp)
            .then((resp2) => {
                promise3(resp2)
                    .then((resp3) => {
                        if(resp3.something) {
                            // do something
                        } else {
                            // do something else
                        }
                    });
            });
    });
```

Instead, do the following:

```
promise1()
    .then((resp) => {
        return promise2(resp);
    })
    .then((resp2) => {
        return promise3(resp2);
    })
    .then((resp3) => {
        if(resp3.something) {
            // do something
        } else {
            // do something else
        }
    })
```

Keeping DOM access to a minimum

DOM access is an expensive operation, and we need to reduce it as much as we can to avoid our page from dying. Try caching the DOM elements once they are accessed in some local variables or leverage virtual DOM, which is more efficient, as it batches all the DOM changes and dispatches them all together.

Validating all data

Registering a new user? Ensure that all the fields entered are validated on both the UI and the backend. Doing it in both the places makes it twice as good, and validations on the UI help get the error message to the user a lot quicker than that of server-side validation.

Do not reinvent the wheel

JavaScript community is very generous when it comes to open source software and projects. Leverage them; do not rewrite something that is already available someplace else. It is not worth the time and effort to rewrite some of the community-tested software that is freely available. If a software does only 90% of what you need, consider contributing the remaining 10% of that functionality yourself to the open source project.

HTML optimizations

As web developers, we are well versed in creating templates. In this section, we will explore ways in which we can make this process as efficient as possible.

DOM structuring

As obvious as this might seem, DOM structuring can make quite a big difference when it comes to rendering the UI. For an HTML template to become DOM, it goes through a series of steps:

1. **Template Parsing** : Parser reads the HTML file
2. **Tokenization**: Parser identifies the tokens, such as html and body
3. **Lexing**: Parser converts the tokens to tags, such as <html> and <body>
4. **DOM Construction**: This is the last step where the browser converts the tags into a tree while applying the applicable styles and rules for the element

With that in mind, it becomes important that we do not nest our elements unnecessarily. Try to apply styles to elements rather than nest them in other elements. With that being said, one might wonder, how much does this really matter? The browsers are pretty good at doing this, so would it really matter if I have an extra element in my DOM? Truthfully, no, it would not matter if you do have an extra element. However, think about all the different browsers that are out there. Also, how many places you are adding this additional element; consider the precedent that such a practice would set. Over time, your overhead is going to start to matter.

Prefetching and preloading resources

Some of the lesser-known properties of the <link> tag are the rel=prefetch and rel=preload options. They allow the browser to preload some of the content that will be required in the subsequent or, sometimes, even the current page.

<link rel=prefetch >

Let's discuss a rather simple example to understand prefetching: loading images. Loading images is one of the most common actions a web page performs. We decide which image we want to load using either an `img` tag in the HTML template or the `background-image` property in CSS.

Either way, the image does not get loaded until the element is parsed. Also, let's say that your image is very large and takes a lot of time to download, then you would have to rely on a bunch of fallbacks, such as providing the image dimension so that the page does not flicker or using the `alt` attribute in case the download fails.

One possible solution is to prefetch your resources that will be needed in the near future. That way, you can avoid downloading the resources until the user lands on that page. A simple example would look as follows:

```
<!DOCTYPE html>
<html lang="en">
<head>
    <!-- a very large image -->
    <link rel="prefetch"
href="http://gfsnt.no/oen/foto/Haegefjell_Jan_2013_Large.jpg">
</head>

<body>
    <script>
        window.onload = function() {
            setTimeout(function() {
                var x = document.createElement("IMG");
                x.setAttribute("src",
            "http://gfsnt.no/oen/foto/Haegefjell_Jan_2013_Large.jpg");
                document.body.appendChild(x);
            }, 5000);
        }
    </script>
</body>
</html>
```

We are intentionally delaying the load of the `img` tag until the prefetch is done. Ideally, you would prefetch the resources needed for the next page, but this accomplishes the same.

Once we run this page, we can see the requests for the image as follows:

Name	Method	Status	Type	Initiator	Size	Time	Waterfall ▲
prefetch.html?_ijt=5c5be16e8vp5e0t8och47pctie	GET	200	document	Other	834 B	70 ms	
Haegefjell_Jan_2013_Large.jpg	GET	200	jpeg	prefetch.html?...	13.2 MB	4.20 s	
Haegefjell_Jan_2013_Large.jpg	GET	200	jpeg	prefetch.html?...	(from disk cache)	56 ms	

This sounds too good to be true, right? Right, as useful as this feature is, there are issues that we run into when dealing with prefetch across multiple browsers. Firefox only prefetches when it is idle; some browsers are capable of pausing the download if the user triggers another action and then redownload the rest of the image when the browser is idle again, but again that depends on how the server is serving the cacheable content (that is, server needs to support serving multipart file). Then, there are browsers which can, and will, abandon the prefetch because the network is too slow.

<link rel=preload >

Preload is very similar to prefetch, with the difference that the browser does not have a choice to abandon the download for any reason at any point once the resource download is triggered.

The syntax is also very similar, except that we define the type of the resource that we are trying to preload:

```
<link rel="preload"
href="http://gfsnt.no/oen/foto/Haegefjell_Jan_2013_Large.jpg" as="image">
```

Prefetching and preloading are also a very common choice when it comes to downloading fonts and font families because the request to load fonts is not triggered until both the CSSOM and DOM are ready to go.

Layout and layering of HTML

Coming up with an HTML template for rendering your elements on the UI is one of the simplest tasks of being a web developer. In this section, we will talk about how Chrome handles the template and renders it onto the UI. There are two crucial parts of the HTML template, layout and layers, and we will take a look at examples of each of these and how they affect the page performance.

The HTML layout

Let's start with an extremely simple web page and take a look at how chrome handles rendering this page:

```
<!DOCTYPE html>
<html>
    <head></head>

    <body>
        <div>test</div>
    </body>
</html>
```

Once we load the page, we will use Chrome **Developer tools** (**DevTools**) to generate the performance snapshot of this templates load. To do so, navigate to the CDT on your Chrome browser (**Settings -> More tools -> Developer tools**).

Once we are there, let's record a new snapshot by clicking on the record button on the top-left corner of the panel that just opened. Once your page loads, stop the recording and let the snapshot load in the panel. The result of that would look as follows:

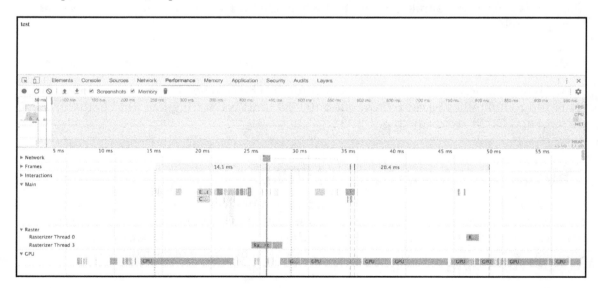

Incomprehensible, right? Well, let's break this down into small pieces that we can understand. Our main focus will be on the `main` section (expanded in the screenshot). Let's zoom into that a bit to take a look at what the events are from left to right.

First, we will see the **beforeunload** event:

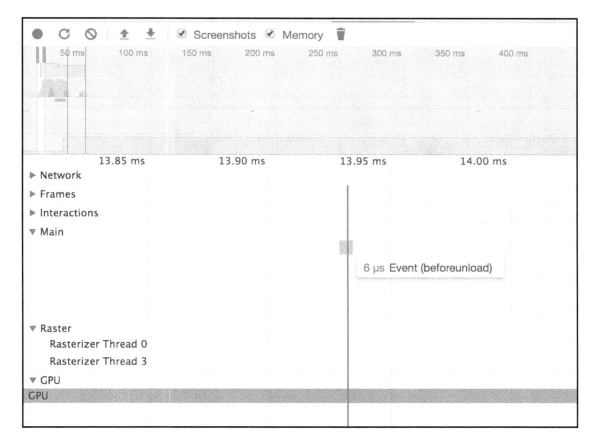

Next, we will see the update layer tree (which we will discuss later):

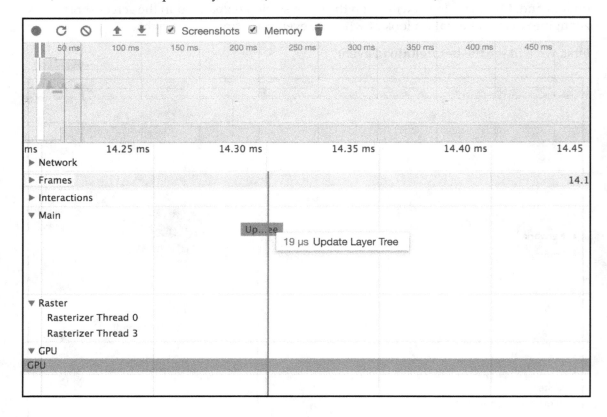

We now note a **Minor GC**, which is a browser-specific event (we will discuss this in a later section):

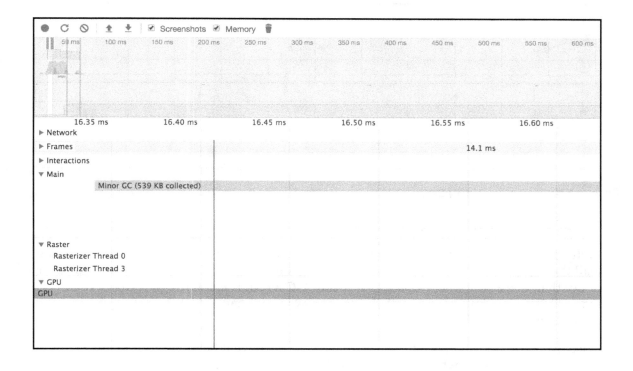

Then, we will note the `DOMContentLoaded` event followed by the `Recalculate Style` event, which is when our page is ready to be interacted with:

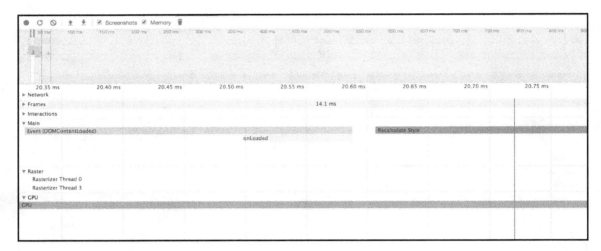

Pretty cool, right? This syncs exactly with what we have heard about browsers before. They load the page, then `DOMContentLoaded` gets triggered when everything is ready. However, notice that, there is another event called **Minor GC** which is being triggered too. We can ignore this, as it is internally handled by the browser and has very little to do with the way our code is structured.

Once the DOM is loaded, we note that we have another event being triggered called `Recalculate Style`, which is exactly what it sounds like. The DOM is ready, and the browser checks and applies any and all styles that need to be applied to this element. However, you may wonder, we did not add any styles to our template, right? Then, what styles are we talking about? By default, all browsers apply styles to all the elements they render, and these are known as User Agent Stylesheets. The browser still has to add the user agent style sheet styles to the CSSOM.

We still haven't really discussed what `Layout` is, apart from it being the geometrical structure in which the browser will arrange the elements including, but not limited to, their size, shape, and position on the page. `Layout` is also an event, which will be recorded by the CDT, to show you how long the browser is spending in trying to rearrange your layout. It is very important that we try to keep the layout event to a minimum. Why? Because `Layout` is not an isolated event. It is chained by a sequence of other events (such as updating the layer tree and painting the UI), which are required to complete the arrangement of the elements on the UI.

Another important thing to consider is that the Layout event is triggered for all the elements that are effected on the page, that is, even when one deeply nested element is changed, your entire element (or event surrounding elements based on the change) is re-laid out. Let's take a look at an example:

```html
<!DOCTYPE html>
<html>
    <head>

        <style>
            .parent {
                border: 1px solid black;
                padding: 10px;
            }

            .child {
                height: 20px;
                border: 1px solid red;
                padding: 5px;
            }
        </style>

    </head>

    <body>
        <div class="parent">
            <div class="child">
                child 1
            </div>
            <div class="child">
                child 2
            </div>
            <div class="child">
                child 3
            </div>
            <div class="child">
                child 4
            </div>
        </div>

        <button onclick="updateHeight();">update height</button>

        <script>
            function updateHeight() {
                var allEl = document.getElementsByTagName('div');
                var allElemLength = allEl.length;
```

```
                    for(var i = 0; i < allElemLength; i++) {
                        allEl[i].style.height = '100px';
                    }

            }
        </script>
    </body>
</html>
```

It is pretty straightforward; we have one page with a very small parent consisting of four child elements. We have a button which sets the height of all elements to 100px. Let's now run this page and track the performance when we click on the button update height to change the height of the elements we see the following on the UI:

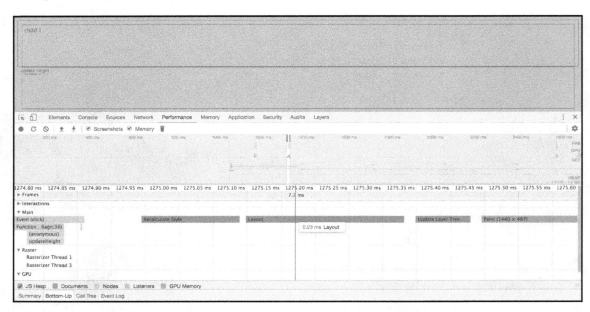

We can see from preceding screenshot that once the click event starts, it triggers our function, which then sets off a chain of events, including Layout that takes **0.23ms**. However, one might wonder, why do we have a Recalculate Style event in between the Function and the Layout? Remember our old friend User Agent Stylesheet? It sets a few styles on the button when it is active, which triggers the Recalculate Style event.

If you want to remove all the styles of an element (such as a button in the case described earlier), you can do so by applying the `all:unset;` property to the element of your choice. This will completely un-style the element. However, it will reduce the `Recalculate Style` event to a fraction of what it is with the User Agent Styles applied.

Let's now change the JavaScript function to only change the style of the first child element instead of all the elements on the page and take a look at how that affects the `Layout` events execution in our case:

```
function updateHeight() {
    var allEl = document.getElementsByTagName('div');
    allEl[1].style.height = '100px';
}
```

Now, when we run the page and profile the execution of the click method, we will see the following in the profiler:

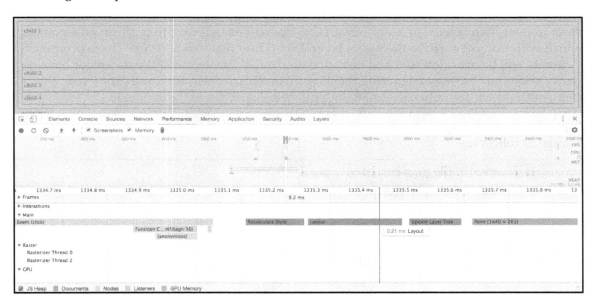

As you can see in the preceding screenshot, it still takes **0.21ms** to layout the entire page, which is not very different from our previous value. In our preceding example, we have five more elements. However, in a production application, this can, and will, scale to **1000s** of elements, and, for a smooth transition, we want to keep our `Layout` event under **16ms** (**60fps**).

In all probability, you may not ever come across this issue, but if you do, the simplest way to handle it would be to first check that you are using the latest layout model supported by your browser. In most of the browsers, it would be flexbox or grid, so prefer that over floats, percentages, or positioning.

HTML layers

As we have seen in the earlier example, once the element is re-laid out, we `Paint` the element, that is, fill the pixels with the color, which is supposed to be a part of the element at the given position (determined by `Layout`).

Once the `Paint` event is complete, the browser then performs `Composition`, which is basically our browser putting together all the parts of the page. The lesser these parts, the faster the page load will be. Also, if a certain section of the `Composition` takes too long, then the entire page load is delayed.

How do we handle these operations which take too long? We can handle it by promoting them to their own layer. There are certain CSS operations that we can perform on elements, which will promote them to their own layer. What does that mean for us? These promoted elements will be now deferred and executed on the GPU as textures. We no longer have to worry about our browser triggering the `Layout` or `Paint` event for these promoted elements, and we are only concerned with the `Composition` of the element.

From the example earlier, so far we have established the first four steps of the flow of any change as follows:

1. JavaScript file gets executed
2. Recalculation of styles
3. The `Layout` event
4. The `Paint` event

Now, to that list, we can add the following steps to completely render the element on the UI:

5. `Composition`

6. Multithread Rasterization

Step 6 merely renders our pixels onto the UI, which can be batched and run on parallel threads. Let's create a simple HTML and take a look at how it renders onto a single layer on the UI:

```
<!DOCTYPE html>
<html>
<head>

</head>

<body>
    <div>
         Default Layer
    </div>
</body>
</html>
```

We can access the **Layers** from the DevTool by navigating to the **Settings** option and then selecting **More tools** and **Layers**. On loading the page shown previously, we will see the following in the **Layers**:

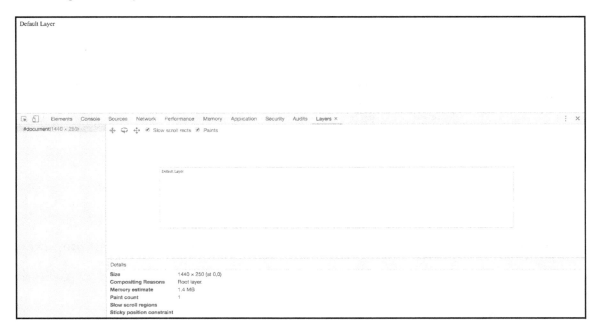

When we profile the preceding page, we can see, as expected, that the page loads and renders the UI on the `Main` thread:

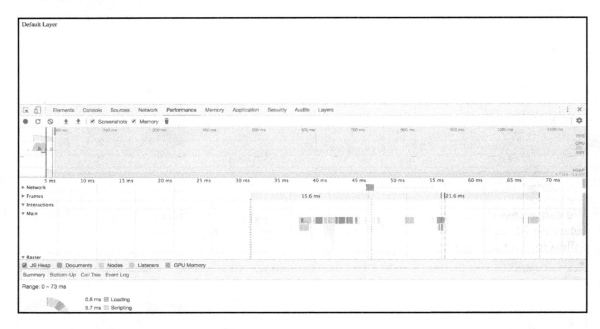

Let's now change this example to load onto its own layer so that we can completely skip both the `Layout` and the `Paint` sections altogether. To load an element onto a layer of its own, all we need to do is either give it a CSS transform or set the `will-change` property to transform:

```
.class-name {
    will-change: transform:
    // OR
    transform: translateZ(0); <- does nothing except loading to a new Layer
}
```

The following is an updated example template, which uses the CSS3 `transform` property:

```
<!DOCTYPE html>
<html>
<head>
    <style>
        div {
            width: 100px;
            height: 100px;
            margin: 200px;
```

```
            border: 1px solid black;
            animation: spin 1s infinite;
            transition: all 0.35s ease;
        }

        @keyframes spin {
            from {
                transform: rotate(0deg);
            }

            to {
                transform: rotate(360deg);
            }
        }
    </style>
</head>

<body>
    <div></div>
</body>
</html>
```

In the preceding code, we added a very small animation, which will infinitely rotate the element. When we reload the page, we can see that it has been added to its own layer:

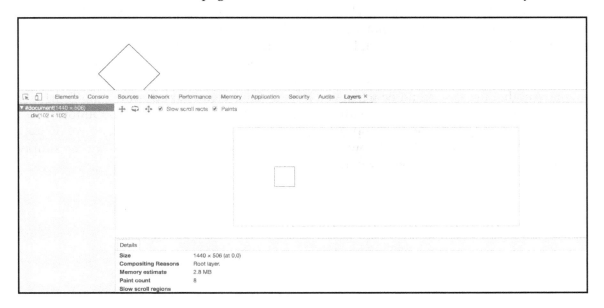

Not just that, when we record the performance of our modified template, we can see something quite interesting:

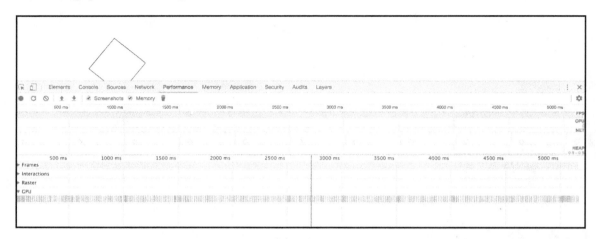

As we can see in the preceding screenshot, the browser completely defers the Layer onto the GPU as a new texture, and, from then on, the GPU handles the rendering/updating of the element and not the browser.

Okay, so, does that mean we load each element onto its own Layer and then let the GPU take it from there? No, certainly not, because each Layer internally requires memory, and loading 1,000s of elements onto each Layer would be counterproductive. For example, the only time when we should intentionally promote elements to their own Layer is when an element is taking too long during Composition and is choking operations, such as scroll or swipe. Another use case could be when you have a single element performing multiple changes, such as animating height, width, and background color. This will continuously invoke all the steps of the rendering process (from Layout to Rasterization), and we do not really need to do all of that if we know that it is limited to these few changes. We can simply promote this element to its own layer and be done with it.

CSS optimizations

CSS optimizations are extremely easy and kind of obvious if you have experience developing with any preprocessor frameworks, such as SCSS/LESS. When we discuss CSS optimization, we are really talking about two different yet dependent things:

- Loading the style sheets
- Rendering and applying styles

Coding practices

There are a number of coding practices that we can adapt and learn to make our application perform better. Most of them might seem insignificant, but they do matter when scaled to a large application. We will discuss a few of these techniques with examples.

Using smaller values for common ENUM

As we are talking about reducing the page load time, one quick way to do so is by removing redundancies in the CSS file itself:

- Using #FFFFFF ? Switch to #FFF, which is the same RGB value represented in short.
- Do not add px after a properties value if the value is 0.
- Use minification if not being used already. This concatenates all the CSS files in use and removes all the whitespace and newlines.
- Use GZip to compress the minified file while transferring it over the network. It is very easy, and browsers are very good at unzipping the files efficiently.

- Be aware of browser-specific optimizations at hand. For example, in case of Chrome, we do not have to apply styles in the `rgba(x,y,z,a)` format. We can apply it as `rgba` during dev and extract the corresponding HEX value using the DevTool. Simply, inspect the element in question and click on the small rectangle while pressing *Shift*:

```
<!DOCTYPE html>
<html>
  <head>
  </head>
  ▼ <body>
      <div style="
          color: rgba(255, 0, 0, 0.3);
        ">Color me red</div> == $0
    </body>
  </html>
```

```
Styles   Computed   Event Listeners   DOM

Filter

element.style {
    color: ▇#ff00004d;
}

div {
    display: block;
}
```

Using shorthand properties

Using shorthand properties is one way in which the page load can be sped up. As obvious as it may sound, sometimes, we take the browser and network for granted when we are working on our cozy laptop, and we forget to take into consideration the poor 3G-based devices. So, the next time you want to style the background or border of an element, ensure that they are all collapsed and written using shorthand.

Sometimes, you may run into a situation where you want to override only one property of a certain element's style. For example, if you want to apply border on three sides of an element, use the following:

```
.okay {
    border-left: 1px solid black;
    border-right: 1px solid black;
    border-bottom: 1px solid black;
} // 114 characters including spaces

.better {
    border: 1px solid black;
    border-top: 0;
} // 59 characters including spaces
```

Avoiding complex CSS selectors

Whenever you are creating your CSS styles, it is imperative to understand that there is a cost associated with the browser to apply these styles to any element. We can analyze our CSS selectors the same way we do our JavaScript and come up with the best and worst case runtime performance of each of the styles we apply.

For instance, consider that we have a style as follows:

```
.my-class > div > ul.other-class .item:nth-child(3) {
```

The complexity of this would be much higher than simply creating a class and assigning it directly to the element itself:

```
.my-class-child {
```

Our browser no longer has to check whether each and every element falls into the hierarchy of the style defined previously. A technique developed out of this concept is called **Block-Element-Modifier** (**BEM**), which is quite easy to understand. Give a single class name to your elements, and try not to nest them:

So, consider that your template looks as follows:

```
<div class="nav">
  <a href="#" class="nav__trigger">hamburger_icon</a>

  <ul class="nav__items">
    <li class="nav__item">
      <a href="#" class="nav__link">About</a>
    </li>

    <li class="nav__item">
      <a href="#" class="nav__link">Blog</a>
    </li>

    <li class="nav__item">
      <a href="#" class="nav__link">Contact</a>
    </li>
  </ul>
</div>
```

You could apply styles using BEM as follows:

```
.nav {
    /* styles */
}
```

```
.nav__items {
    /* styles */
}

.nav__item {
    /* styles */
}

.nav__link {
    /* styles */
}

.nav__link--active {
    /* styles */
}
```

If you ever need to add a custom styling to an element, you can either create a new class and apply it directly, or you can combine the nesting with the current level:

```
.nav__item--last-child--active {
    /* styles */
}
```

Understanding the browser

Similar to HTML rendering, CSS parsing and rendering are also complex processes, which browsers very effortlessly hide. It is always good to know what we can avoid to make things better for us. Let's take the same example as HTML and discuss how Chrome handles these.

Avoiding repaint and reflow

Let's first briefly talk about what a repaint and reflow are:

Repaint: An action performed by the browser when the non-geometric properties of an element change, for example, background color, text color, and so on.

Reflow: An action performed by the browser because of the geometric change to an element (or its parent) directly or via a computed property. This process is same as the Layout discussed earlier.

While we cannot completely prevent Repaint and Reflow events completely, we can certainly play our part in minimizing the changes that trigger these operations. Almost all DOM read operations (such as offsetWidth and getClientRects) trigger a Layout event because the values of such read operations are done on demand, and the browser does not care about their values until explicitly requested. Also, anytime we modify the DOM, the Layout is invalidated and it will have to be recalculated if we need to read the DOM elements properties the next time.

Critical rendering path (CRP)

So far, we have seen how to optimize the page load (reducing payload, size, and so on), and then we talked about the things which we will need to account for to keep the page performant once it is rendered. Critical rendering path is the technique of optimizing the initial load of the page above the fold (that is, the top part of the page that shows up on the initial load prior to any scroll). This is also known as **time to interact** (**TTI**) or **time to first byte** (**TTFB**), which we want to reduce to keep the page load fast.

Technically, CRP includes the following steps:

1. Receive and start parsing HTML.
2. Download and construct CSSOM.
3. Download and execute JS.
4. Finish constructing DOM.
5. Create Render Tree.

So if we want our TTI to be low, it's quite obvious that we will need to have our DOM and CSSOM constructed as quickly as possible without any render-blocking CSS or parser-blocking JS files. One of the indications for our TTI to be low is that our DOMContentLoaded event fires quickly because DCL is fired only when DOM and CSSOM are ready. Let's take the following example template:

```
<html>
<head>
    <title>CRP Blank</title>
</head>
<body>
    <div>Blank</div>
</body>
</html>
```

We can see that it is pretty lean and does not even load any external styles or scripts. This is pretty unusual for a web page, but it serves as a good example. When we run this page and open the **Network** tab, we can see the following:

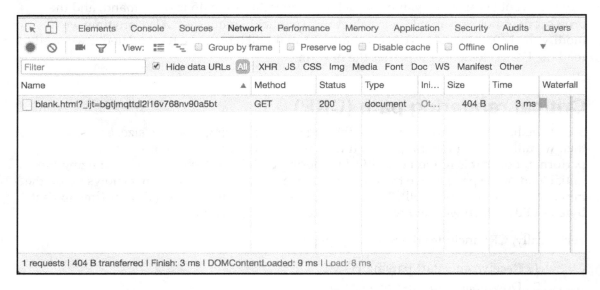

However, the HTML we mentioned is pretty unusual. In all possibility, we will have more than one external CSS and JS file being loaded into our page. In situations like that, our DCL event gets delayed. Let's add blank CSS and JS files to be loaded in our `blank.html` file:

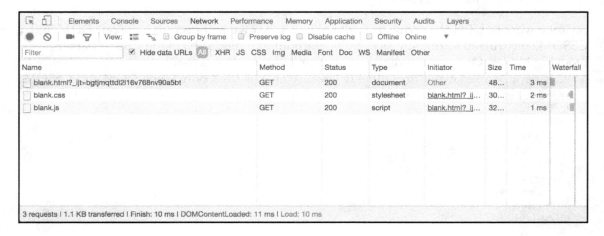

Here, we can see that, even though there isn't much to be loaded, the DCL event has been pushed until the browser downloads and runs the JS file because the JS files fetching and execution are render blocking operations. Our goal is now much clearer: we will need to reduce the DCL to a minimum, and, from what we have seen so far, we will need to load the HTML ASAP while everything else can be loaded once the initial page is rendered (or at least is being rendered). Earlier we have seen that we can use the `async` keywords along with the script tags to make the JavaScript load and execute asynchronously. Let's use the same now to make our page load faster:

```html
<html>
<head>
    <title>CRP Blank</title>
    <link rel="stylesheet" href="blank.css">
</head>
<body>
    <div>Blank</div>

    <script async src="blank.js"></script>
</body>
</html>
```

Now, when we run this page with the **Network** tab open, we will see the following:

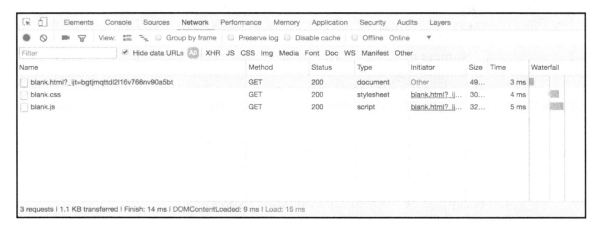

We can see that the DCL (represented by the blue vertical line under the *waterfall* tab) occurs way before the CSS and JS files are downloaded and executed. Another advantage of using the `async` attribute is that the `async` attribute indicates that the JavaScript is not dependent on CSSOM, and hence it does not have to be blocked by the CSSOM construction.

JavaScript optimizations

There are tons of resources available online to discuss the various optimizations that can be applied to JavaScript. In this section, we will take a look at some of these micro-optimizations and determine how we can take small steps toward making our JavaScript more performant.

Truthy/falsy comparisons

We have all, at some point, written if conditions or assigned default values by relying on the truthy or falsy nature of the JavaScript variables. As helpful as it is most of the times, we will need to consider the impact that such an operation would cause on our application. However, before we jump into the details, let's discuss how any condition is evaluated in JavaScript, specifically an `if` condition in this case. As a developer, we tend to do the following:

```
if(objOrNumber) {
    // do something
}
```

This works for most of the cases, unless the number is 0, in which case it gets evaluated to false. That is a very common edge case, and most of us catch it anyway. However, what does the JavaScript engine have to do to evaluate this condition? How does it know whether the objOrNumber evaluates to true or false? Let's return to our ECMA262 specs and pull out the IF condition spec (https://www.ecma-international.org/ecma-262/5.1/#sec-12.5). The following is an excerpt of the same:

Semantics

The production IfStatement : If (Expression) Statement else Statement

Statement is evaluated as follows:

1. Let exprRef be the result of evaluating Expression.
2. If ToBoolean(GetValue(exprRef)) is true, then
    • Return the result of evaluating the first Statement.
3. Else,
    • Return the result of evaluating the second Statement.

Now, we note that whatever expression we pass goes through the following three steps:

1. Getting the `exprRef` from `Expression`.
2. `GetValue` is called on `exprRef`.
3. `ToBoolean` is called as the result of *step 2*.

Step 1 does not concern us much at this stage; think of it this way—an expression can be something like a `==` b or something like the `shouldIEvaluateTheIFCondition()` method call, that is, something that evaluates your condition.

Step 2 extracts the value of the `exprRef`, that is, 10, true, undefined. In this step, we differentiate how the value is extracted based on the type of the `exprRef`. You can refer to the details of `GetValue` at `https://www.ecma-international.org/ecma-262/5.1/#sec-8.7.1`.

Step 3 then converts the value extracted from *Step 2* into a Boolean value based on the following table (taken from `https://www.ecma-international.org/ecma-262/5.1/#sec-9.2`):

9.2 ToBoolean

The abstract operation ToBoolean converts its argument to a value of type Boolean according to Table 11:

Table 11 — ToBoolean Conversions

Argument Type	Result
Undefined	false
Null	false
Boolean	The result equals the input argument (no conversion).
Number	The result is false if the argument is +0, −0, or NaN; otherwise the result is true.
String	The result is false if the argument is the empty String (its length is zero); otherwise the result is true.
Object	true

At each step, you can see that it is always beneficial if we are able to provide the direct boolean value instead of a truthy or falsy value.

Looping optimizations

We can do a deep-down dive into the for loop, similar to what we did with the if condition earlier (`https://www.ecma-international.org/ecma-262/5.1/#sec-12.6.3`), but there are easier and more obvious optimizations which can be applied when it comes to loops. Simple changes can drastically affect the quality and performance of the code; consider this for example:

```
for(var i = 0; i < arr.length; i++) {
    // logic
}
```

The preceding code can be changed as follows:

```
var len = arr.length;

for(var i = 0; i < len; i++) {
    // logic
}
```

What is even better is to run the loops in reverse, which is even faster than what we have seen previously:

```
var len = arr.length;

for(var i = len; i >= 0; i--) {
    // logic
}
```

The conditional function call

Some of the features that we have within our applications are conditional. For example, logging or analytics fall into this category. Some of the applications may have logging turned off for some time and then turned back on. The most obvious way of achieving this is to wrap the method for logging within an if condition. However, since the method could be triggered a lot of times, there is another way in which we can make the optimization in this case:

```
function someUserAction() {

    // logic

    if (analyticsEnabled) {
        trackUserAnalytics();
```

```
    }
}


// in some other class

function trackUserAnalytics() {

    // save analytics

}
```

Instead of the preceding approach, we can instead try to do something, which is only slightly different but allows V8-based engines to optimize the way the code is executed:

```
function someUserAction() {

    // logic

    trackUserAnalytics();
}


// in some other class

function toggleUserAnalytics() {
    if(enabled) {
        trackUserAnalytics =  userAnalyticsMethod;
    } else {
        trackUserAnalytics = noOp;
    }
}

function userAnalyticsMethod() {

    // save analytics

}

// empty function
function noOp   {}
```

Now, the preceding implementation is a double-edged sword. The reason for that is very simple. JavaScript engines employ a technique called **inline caching** (**IC**), which means that any previous lookup for a certain method performed by the JS engine will be cached and reused when triggered the next time; for example, if we have an object that has a nested method, a.b.c, the method a.b.c will be only looked up once and stored on cache (IC); if a.b.c is called the next time, it will be picked up from IC, and the JS engine will not parse the whole chain again. If there are any changes to the a.b.c chain, then the IC gets invalidated and a new dynamic lookup is performed the next time instead of being retrieved from the IC.

So, from our previous example, when we have noOp assigned to the trackUserAnalytics() method, the method path gets tracked and saved within IC, but it internally removes this function call as it is a call to an empty method. However, when it is applied to an actual function with some logic in it, IC points it directly to this new method. So, if we keep calling our toggleUserAnalytics() method multiple times, it keeps invalidating our IC, and our dynamic method lookup has to happen every time until the application state stabilizes (that is, toggleUserAnalytics() is no longer called).

Image and font optimizations

When it comes to image and font optimizations, there are no limits to the types and the scale of optimization that we can perform. However, we need to keep in mind our target audience, and we need to tailor our approach based on the problem at hand.

With both images and fonts, the first and foremost important thing is that we do not overserve, that is, we request and send only the data that is necessary by determining the dimensions of the device that our application is running on.

The simplest way to do this is by adding a cookie for your device size and sending it to the server along with each of the request. Once the server receives the request for the image, it can then retrieve the image based on the dimension of the image that was sent to the cookie. Most of the time these images are something like a user avatar or a list of people who commented on a certain post. We can agree that the thumbnail images do not need to be of the same size as that of the profile page, and we can save some of the bandwidth while transmitting a smaller image based on the image.

Since screens these days have very high **Dots Per Inch** (**DPI**), the media that we serve to screens needs to be worthy of it. Otherwise, the application looks bad and the images look all pixelated. This can be avoided using Vector images or SVGs, which can be GZipped over the wire, thus reducing the payload size.

Another not so obvious optimization is changing the image compression type. Have you ever loaded a page in which the image loads from the top to bottom in small, incremental rectangles? By default, the images are compressed using a baseline technique, which is a default method of compressing the image from top to bottom. We can change this to be progressive compression using libraries such as `imagemin`. This would load the entire image first as blurred, then semi blurred, and so on until the entire image is uncompressed and displayed on the screen. Uncompressing a progressive JPEG might take a little longer than that of the baseline, so it is important to measure before making such optimizations.

Another extension based on this concept is a Chrome-only format of an image called `WebP`. This is a highly effective way of serving images, which serves a lot of companies in production and saved almost 30% on bandwidth. Using `WebP` is almost as simple as the progressive compression as discussed previously. We can use the `imagemin-webp` node module, which can convert a JPEG image into a `webp` image, thus reducing the image size to a great extent.

Web fonts are a little different than that of images. Images get downloaded and rendered onto the UI on demand, that is, when the browser encounters the image either from the HTML 0r CSS files. However, the fonts, on the other hand, are a little different. The font files are only requested when the Render Tree is completely constructed. That means that the CSSOM and DOM have to be ready by the time request is dispatched for the fonts. Also, if the fonts files are being served from the server and not locally, then there are chances that we may see the text without the font applied first (or no text at all) and then we see the font applied, which may cause a flashing effect of the text.

There are multiple simple techniques to avoid this problem:

- Download, serve, and preload the font files locally:

  ```
  <link rel="preload" href="fonts/my-font.woff2" as="font">
  ```

- Specify the unicode-range in the font-face so that browsers can adapt and improvise on the character set and glyphs that are actually expected by the browser:

  ```
  @font-face(
      ...
      unicode-range: U+000-5FF; // latin
      ...
  )
  ```

- So far, we have seen that we can get the unstyled text to be loaded on to the UI and the get styled as we expected it to be; this can be changed using the font loading API, which allows us to load and render the font using JavaScript:

```
var font = new FontFace("myFont", "url(/my-fonts/my-font.woff2)", {
    unicodeRange: 'U+000-5FF'
});

// initiate a fetch without Render Tree
font.load().then(function() {
    // apply the font
    document.fonts.add(font);

    document.body.style.fontFamily = "myFont";
});
```

Garbage collection in JavaScript

Let's take a quick look at what **garbage collection** (**GC**) is and how we can handle it in JavaScript. A lot of low-level languages provide explicit capabilities to developers to allocate and free memory in their code. However, unlike those languages, JavaScript automatically handles the memory management, which is both a good and bad thing. Good because we no longer have to worry about how much memory we need to allocate, when we need to do so, and how to free the assigned memory. The bad part about the whole process is that, to an uninformed developer, this can be a recipe for disaster and they can end up with an application that might hang and crash.

Luckily for us, understanding the process of GC is quite easy and can be very easily incorporated into our coding style to make sure that we are writing optimal code when it comes to memory management. Memory management has three very obvious steps:

1. Assign the memory to variables:

   ```
   var a = 10; // we assign a number to a memory location referenced
   by variable a
   ```

2. Use the variables to read or write from the memory:

   ```
   a += 3; // we read the memory location referenced by a and write a
   new value to it
   ```

3. Free the memory when it's no longer needed.

Now, this is the part that is not explicit. How does the browser know when we are done with the variable a and it is ready to be garbage collected? Let's wrap this inside a function before we continue this discussion:

```
function test() {
    var a = 10;
    a += 3;
    return a;
}
```

We have a very simple function, which just adds to our variable a and returns the result and finishes the execution. However, there is actually one more step, which will happen after the execution of this method called **mark and sweep** (not immediately after, sometimes this can also happen after a batch of operations is completed on the main thread). When the browser performs mark and sweep, it's dependent on the total memory the application consumes and the speed at which the memory is being consumed.

Mark and sweep algorithm

Since there is no accurate way to determine whether the data at a particular memory location is going to be used or not in the future, we will need to depend on alternatives which can help us make this decision. In JavaScript, we use the concept of a **reference** to determine whether a variable is still being used or not—if not, it can be garbage collected.

The concept of mark and sweep is very straightforward: what all memory locations are reachable from all the known active memory locations? If something is not reachable, collect it, that is, free the memory. That's it, but what are the known active memory locations? It still needs a starting point, right? In most of the browsers, the GC algorithm keeps a list of the roots from which the mark and sweep process can be started. All the roots and their children are marked as active, and any variable that can be reached from these roots are also marked as active. Anything that cannot be reached can be marked as unreachable and thus collected. In most of the cases, the roots consist of the window object.

So, we will go back to our previous example:

```
function test() {
    var a = 10;
    a += 3;
    return a;
}
```

Our variable a is local to the `test()` method. As soon as the method is executed, there is no way to access that variable anymore, that is, no one holds any reference to that variable, and that is when it can be marked for garbage collection so that the next time GC runs, the `var a` will be swept and the memory allocated to it can be freed.

Garbage collection and V8

When it comes to V8, the process of garbage collection is extremely complex (as it should be). So, let's briefly discuss how V8 handles it.

In V8, the memory (heap) is divided into two main generations, which are the **new-space** and **old-space**. Both new-space and old-space are assigned some memory (between *1 MB* and *20 MB*). Most of the programs and their variables when created are assigned within the new-space. As and when we create a new variable or perform an operation, which consumes memory, it is by default assigned from the new-space, which is optimized for memory allocation. Once the total memory allocated to the new-space is almost completely consumed, the browser triggers a **Minor GC**, which basically removes the variables that are no longer being referenced and marks the variables that are still being referenced and cannot be removed yet. Once a variable survives two or more **Minor GC**s, then it becomes a candidate for old-space where the GC cycle is not run as frequently as that of the new-space. A Major GC is triggered when the old-space is of a certain size, all of this is driven by the heuristics of the application, which is very important to the whole process. So, well-written programs move fewer objects into the old-space and thus have less Major GC events being triggered.

Needless to say that this is a very high-level overview of what V8 does for garbage collection, and since this process keeps changing over time, we will switch gears and move on to the next topic.

Avoiding memory leaks

Well, now that we know on a high level what garbage collection is in JavaScript and how it works, let's take a look at some common pitfalls which prevent us from getting our variables marked for GC by the browser.

Assigning variables to global scope

This should be pretty obvious by now; we discussed how the GC mechanism determines a root (which is the window object) and treats everything on the root and its children as active and never marks them for garbage collection.

So, the next time you forget to add a `var` to your variable declarations, remember that the global variable that you are creating will live forever and never get garbage collected:

```
function test() {
    a = 10; // created on window object
    a += 3;
    return a;
}
```

Removing DOM elements and references

It's imperative that we keep our DOM references to a minimum, so a well-known step that we like to perform is caching the DOM elements in our JavaScript so that we do not have to query any of the DOM elements over and over. However, once the DOM elements are removed, we will need to make sure that these methods are removed from our cache as well, otherwise, they will never get GC'd:

```
var cache = {
    row: document.getElementById('row')
};

function removeTable() {
    document.body.removeChild(document.getElementById('row'));
}
```

The code shown previously removes the `row` from the DOM but the variable cache still refers to the DOM element, hence preventing it from being garbage collected. Another interesting thing to note here is that even when we remove the table that was containing the `row`, the entire table would remain in the memory and not get GC'd because the row, which is in cache internally refers to the table.

Closures edge case

Closures are amazing; they help us deal with a lot of problematic scenarios and also provide us with ways in which we can simulate the concept of private variables. Well, all that is good, but sometimes we tend to overlook the potential downsides that are associated with the closures. Here is what we do know and use:

```
function myGoodFunc() {
    var a = new Array(10000000).join('*');
    // something big enough to cause a spike in memory usage

    function myGoodClosure() {
        return a + ' added from closure';
    }

    myGoodClosure();
}

setInterval(myGoodFunc, 1000);
```

When we run this script in the browser and then profile it, we see as expected that the method consumes a constant amount of memory and then is GC'd and restored to the baseline memory consumed by the script:

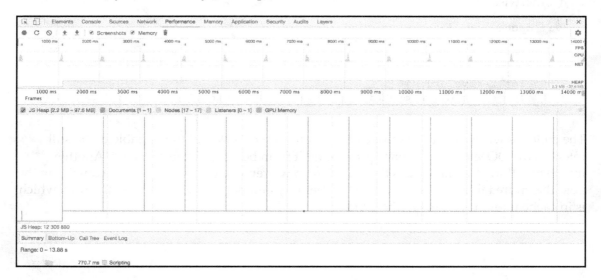

Now, let's zoom into one of these spikes and take a look at the call tree to determine what all events are bring triggered around the time of the spikes:

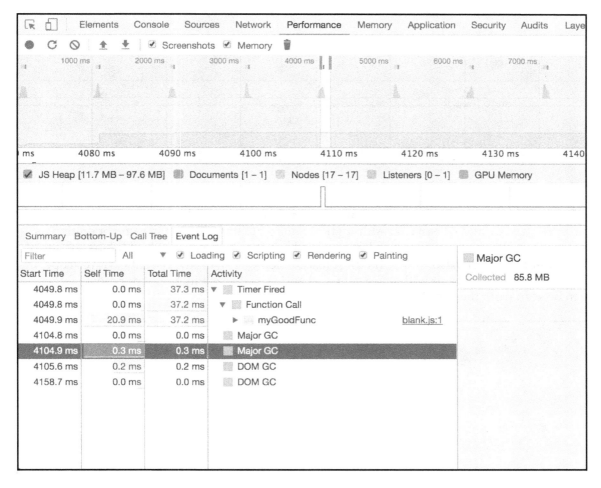

We can see that everything happens as per our expectation here; first, our `setInterval()` is triggered, which calls `myGoodFunc()`, and once the execution is done, there is a GC, which collects the data and hence the spike, as we can see from the preceding screenshots.

Now, this was the expected flow or the happy path when dealing with closures. However, sometimes our code is not as simple and we end up performing multiple things within one closure, and sometimes even end up nesting closures:

```
function myComplexFunc() {
    var a = new Array(1000000).join('*');
    // something big enough to cause a spike in memory usage

    function closure1() {
```

```
        return  a + ' added from closure';
    }

    closure1();

    function closure2() {
        console.log('closure2 called')
    }

    setInterval(closure2, 100);
}

setInterval(myComplexFunc, 1000);
```

We can note in the preceding code that we extended our method to contain two closures now: closure1 and closure2. Although closure1 still performs the same operation as before, closure2 will run forever because we have it running at 1/10th of the frequency of the parent function. Also, since both the closure methods share the parent closure scope, in this case the variable a, it will never get GC'd and thus cause a huge memory leak, which can be seen from the profile as follows:

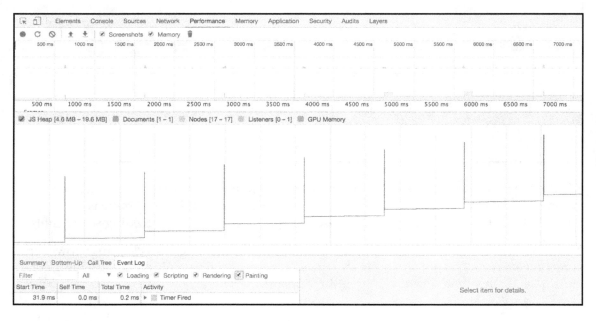

On a closer look, we can see that the GC is being triggered but because of the frequency at which the methods are being called, the memory is slowly leaking (lesser memory is collected than being created):

Well, that was an extreme edge case, right? It's way more theoretical than practical—why would anyone have two nested `setInterval()` methods with closures. Let's take a look at another example in which we no longer nest multiple `setInterval()`, but it is driven by the same logic.

Let's assume that we have a method that creates closures:

```
var something = null;

function replaceValue () {
   var previousValue = something;

   // `unused` method loads the `previousValue` into closure scope
   function </span>unused() {
      if (previousValue)
         console.log("hi");
   }

   // update something

   something = {
      str: new Array(1000000).join('*'),

      // all closures within replaceValue share the same
      // closure scope hence someMethod would have access
      // to previousValue which is nothing but its parent
```

```
        // object (`something`)


        // since `someMethod` has access to its parent
        // object, even when it is replaced by a new (identical)
        // object in the next setInterval iteration, the previous
        // value does not get garbage collected because the someMethod
        // on previous value still maintains reference to previousValue
        // and so on.

        someMethod: function () {}
    };
}

setInterval(replaceValue, 1000);
```

A simple fix to solve this problem is obvious, as we have said ourselves that the previous value of the object `something` doesn't get garbage collected as it refers to the `previousValue` from the previous iteration. So, the solution to this would be to clear out the value of the `previousValue` at the end of each iteration, thus leaving nothing for `something` to refer once it is unloaded, hence the memory profiling can be seen to change:

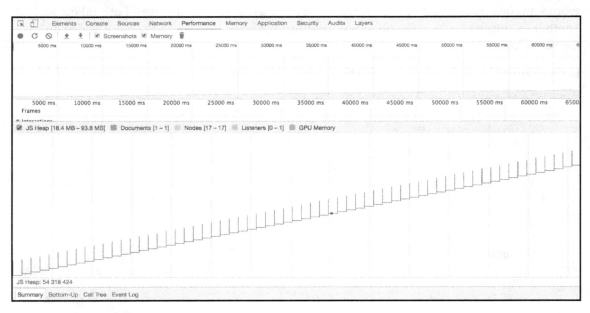

The preceding image changes as follows:

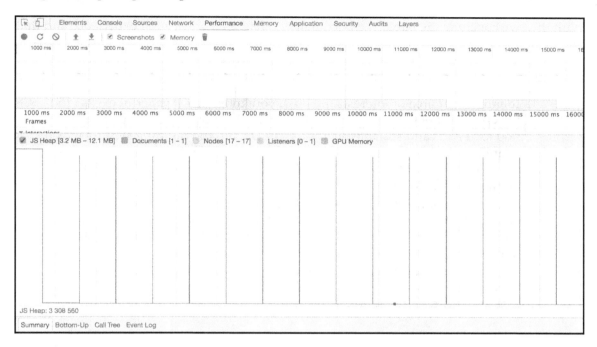

Summary

In this chapter, we explored ways in which the code performance can be improved by making optimizations to HTML, CSS, and JavaScript that we write for our applications. It is very important to understand that these are something that may, or may not, benefit you, based on the application that you are trying to build. The main takeaway from this chapter should be the ability to open up the browser's insides and not be scared to dissect and take a look at how the browsers handle our code. Also, be wary that the ECMA specification guide keeps changing, but it takes time for the browsers to catch up with the changes. Also, last but not the least, never over-optimize or optimize too early. If you run into issues, then measure first and then decide what the bottlenecks are before coming up with a plan for optimization.

What's next?

With this, we conclude the book. We hope that you had a great learning experience and that you benefit from these techniques on a day-to-day basis. JavaScript, being the way it is, is ever growing. Things are changing at a rapid pace, and it gets tough to keep track of things. Here are some suggestions, which you can explore and modify as you try them out:

1. Identify your area of interests. By now, you know that JavaScript exists (and rocks) in a lot of things beyond the browser. Are you more of a UI person? Do you love APIs and scalable microservice? Do you dig building sensors which count how many coffees you consume every day? Find your passion and apply your newly learned JavaScript concepts there. The concepts are same, the applications are different.

2. Subscribe to newsletters and mailing lists from areas of interests. You will be amazed by the amount of information you get from each of these emails on a daily or weekly basis. It helps you to keep on your toes, and you can stay up to date on the latest technologies.

3. Write a blog (or even a StackOverflow answer) for what you know and learn. It always helps when you write down what you learn. Someday, you can even use that for your own reference.

Other Books You May Enjoy

If you enjoyed this book, you may be interested in these other books by Packt:

Isomorphic JavaScript Web Development
Tomas Alabes, Konstantin Tarkus

ISBN: 978-1-78588-976-9

- Build on the client side with the awesomeness of React
- Style your application effectively
- Render the server side using React
- Implement a GraphQL server based on Node, Express, and SQL
- Fetch application data using Relay
- Build an isomorphic router to use in the application
- Deploy your application to a cloud host
- Secure your application with a solid token-based authentication system

JavaScript by Example
Dani Akash S

ISBN: 978-1-78829-396-9

- A strong understanding of web application development with JavaScript and ES6.
- A firm foundation on which to master other JavaScript frameworks and libraries.
- Write maintainable and scalable code by organizing functions into modules.
- Importance of tools such as Node, NPM, Babel, and Webpack in Front-end development
- Work with real-time data such as incoming video streams, texts, and so on
- Integrate React with JavaScript to build large-scale applications.
- Utilize Redux to manage data across React components and greatly speed up the development process

Leave a review - let other readers know what you think

Please share your thoughts on this book with others by leaving a review on the site that you bought it from. If you purchased the book from Amazon, please leave us an honest review on this book's Amazon page. This is vital so that other potential readers can see and use your unbiased opinion to make purchasing decisions, we can understand what our customers think about our products, and our authors can see your feedback on the title that they have worked with Packt to create. It will only take a few minutes of your time, but is valuable to other potential customers, our authors, and Packt. Thank you!

Index

A

Angular application
  Angular CLI, installing 15
  creating 14, 77, 103
  creating, with CLI 15
  stack, creating 16, 18
API
  about 8
  clear 8
  implementing 42
  peek 8
  pop 8
  push 8
  size 8
arrays
  performance, comparing with sets 99
Asymptotic Notations
  about 247
  Big-O notation 248
  Omega notation 249
  theta notation 251
Auxiliary space 257

B

bidirectional graph
  creating 150, 152
Big-O notation 245, 248
Block-Element-Modifier (BEM) 289
branch and bound algorithm
  about 210, 212
  implementing 212, 216, 218
  used, for creating custom shopping list 208, 210
Breadth First Search (BFS)
  about 150, 177
  implementing 188, 193
  pseudocode 187

  used, for determining relationships 183, 187
browser
  about 290
  Critical rendering path (CRP) 291
  reflow, avoiding 290
  repaint, avoiding 290
brute-force algorithm
  avoiding 218
  Fibonacci generator 219
  memoized Fibonacci generator 220
  Recursive Fibonacci generator 220

C

chat endpoint
  creating 51, 56
constant time function 252
credit card approval predictor
  creating 116
  ID3 algorithm 117
  ID3 algorithm, coding 122
critical rendering path (CRP) 291
CSS Object Model (CSSOM) 263
CSS, best practices
  !important, avoiding 266
  inline styles, avoiding 266
  media queries, defining in ascending order 267
  styles, arranging within class alphabetically 266
CSS, optimizations
  about 287
  browser 290
  coding practices 287
  complex CSS selectors, avoiding 289, 290
  shorthand properties, using 288
  smaller values, using for common ENUM 287
custom back button
  application logic 25

application state changes, detecting 22
application, routing 19, 22
application, setting up 19, 22
creating, for web application 19
states, navigating 25
UI, laying out 23
custom keyboard shortcuts
Angular application, creating 79, 81
creating, for application 78
states, creating with keymap 81, 87

D

data 81
decision nodes 117
Developer Tools (DevTools) 274
Dijkstra
about 150
algorithm, implementing 179
implementing 183
pseudocode 178
used, for determining shortest path 177
divide and concur 174
Document Object Model (DOM) 263
DOM structuring 271
Dots Per Inch (DPI) 298
dynamic programming (DP)
implementing 196, 199, 200
pseudo code 195
used, for building financial planner 193, 195

E

ECMAScript
URL 296
evaluator
building 28
Express server
creating 225

F

first-in first-out (FIFO) 41
friend recommendation system
analysis 169
creating, for social media 160
PageRank algorithm 161

Personalized PageRank (PPR) algorithm 162
Personalized PageRank, implementing 166, 169
pseudocode, for personalized PageRank 164
results 169
web server, creating 165

G

garbage collection (GC) 300
graph, use cases
friend recommendation system, creating for social
media 160
Node.js web server, creating 148
reference generator, creating for job portal 149
graph
cyclic graph 146
directed acyclic graph 146
directed graph 145
simple graph 144
types 144
undirected graph 145
use cases 147
weighted graph 147
greedy algorithm
pseudo code 203
spanning trees 203
used, for building travel itinerary 201
used, for implementing minimum spanning tree
204, 208

H

Hoare Partition Scheme 239, 241
HTML, best practices
Accessible Rich Internet Applications (ARIA)
attributes, using 265
DOCTYPE, declaring 262
inline styles, avoiding 264
meta-information, adding to page 262
scripts, loading 265
semantic markup, using 264
style sheets, loading 263
unnecessary attributes, dropping 263
viewport, using 263
HTML, optimizations
DOM, structuring 271

HTML, layering 282, 285, 286
HTML, layout 273, 280, 282
resources, prefetching 271
resources, preloading 271, 273

I

Information Theory
    entropy 117
    information gain 117
inline caching (IC) 298
Insertionsort API
    about 227
    implementing 228, 229, 231
Iterative Dichotomiser 3 (ID3) algorithm
    about 116, 117
    branch entropy, calculating 119
    coding 122
    decision tree, generating 127, 133
    information gain per branch 120
    outcome, predicting of sample inputs 133
    output, visualization 134, 139
    target entropy, calculating 118
    training dataset, generating 122, 126
    tree, visualization 134, 139

J

JavaScript syntax parser
    building 28
    infix, converting to postfix expressions 37
    input, transforming to machine-understandable
        expression 32, 36
    postfix expressions, evaluating 38
    UI, laying out 29
    web worker communication 30
    web worker communications, enabling 31
    web worker, building 28
JavaScript, best practices
    ==, versus === 268
    boolean operators, using 268
    code, modularization 269
    data, validating 270
    DOM access, minimizing 270
    global scope pollution, avoiding 268
    pyramid of doom, avoiding 269
    rewrite, avoiding 270
    ternary operations, using 268
    use strict, using 268
JavaScript, optimizations
    about 294
    conditional function call 296
    font optimization 298
    garbage collection 300, 302
    image optimization 298
    looping, optimizations 296
    mark and sweep algorithm 301
    truthy/falsy comparisons 294
    V8 302

L

last in first out (LIFO) 7
leaf nodes 117
library books data
    mocking 226
linear time 253
logarithmic time function 252
Lomuto Partition Scheme 237, 238

M

map
    API, differences 75
    origin, exploring 71
    performance, comparing with objects 101
    types, analyzing 72
    WeakMap 73
memoization 194
memory leaks
    avoiding 302
    closures edge case 304, 308
    DOM elements, removing 303
    references, removing 303
    variables, assigning tp global scope 303
Mergesort API
    about 231
    implementing 232
    pseudo code 232
minimum spanning tree (MST) 203
multithreading 29

N

Node.js application
  creating 49, 50, 174
Node.js web server
  creating 148
Node.js
  URL 49

O

object-oriented programming (OOP) 7
objects
  performance, comparing with maps 101
Omega notation 249

P

performance
  benchmark tests, executing 66, 70
  comparing 61, 66
  comparison 98, 241, 243
Personalized PageRank (PPR) algorithm
  about 161, 162
  implementing 166, 169
polynomial time
  about 254
  complexity classes 255
priority queue
  about 45
  testing 46, 49
  used, for implementing log 57
programming paradigm 174

Q

quadratic time algorithms 254
queue, operations
  add() 42
  clear() 42
  front() 42
  peek() 42
  remove() 42
  size() 42
queue
  chat endpoint, creating 51, 56
  circular queue 42

creating 42
  Double Ended Queue (Dequeue) 42
  log, implementing with priority queues 57
  Node.js server, beginning 51
  priority queue 42, 45
  simple queue 42, 43
  testing 44
  types 42
  use cases 49
Quicksort API
  about 234, 235
  Hoare Partition Scheme 239, 241
  implementing 235, 237
  Lomuto Partition Scheme 237, 238
  pseudo code 235

R

recursion
  data, serializing 175
  pseudo code 175, 177
  using, to serialize data 174
reference 301
reference generator
  bidirectional graph, creating 150, 152
  creating, for job portal 149
  executing 159
  pseudo code, generating for shortest path
    generation 152
  shortest path generation, implementing 153, 158
  web server, creating 158

S

sets
  API, difference 77
  origin, exploring 71
  performance, comparing with arrays 99
  types, analyzing 72
  versus WeakSets 75
shortest path generation
  implementing 153, 158
  pseudo code, generating 152
sorting algorithms, use cases
  Express server, creating 225
  Insertionsort API 227

library books data, mocking 226
Mergesort API 231
performance comparison 241, 243
Quicksort API 234
sorting algorithms
types 224
use cases 224
Space complexity
about 257
constant space 258
examples 258
linear space 258
spanning trees 203
stack, use cases
Angular application, creating 14
custom back button, creating for web application
19
evaluator, building 28
JavaScript syntax parser, building 28
stack
comparing, with array 9
creating 10
methods, implementing 10
prerequisites 8
terminology 8
testing 13
use cases 14
using 13

T

theta notation 251
time complexity
additive complexity 256

constant time 252
examples 252
linear time 253
logarithmic time 252
polynomial time 254
quadratic time 254
recursion 256
time to first byte (TTFB) 291
time to interact (TTI) 291
trie tree
about 103
creating 106
typeahead lookup
add() method, implementing 107, 108
creating 104, 105
final form 114
remainders, retaining at nodes 111, 113
search() method, implementing 109, 111
trie tree, creating 106

W

WeakMap
about 73
memory management 73
URL 73
WeakSets
about 76
API, differences 77
versus sets 75
web applications
activity, tracking 88
analytics 88
Angular application, creating 88, 94, 97, 98

* 9 7 8 1 7 8 8 3 9 8 5 5 8 *